Colonel of the Argyll and Sutherland Highlanders.
Portrait by Leonard Boden, A&SH Museum, Stirling Castle

Ma in later life and as a young girl

General Sir Gordon MacMillan
of
MacMillan and Knap

KCB KCVO CBE DSO MC LLD

The Babe

(1897 – 1986)

by

His Children

George, John, David & Andrew MacMillan, and Judy Hutton

An environmentally friendly book printed and bound in England by
www.printondemand-worldwide.com

This book is made entirely of chain-of-custody materials

www.fast-print.net/store.php

General Sir Gordon MacMillan
of MacMillan and Knap
KCB KCVO CBE DSO MC LLD
The
Babe
(1897-1986)

A catalogue record for this book is available from the British Library

ISBN 978-178035-577-1

First published 2013 by
FASTPRINT PUBLISHING
Peterborough, England.

*We have written this book
in fond memory
of
our parents
Gordon and Marian MacMillan*

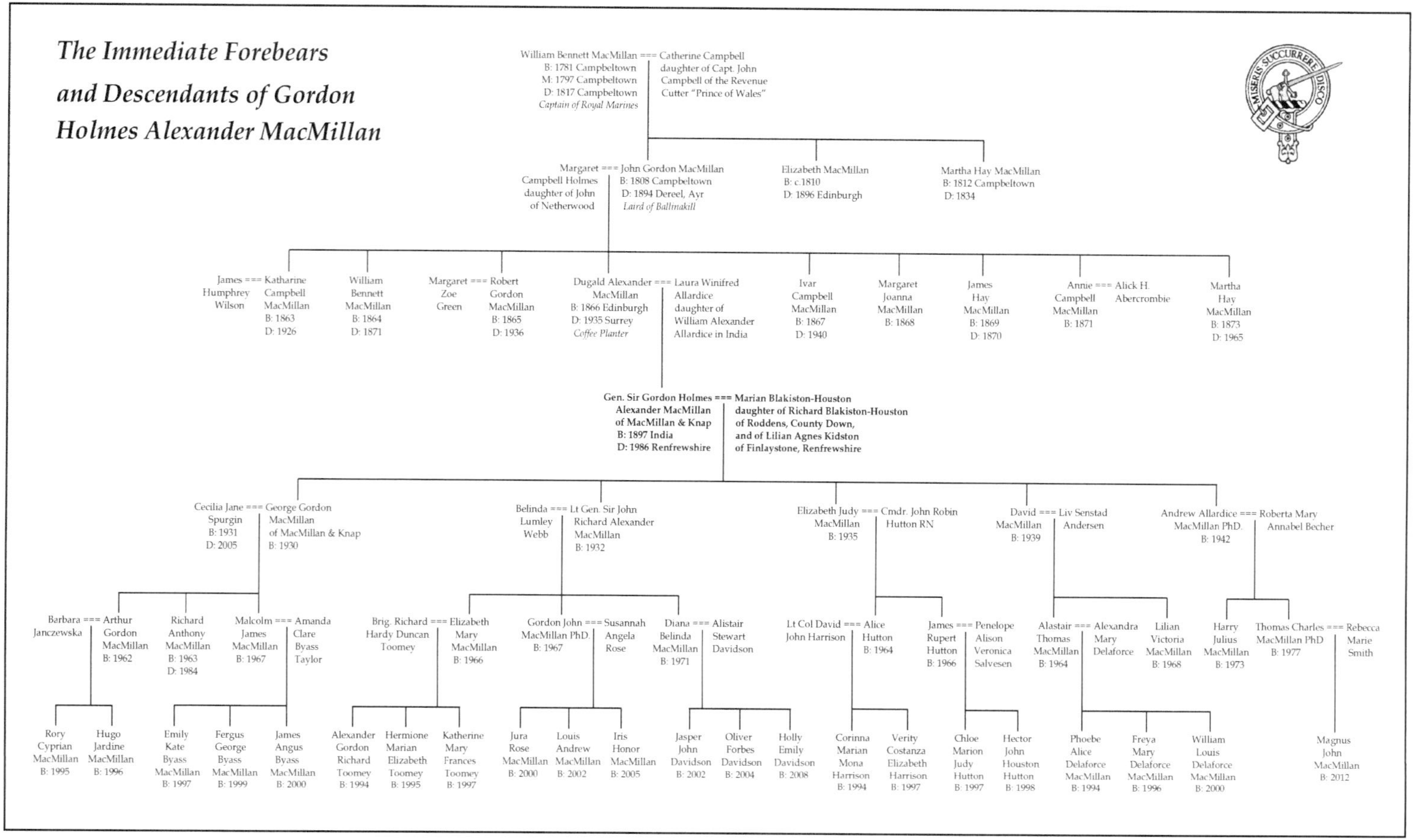

The Immediate Forebears and Descendants of Gordon Holmes Alexander MacMillan

William Bennett MacMillan === **Catherine Campbell**
B: 1781 Campbeltown / daughter of Capt. John
M: 1797 Campbeltown / Campbell of the Revenue
D: 1817 Campbeltown / Cutter "Prince of Wales"
Captain of Royal Marines

Children:

- **Margaret Campbell Holmes** (daughter of John of Netherwood) === **John Gordon MacMillan** — B: 1808 Campbeltown, D: 1894 Dereel, Ayr, *Laird of Ballmakill*
- **Elizabeth MacMillan** — B: c.1810, D: 1896 Edinburgh
- **Martha Hay MacMillan** — B: 1812 Campbeltown, D: 1834

Children of Margaret & John Gordon MacMillan:

- **James Humphrey Wilson** === **Katharine Campbell MacMillan** — B: 1863, D: 1926
- **William Bennett MacMillan** — B: 1864, D: 1871
- **Margaret Zoe Green** === **Robert Gordon MacMillan** — B: 1865, D: 1936
- **Dugald Alexander MacMillan** — B: 1866 Edinburgh, D: 1935 Surrey, *Coffee Planter* === **Laura Winifred Allardice** — daughter of William Alexander Allardice in India
- **Ivar Campbell MacMillan** — B: 1867, D: 1940
- **Margaret Joanna MacMillan** — B: 1868
- **James Hay MacMillan** — B: 1869, D: 1870
- **Annie Campbell MacMillan** — B: 1871 === **Alick H. Abercrombie**
- **Martha Hay MacMillan** — B: 1873, D: 1965

Child of Dugald Alexander & Laura Winifred:

Gen. Sir Gordon Holmes Alexander MacMillan of MacMillan & Knap — B: 1897 India, D: 1986 Renfrewshire === **Marian Blakiston-Houston** — daughter of Richard Blakiston-Houston of Roddens, County Down, and of Lilian Agnes Kidston of Finlaystone, Renfrewshire

Children:

- **Cecilia Jane Spurgin** — B: 1931, D: 2005 === **George Gordon MacMillan of MacMillan & Knap** — B: 1930
- **Belinda Lumley Webb** === **Lt Gen. Sir John Richard Alexander MacMillan** — B: 1932
- **Elizabeth Judy MacMillan** — B: 1935 === **Cmdr. John Robin Hutton RN**
- **David MacMillan** — B: 1939 === **Liv Senstad Andersen**
- **Andrew Allardice MacMillan PhD.** — B: 1942 === **Roberta Mary Annabel Becher**

Children of Cecilia Jane & George Gordon MacMillan:

- **Barbara Janczewska** === **Arthur Gordon MacMillan** — B: 1962
- **Richard Anthony MacMillan** — B: 1963, D: 1984
- **Malcolm James MacMillan** — B: 1967 === **Amanda Clare Byass Taylor**

Children of Belinda & John Richard Alexander MacMillan:

- **Brig. Richard Hardy Duncan Toomey** === **Elizabeth Mary MacMillan** — B: 1966
- **Gordon John MacMillan PhD.** — B: 1967 === **Susannah Angela Rose**
- **Diana Belinda MacMillan** — B: 1971 === **Alistair Stewart Davidson**

Children of Elizabeth Judy & John Robin Hutton:

- **Lt Col David John Harrison** === **Alice Hutton** — B: 1964
- **James Rupert Hutton** — B: 1966 === **Penelope Alison Veronica Salvesen**

Children of David & Liv Senstad Andersen:

- **Alastair Thomas MacMillan** — B: 1964 === **Alexandra Mary Delaforce**
- **Lilian Victoria MacMillan** — B: 1968

Children of Andrew Allardice & Roberta Mary Annabel Becher:

- **Harry Julius MacMillan** — B: 1973
- **Thomas Charles MacMillan PhD** — B: 1977 === **Rebecca Marie Smith**

Youngest generation:

Children of Barbara & Arthur Gordon MacMillan:
- **Rory Cyprian MacMillan** — B: 1995
- **Hugo Jardine MacMillan** — B: 1996

Children of Malcolm & Amanda Clare Byass Taylor:
- **Emily Kate Byass MacMillan** — B: 1997
- **Fergus George Byass MacMillan** — B: 1999
- **James Angus Byass MacMillan** — B: 2000

Children of Brig. Richard Hardy Duncan Toomey & Elizabeth Mary MacMillan:
- **Alexander Gordon Richard Toomey** — B: 1994
- **Hermione Marian Elizabeth Toomey** — B: 1995
- **Katherine Mary Frances Toomey** — B: 1997

Children of Gordon John MacMillan & Susannah Angela Rose:
- **Jura Rose MacMillan** — B: 2000
- **Louis Andrew MacMillan** — B: 2002
- **Iris Honor MacMillan** — B: 2005

Children of Diana Belinda MacMillan & Alistair Stewart Davidson:
- **Jasper John Davidson** — B: 2002
- **Oliver Forbes Davidson** — B: 2004
- **Holly Emily Davidson** — B: 2008

Children of Lt Col David John Harrison & Alice Hutton:
- **Corinna Marian Mona Harrison** — B: 1994
- **Verity Costanza Elizabeth Harrison** — B: 1997

Children of James Rupert Hutton & Penelope Alison Veronica Salvesen:
- **Chloe Marion Judy Hutton** — B: 1997
- **Hector John Houston Hutton** — B: 1998

Children of Alastair Thomas MacMillan & Alexandra Mary Delaforce:
- **Phoebe Alice Delaforce MacMillan** — B: 1994
- **Freya Mary Delaforce MacMillan** — B: 1996
- **William Louis Delaforce MacMillan** — B: 2000

Child of Thomas Charles MacMillan & Rebecca Marie Smith:
- **Magnus John MacMillan** — B: 2012

4

Contents

This Book

Around New Year's Day 2011, we – George, John, Judy, David and Andrew – decided that we would jointly write a short book in which to record the life of our father, General Sir Gordon MacMillan of MacMillan and Knap, KCB, KCVO, CBE, DSO, MC (and 2 bars), LLD. The intended readers would be his grandchildren and great-grandchildren and some family friends. We would try to present a mix of well-documented historical information and anecdotal material. We also agreed that, following his marriage, the focus would widen to include, but to a lesser extent, his bride and the broader family, as we were born and grew up.

The Authors, September 1944

One of the reasons for writing the book was to correct our own woeful ignorance about Pa's life. He seldom displayed any sense of self-importance, but occasionally, when exasperated by bureaucratic pettiness or seeming impertinence, he would raise his voice and angrily ask the unwitting offender "Don't you realise who I am?" He never asked this question of us, but, had he done so, we would have had to admit that we knew very little about much of his life: we had almost no knowledge of his childhood and none of us had a full picture of his army career, especially of the details of his service during the two world wars. And so the writing of this book has been an eye opener for all of us, and an enormously interesting process that has led us to come to know Pa better than we did when he was still alive.

Like almost all his brother officers during the First World War, Pa seems to have quickly acquired a nick-name. He was known as "The Babe", or "Babe MacMillan". We have not been able to trace its origins but we have discovered how, as a very young officer, plunged into the horrors of trench warfare in North-East France, he acted with immense bravery and complete disregard for his own survival. This remarkable capacity for fearless leadership by example was equally in evidence when he held positions of command during the Second World War and subsequently in Palestine.

––––––

It may help readers to understand the setting of the book, if we provide a brief description of Finlaystone, the family home in Scotland, and then introduce ourselves.

Painting by Nicola Leader

Finlaystone is a large, four-storeyed country house, built on a ledge of the steep bank that rises from the southern shore of the River Clyde, about 20 miles to the west of Glasgow, a few miles before westbound travellers reach Port Glasgow. A keep, belonging to the Dennistoun family, is recorded at this location in the 13th century. Through marriage, the house passed to the Cunninghame family, of which a member was created Earl of Glencairn in 1488. When the 15th Earl died childless in 1796, ownership passed to his cousins, the Cunninghame Grahams, who sold it in 1863, to pay off debts, to Sir David Carrick Buchanan. Ten years later he leased it to his friend, George Jardine Kidston, the chairman of the Clyde Shipping Company and our mother's maternal grandfather, who subsequently bought the house in 1897. Our grandmother, Lilian Kidston and her husband, Richard Blakiston-Houston (known to his children as 'Flath'), acquired ownership of the house from the rest of her brothers and sisters. It was left by 'Granny Houston' to George who became laird of Finlaystone in 1955 after her death, and it now belongs to Arthur, his eldest son.[i]

Granny Houston

Finlaystone grew in size over the years and was remodelled at various times, most notably in 1746 and 1900. The latter resulted in the raising of the roof to make space for a nursery floor, later to be known as the 'top flat'.

The house is imposing and very well positioned but not particularly beautiful when seen from the outside. The northern end of the building contains the spacious dining room on the ground floor and the drawing room immediately above. Both have bow windows, with magnificent views looking northwards across the Clyde, stretching from the Tail of the Bank on the left to Dumbarton on the right, with the peaks of mountains – usually snow-covered in winter – reminding us how close the highlands are. The western windows in these two rooms, as well as in the library, have commanded excellent views of the ornamental garden since 1900 when the John Knox tree – a very large yew next to which Knox delivered his first sermon in the West of Scotland in 1556 – was moved away from the house by G.J. Kidston in a complex operation to allow more daylight to enter the drawing room to illuminate his sister's embroidery work.

Much of the southern part of the house consisted of the cooking area, including a massive kitchen with a giant *Esse* stove, a bake-house, scullery and boiler room, larders, game-larder, beer cellar, coal and wood cellars, an apple-house and so on. There was a linen room and ample live-in space for cooks and house-maids upstairs. Many of the original rooms remain intact but others have been converted into a couple of flats, with George now living in one centred around the old servants' hall on the ground floor.

———

George is the eldest of us, born in London in 1930. He went to school at Aysgarth and Eton, as did his brothers. He entered Eton as a King's Scholar and was Captain of the School in his final year. He then took a degree in Classics and Theology when at Trinity College, Cambridge. His first job was as an 'usher' at Wellington College, where he taught classics, after which he spent a year teaching at Toronto University and then moved to Bede College at Durham University as a lecturer in theology. He and Jane Spurgin were married in 1961, and had 3 children, Arthur, Richard (who sadly died as a result of a car accident when he was 21 years old) and Malcolm. George retired in 1974, and the family moved to Finlaystone, occupying the 'top flat' while our parents lived in the main part of the house as his tenants. George and Jane gradually took over the running of the house and the estate, opening the woodlands and gardens to paying visitors, and doing a huge amount of work to maintain the house and its surroundings in good condition. Sadly, Jane died in 2005. George continues to do a great deal of manual work at Finlaystone, combining this with his duties as Chief of the Clan.

John was born in London in 1932. He was the only one of us to follow in our father's footsteps, spending his working life in the Army. At Eton, he was Captain of the Boats. He took a history degree while at Trinity, Cambridge, where he was in the winning Cambridge crew for the boat race: he also rowed in a double scull for Great Britain in the 1952 Helsinki Olympics. He was commissioned into the Argyll and Sutherland Highlanders, and served in many parts of the world – from Guyana to the Gulf, Cyprus to Borneo – before ending his military career as a Lieutenant General, serving as GOC Scotland, and living at Gogar Bank, which had been our home when Pa had the same job in 1949-52. John and Belinda Webb (a.k.a. *Blynda* or, occasionally, *Auntie Batty*) – a former 'slave'[ii] at Finlaystone and daughter of a brother officer of Pa – married in 1964 and have 3 children, Liza, Gordon and Diana. After retiring, John settled down in the countryside near Stirling, growing soft fruits and vegetables.

Judy was the only child to have been born abroad, in Kingston, Ontario in Canada, in 1935. After having lessons from a governess, she went to Ma's old school, West Heath, in Kent. After Pa retired, she stayed at home, helping Ma to develop a flower arranging business. She married Robin Hutton in 1963. Robin was an officer in the Royal Navy, and so they moved around from place to place including Malaysia and Virginia Beach in the USA, as well as several assignments in Scotland. When the "Commander" retired from the Navy in 1986, they returned to Finlaystone and live in Auchenclava, a house that they built, looking out over the garden towards the highlands. Judy has spent many years helping to maintain and enhance the garden and to pick flowers for sale to boost its income. Their children are Alice (who provides a young child's view of her grandparents in the last chapter of this book) and James.

David was born in London in 1939 but, before he was one year old, had moved to live at Finlaystone with the rest of the family, while Pa was taken up with the Second World War. After leaving Eton, where he rowed in the first VIII, he spent a period of practical work on farms in New Zealand and Australia. He studied agriculture at Edinburgh and took over the running of Bogside and Langside farms at Finlaystone. He and Liv Andersen – a sewing 'slave'– married in 1962 and, since then, have lived in the Gardener's Cottage which they expanded and renamed The White House. Their children are Alastair and Lilian. David combined farming with a penchant for inventing machines that would make his life – and that of other farmers – easier. This eventually led to the creation of White House Products, a supplier of hydraulic equipment, which began in a converted barn at Finlaystone but which he and Alastair now run out of a large building in Port Glasgow.

Andrew was the only one of us to have been born at Finlaystone, in 1942. Like John and David, he also rowed in the Eton first VIII. He then studied agriculture at Cambridge and tropical agriculture in Trinidad. For many years he worked in the United Nations Food and Agriculture Organization, based in Rome, assisting developing countries in designing and implementing agricultural and rural development programmes. He and Roberta Becher (a.k.a *Berta*) – also a former 'slave' – were married in 1972. Since Andrew retired in 2005, they have continued to live in Italy, maintaining a few acres of land in the south-western corner of Tuscany. Their children are Harry and Thomas.

Jane decreed that we should all try to meet up, together with our children and grand-children, at Finlaystone for at least one day around Christmas time every four years – in Olympic Games years. This helps to hold our growing extended family together and to link all its members to the place that was, for our generation, a real home to which we all became very attached.

To write this book, we each took lead responsibilities for recounting different periods of Pa's life. We have tried to compile as complete a record as possible, which inevitably means that some parts are more interesting than others – for life is like that! Andrew was given the role of editor. He has sought to preserve the distinctive styles of each writer, to fill gaps but avoid repetition, to prevent the text from becoming unduly long, and to ensure that all historical material is properly referenced. John has selected the photographs and arranged for their reproduction.

––––

We wish to express our thanks to Jock Asbury-Bailey and Martin Clifford for information and photos relating to Pa's time at St. Edmund's School; Joyce Steele and Rod Mackenzie of the Regimental Museum of the Argyll and Sutherland Highlanders in Stirling Castle; Debbie Usher, Archivist of the Middle East Centre Archive, St. Antony's College, Oxford; and staff at the Imperial War Museum and the National Archives as well as the Liddle Collection. We thank Arthur MacMillan for helping us to locate and have access to family papers kept at Finlaystone, and Pauline Simpson for her assistance in extracting some of this material. We wish to thank Richenda Miers and her publisher for permission to quote from an article on Finlaystone published in *Scottish Life Magazine* in which she enlightens readers about the life of Finlaystone 'slaves'. We also thank her for helping us in proof reading. We are also most grateful to Lesmoir Edington for letting us read letters written to her parents while she worked as Ma's Personal Assistant in Gibraltar. We want to express our gratitude to Alice Harrison, Judy's daughter, for allowing us to draw on a draft paper in which she sets out her recollections of her grandparents – which she had begun to write for her children before we embarked on this book: both Alice and her husband, David, also kindly helped in the research on Pa's army career and in tracking down historical material for Chapter 9. Many thanks to Graeme Mackenzie of *Highland Roots*, Inverness for kindly preparing a family tree. Finally, we wish to thank Dot Graham for her enthusiasm and professionalism in arranging the layout of our book.

Both of our parents were very conscientious letter writers, writing almost every day to each other when they were in separate places, as well as at least once a week to each of us. We know also that Pa wrote to his parents every day. Few of these letters have survived and so we have not been able to draw on what must have been very graphic and personal accounts of some of the events to which we refer in the book. We have, however, benefitted from access to a number of files in which Pa had assembled key documents relating to his life, as well as to a scrap-book and many photograph albums, all of which are preserved at Finlaystone.

CHAPTER 1

The Early Years (1897-1915)

by
George

Gordon Holmes Alexander MacMillan was born on 7th January 1897 (though most official records say it was the 6th) in Bangalore, Madras State, India. His parents were Laura Winifred (*née* Allardice) and Dugald Alexander MacMillan. Dugald was the owner of a coffee plantation about seventy miles from Bangalore, which he had named *Dereel* after a house that his father, John Gordon MacMillan, had built in Ayr. The name appears to have been brought back from Australia by John, who, together with his two sisters, had been taken there by his mother, following the early death of his father, William Bennett MacMillan. John is listed as one of a number of 'staunch Presbyterians' who settled in the 1830s on large tracts of pastoral land near Rokewood, Victoria, where a street and a road bridge still bear his name.[iii] One of his properties, over 25,000 acres in extent, was known as Dereel. It seems reasonable to assume that he named his Ayr home – a substantial building which in later days became the Ayr Ex-Servicemen's Club – to commemorate a successful sojourn in Australia: whether he made money from sheep or from one of the gold rushes that engulfed Rokewood is not known.

The Allardices were a Scottish family with connections in India that spanned several generations, with involvement in trade and coffee planting. Gordon's parents, however, felt it inadvisable to raise him there, so they returned to Britain by P&O liner in 1900. His only memory of India was of a night when a number of Indians with flaming torches brought the body of a tiger that his father had shot into the plantation compound. His next mental snapshot was of games played on the deck of the liner.

The family settled into a semi-detached house (27, Ravensbourne Gardens) in leafy Ealing, from where his father commuted to work in London as a Lloyds underwriter, like his older brother, Robert Gordon (known as *Judy*). Meanwhile, young Gordon attended Hamilton House Preparatory School in Ealing, run by Messrs. Driffield and Chawner, of whom he approved. He left it for the Junior House of St. Edmund's School, Canterbury, arriving there in May 1907. St. Edmund's was – and still is – a small, but high-achieving, school with an intake of about twenty boys per year.

Academically, the boy was no slouch. He was twice winner of the Payne-Smith prize for Old Testament studies and of the V.A. Thrupp prize for English. He also bagged the Stocks Memorial prize for Mathematics. He won a 'distinction' for his English Higher Certificate papers. He is recorded as having studied Greek and gained a Higher Certificate in Latin. He sat for a scholarship at St. John's College Oxford in 1914. Aside from class work, he was active in the Debating Society: at fourteen, he opposed the motion that 'Life is too short'; he proposed (vainly) that 'Most crimes of brutality are the result of drink'. He spoke against the execution of Charles I and nationalisation of the railways. He edited the school magazine and acted the part of Mrs. Pippin in a farce called *What next?*.

Gordon was Secretary of the Games Committee – not, perhaps, surprisingly, because he represented his house and the school in all sports throughout his last two years at St. Edmund's. That included fives in which he had a successful three-year partnership with J.R. Peacey, beating other larger schools in the area.

Comments on his sporting performance are amazingly detailed. In soccer he was "useful with his head, but lacked ball control on the ground; but always played to the limits of his powers". In hockey he was "hard-working and plucky, but a bit slow at centre-half" – which may explain why he found himself in goal as captain of the 2nd Hockey XI in his last year. In cricket he "funked nothing", was "a good – sometimes brilliant – fielder" and "a very useful bat". He was also a Sergeant in the Officers' Training Corps, a school monitor and captain of his house football and hockey teams.[iv]

St. Edmund's School Football Team, 1912: Pa at left of back row

John Peacey (by then The Rev. Canon J.R. Peacey) came to preach at Wellington during my time there as a teacher. He told me two things for which I have no other evidence. The first was that, at one point, he and Pa had a monumental row which culminated in a set-piece bare-knuckle fight, after which they were firm friends, presumably with all their fives-playing hands intact. His second recollection was that their house-master made them joint head of East House because he was reluctant to distinguish between them. They were confirmed simultaneously in Canterbury Cathedral. A hymn composed by Canon Peacey was sung at Pa's memorial service.

The scholarship attempt at St. John's had been a trial run, a year ahead of an intended serious effort. At that point, his sights were on the Indian Civil Service. His failure to pass into Oxford caused a change of plan: without consulting his parents, he persuaded his Headmaster to let him apply for a Prize Cadetship at the Royal Military College, Sandhurst, with a view to gaining an army commission. In those days, one had to pay for training at Sandhurst, but he gained the 5th place pass into the College and was awarded a Cadetship. He joined Sandhurst in April 1915, aged eighteen.

Being aware of family links with Argyll, he went for a commission in the Argyll & Sutherland Highlanders, and was interviewed by Lt. Col. Leonard Wheatley who was serving as an instructor at what later became the Staff College in neighbouring Camberley. *Wheatles*, as he was known, was later to be his Commanding Officer in France and a good friend thereafter. His wife (born Esther Fairbairn) came of the first family in Australia to own a million sheep. I think another member of her family, Steve Fairbairn, was a notable Cambridge oar, after whom the Fairbairn race is named. Their daughter, *Bizzie* Wheatley, was my Godmother.

CHAPTER 2

The First World War (1915-1918)

by
John

When Pa applied to go to Sandhurst the course would have lasted two years, but the need for vast numbers of platoon commanders to swell the ranks of an expanding army, and to keep pace with the very high mortality among infantry subalterns, meant that it was restricted to just four months. He was, therefore, commissioned from Sandhurst in 1915 and posted to the 3rd Battalion of the Argyll and Sutherland Highlanders, stationed near Edinburgh. This was a holding battalion, training and despatching drafts for the battalions which were already serving in France. He described his arrival in an interview with Peter Liddle[v] in 1977:

"I was interviewed at Sandhurst by Colonel Leonard Wheatley, who was later my CO. I chose to join the Argylls because that was where my family were originally from. I was commissioned into the 3rd Reserve Battalion, stationed in a tented camp at Mortonhall outside Edinburgh. I arrived in August 1915, but was frustrated as a ruling had just been made that no one should go to the front until they were 19. In the event I did not join the 2nd Battalion until April, 1916.

"On leaving RMC we were all told by our Company Commander that we must report to the Adjutant of our unit on arrival, wearing our swords. I therefore travelled all day from London to Mortonhall, clutching my claymore. When I went to report to the Adjutant, he surprised me by saying, "What is that you are wearing? Take the bloody thing off."

"He was a particularly stupid chap, and when he joined the 93rd in 1917 and I was Adjutant I was able once or twice to put him in his place."

During his time kicking his heels in Scotland while the war was being fought in France, he was sent on courses in musketry and the

Lewis gun as well as a machine gun refresher course, and a range finding course. On the latter he got 98% and a special certificate.

Map 1. **France** (1916 to 1919)

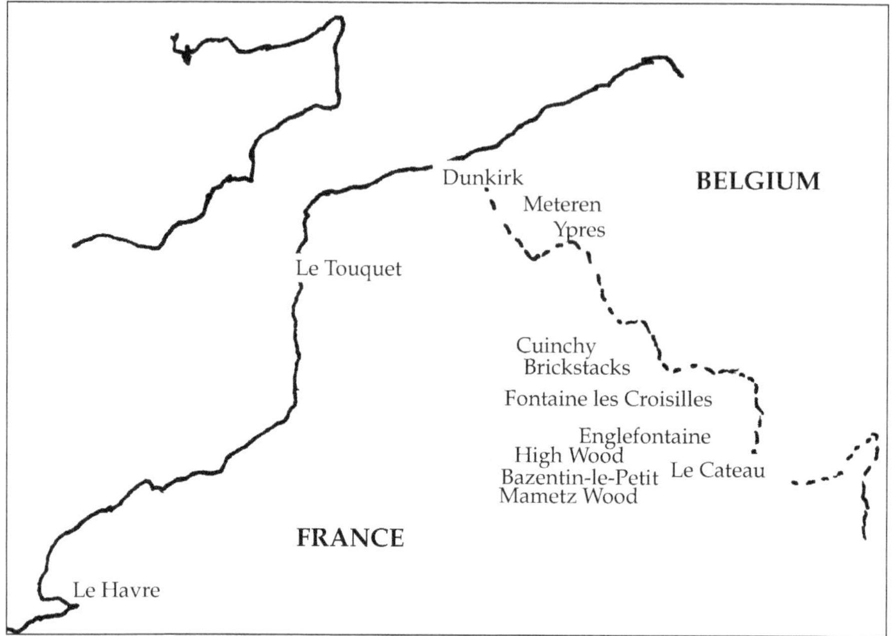

He crossed to France in 1916 and joined the 2nd Battalion the Argyll and Sutherland Highlanders (the 93rd) on 18th April.[vi]

His introduction to what turned out to be two and a half years of combat was an eye opener.

At this time the Battalion was spending almost equal periods in the trenches and in reserve in billets not far behind the line. He was thrown in at the deep end, as the Battalion moved into the line in the vicinity of Auchy, some 100 km south-east of Calais, quite close to the Belgian border, and immediately came under heavy artillery fire.

"I joined the 2nd Battalion at Bethune, near Brickstacks, an area originally the left flank of the battle of Loos. This was an area where a lot of mining and countermining was going on, and on the first night there my platoon had to go and man three listening posts at the end of three saps. I had just returned to the Company HQ to report all was well when there was a huge explosion directly under one of these saps, which made a huge crater, but luckily only two were injured and neither of them very seriously."

He recalled later that the artillery was particularly unpleasant during this action because, wherever a shell fell, it threw up a shower of bricks.[vii]

This seems to have been a fairly quiet deployment, but on 8th May they were back once more, this time at Cuinchy, very close to Brickstacks. Robert Graves, the poet, who was stationed at Cuinchy several times, was appalled by the ubiquitous rats there, writing in *Goodbye to all that,* that "Cuinchy bred rats. They came up from the canal, fed on the plentiful corpses, and multiplied exceedingly." During the twelve days spent by Pa in the line, two German mines, tunnelled under the British lines, were blown, and, combined with heavy machine gun fire while the situation was being restored, the Battalion suffered 9 killed and 27 wounded.[viii]

Pa had the first of many changes of Commanding Officer in the short break after the Cuinchy deployment, when Captain (acting Lieutenant Colonel) Sprot was gassed and handed over to Captain H.M.B. Purves. This probably had little impact on a 2nd Lieutenant serving with a rifle company, though Captain Purves' death from a bullet through the heart soon afterwards must have been hard felt by everyone in the Battalion. Major Thorburn became the third Commanding Officer that Pa experienced within three months.

The main activity reported during the periods in the trenches was the shelling, which caused a steady trickle of casualties. When asked whether mining (in which the enemy, after tunnelling deep below no-man's land, would set off explosives below the trenches) was more alarming than the shelling, Pa said "At the time, yes, but after the Somme, no. The shelling really was, I think, a great deal more frightening than the mining, because it was so intense and so prolonged that it did wear one down. Shelling in the 2nd World War was never as continuous nor went on for as long as 3 months as it did on the Somme."

No doubt there were many patrols against the opposing lines, but no major battle is reported until 15th July when the Battalion was involved in securing the flanks for an offensive in the area of Bazentin-le-Petit. This was their first commitment to the Battle of the Somme, which occupied them through the autumn, and was where they spent a miserable winter. Colonel Scott, who had previously been evacuated when wounded, had returned to his command shortly before the battle, but was once again evacuated through illness, and Major C.B. Purves took over at the beginning of this operation.

Pa had been appointed Battalion Bombing Officer, and therefore would have been close to Battalion HQ, ready to go to the place where the action was hottest. By the time the Battalion was relieved after 48 hours they had lost 11 killed, 99 wounded and 1 missing. Before being permitted to withdraw to billets, they had the satisfaction of shooting down an enemy aircraft, though they suspected it had already been winged by someone else.[ix]

His recollections of the Somme, which, in the following 5 months, claimed 420,000 British casualties, are expressed vividly in his own words: "When we received orders to go to the Somme at the end of July, I had the moving experience of collecting 250 Argylls, who had been miners by profession and were attached to one of our tunnelling companies, and marching them to Bethune to rejoin us. They were the most splendid chaps, but I fear that very few of them survived the war."

He was away from the front during the main engagement of the Battalion in the battle of High Wood, which began soon after the attack on Bazentin-le-Petit and lasted until the British eventually captured the wood from the Germans on 15th September. Otherwise he was there for all engagements and "one was pretty much like another." One incident that he recollected was "Waiting to go up to take over the line from the Indian Cavalry, which had been mistakenly launched against the enemy, which was supposed to have been defeated there. They ran into barbed wire and had very serious casualties. We saw these chaps going up to charge the enemy and we were still lying by the roadside waiting to move forward to our positions ourselves, when the poor wretched remnants of officers, men and horses came straggling back to us, and that was a more vivid recollection than the subsequent action which we had the next day or two in the Bazentin-le-Petit area."

Typically, he makes light of the engagement for which he was recommended for the Military Cross (MC), just 3 months after arriving at the front. The citation, written by Major Purves, reads:

For conspicuous gallantry and devotion to duty during the period 15th July to 22nd July and especially on the morning of the 20th July 1916 when no information had been received from a company that had been despatched to get communication with the troops then occupying the North West corner of High Wood, 2Lt MacMillan was sent to locate them and bring the required information. He found the company about 1,000 yards away from their objective, held up by machine gun fire. He reorganised them and led them to within 100 yards of a hostile barricade and about 600 yards from their objective and had Lewis Guns and bombers brought up to the front to deal with the barricade.[x]

Pa, 1917

The next deployment was to the nearby Mametz Wood, which lasted till 11th August, when Lieutenant Colonel Percy Brown came to take over command. Pa told me once that the Battalion was very shaken after a battle which had depleted them seriously through deaths and woundings, and he was with the few other officers in the bunker which served as Battalion HQ when a new face peered round the gas blanket and said "My name's Brown. I've come to command you". There was a sigh of relief all round, and the sixth Commanding Officer in as many months took over.

Pa told me this story when I was informed that I would take over command of the Gordon Highlanders from Percy Brown's son, Derek, in 1971. His admiration for Colonel Brown was recorded in the Liddle interview: "Lt. Col. Percy Brown, a Gordon, arrived as CO. The 93rd had never had someone from another regiment in that capacity! He was a quite splendid person. Arriving as he did when we had suffered very severe casualties, he put new heart into the Battalion... Strangely enough Percy Brown's eldest son, Tony, was my ADC when I commanded 51st Highland Division at the end of the (second world) war."

Three days after Colonel Brown took over, the Battalion was back in serious combat, at Mametz Wood once more, and very shortly afterwards again at High Wood. All of the many British army units involved in this long battle suffered massive casualties and had to live and fight in the most appalling circumstances. The 93rd always seemed to achieve their objectives, but, as on so many occasions the neighbouring formations were less successful, ground that had been won at great cost in blood too often had to be given up again.

Early in August Pa was sent on a machine gun course at Le Touquet which meant he was away for the most violent phase of the battle for High Wood. He describes his return to the Battalion as a sad occasion, as all the Officers in his Company had been killed. He admitted that he was lucky, but he also felt guilty that he had been away when most needed.

The records show that Pa was appointed Battalion Machine Gun Officer some time before the end of September 1916, and the list of officers on strength at the end of October shows that the award of his MC had come through.

On his return from the course, the Lewis Gun Platoon was formed, but the weapons were not used properly until 1917, when there was one Lewis gun section in each Infantry Platoon. "My role was to help the companies which needed support, but my chief recollection is of dragging the guns about in the most futile hand-pulled carriages with spindly wheels. As by that time the whole Somme area was a sea of mud, it became obvious that the guns should be carried by the men and not hauled about up to their axles in slime."

His time as Machine Gun Officer was brief, as he is shown as 2nd Lieutenant Acting Adjutant in the return of officers' appointments at the end of November 1916. It was not until July 1917 that he was recorded as Lieutenant in this post that was more usually filled by a Captain. He continued to fill this responsible position from that date until December 1920, spanning more than four years of war and peace. For a short time in 1918 he was described as Captain, but his substantive promotion did not come through until August 1924 nearly four years after he had relinquished the Adjutant's position.[xi]

The Adjutant is the staff officer to the Commanding Officer, and so his continuity in the Adjutant's post must have been invaluable, since Commanding Officers came and went at a confusing pace. Lieutenant Colonel Brown went away on a course in December 1916 and at the New Year Lieutenant Colonel J.C. Sprot was appointed in his place, only to be succeeded in April 1917 by Lieutenant Colonel Riccard of the Essex Regiment, who was wounded towards the end of the same month. Lieutenant Colonel Wheatley's arrival on 24th April ushered in a period of greater stability in Battalion Headquarters, though the pace of life in the Battalion remained intense. Wheatley left on promotion to

Brigadier after eight months in command, to be followed briefly by Major Colquhoun, the second in command. Lieutenant Colonel Muir took over command in mid-January 1918 during battles around Passchendael, and remained in command for three months. Lieutenant Colonel Ian Campbell was appointed CO in May 1918, and was still commanding when the war ended in November that year.

While Commanding Officers came and went, Pa had the continued support of 2nd Lieutenant H.W. (*Peter*) Pinckney, who was appointed Assistant Adjutant in July 1917. He continued as his Assistant Adjutant, later incorporating the responsibilities of Intelligence Officer, until almost the end of the war. Although the Pinckney family emigrated to farm in New Zealand after the war, Pa and *Peter* (known outside the regiment as Bill) remained extremely close friends. This friendship between the Pinckney and MacMillan families has grown and blossomed over two more generations.

His new role as Adjutant did not keep Pa away from the action. While the rifle companies took it in turn to man the forward trenches, and to lead the advance when offensive action was needed, the Battalion Advanced Headquarters to which he was attached was always close behind. It was when he had been Adjutant for six months that he was commended for his actions once more, at the battle of Arras. The citation reads:

Throughout the 23rd/24th April 1917 near Fontaine les Croisilles for conspicuous gallantry and devotion to duty. When the Commanding Officer had been wounded about 6pm on 23rd the command of the Battalion devolved upon him. At this time the situation was most uncertain and critical. Lieut. MacMillan organised the details near advanced Battalion Headquarters for the defence of the position as the German counterattack had brought them to within 100 yards. His personal example of coolness and total disregard of danger at this time were most noticeable. He maintained touch with all companies except A Company which was isolated in the German line, and finally, when ordered, withdrew the Battalion into support.

This officer has been recommended for special award on two other occasions and has received the Military Cross.[xii]

The recommendation was for a DSO or a French award. Higher authority had its say, and the award was made for the lower distinction of the MC. Since he had already been awarded the MC, this came as a bar to the medal. Incidentally this is the only mention of a recommendation for a second previous award. The citation which gained his MC is the only earlier one that is on record, but it would not be surprising, given the chaotic conditions prevailing at the front, if such recommendations sometimes got lost in the system!

His own description of these events gives a picture of the confusion that must have ensued when a 2nd Lieutenant became the Commanding Officer of a Battalion in the midst of battle. Describing the battle of Arras in April he says: "After the initial success of our attack on 23rd April, we had moved our Battalion HQ into the original front line. Unfortunately the Germans pushed back the troops on our right and infiltrated between us and our forward companies. As we at Battalion HQ were preparing to lead our reserve companies over the top to clear the Germans out, a stonk fell on Battalion HQ, and I found myself to be the only one who was not a casualty. I was in the proud position of being the Battalion Commander until we were withdrawn." This was his only time in command of a Battalion of the Argylls, as he went swiftly from Major to Brigadier at the beginning of the Second World War.

He remembered this battle as the one in which the greatest display of gallantry occurred. Talking to Liddle he said "The most heroic act I saw was in April 1917 at Arras, when 4 companies, 2 from the Middlesex Regiment and 2 from the Argylls, were stranded and encircled. They held out and eventually forced the Germans to withdraw." It made a lasting impression on him as he quoted this as an example of tenacity in his Foreword to the *History of the Reconstituted 93rd in 1944 and 1945.*

Many other battles intervened between this time and the end of the War, but there are few personal reminiscences or documents in which he is named. He was able to get a few days leave in April 1918, and returned to find the Battalion had been rapidly moved to the area of Meteren, to provide a defensive line behind the Portuguese forces who were in disarray. When asked how they set about an operation like this he said they were "given a line on a map when the Portuguese had deserted and then dug holes, 4 or 5 feet deep, using entrenching tools and with any luck a spade or shovel were produced and one dug further and made a section post and then, if you were in the same place for a long time, these were joined up and became trenches."

It sounds simpler than his return to the battle which he described thus: "It was slightly amusing to arrive back in France from leave and be told by an agitated Railway Transport Officer (RTO) at Hazebrouck that the Germans were expected at any moment and I was to take my fellow passengers to hold a certain bit of high ground at all costs. Luckily I saw a divisional vehicle on the road, so deserted the RTO and got back to the 93rd that evening, in time for the battle of Meteren, from where the Germans were unable to advance to attack the RTO and his gallant defenders a good many miles behind us."

It was about this time, in May 1918, that American troops were attached to the 93rd for training in trench warfare. Pa recalled that "While in this area we had to train an American Division by having first of all a platoon, then a company and then a whole battalion attached to us. They were very raw and even carried whole carcasses of lamb uncooked up to the front line in the early stages of their time with us. When they were taken away – the 30th American Division – they actually wept at the thought of having to fight all on their own. As it happened they had very heavy casualties on their first operation, which was carried out on the French Front in the south."

It was about this time that Ian Campbell, his new CO, commented in his diary "On taking command, the Adjutant was G.H.A. MacMillan, I think the best officer of his age I ever met."[xiii]

Pa's third commendation for gallantry was also earned while he was Adjutant. During the final advance of the Allies, before the Germans surrendered, the Battalion was involved in very heavy fighting near Le Cateau, losing 9 officers and 192 other ranks, in exactly the same area as the 93rd had had its first big action of the war in 1914. In his citation, Major Colquhoun, who was in command at that time while Ian Campbell was temporarily absent on leave, wrote:

When the Battalion advanced on the morning of the 10th Oct. they came under <u>exceptionally</u> heavy shell fire crossing the high ground NW of Le Cateau. The enemy's guns were firing chiefly over open sights. There were a large number of casualties and momentarily the Battn. became somewhat disorganised. Capt and Adjt MacMillan with an utter disregard of personal safety at once ran forward and by the absolute fearlessness and gallant leadership which has always been characteristic of this officer was greatly instrumental in rallying the men and enabling the advance to be resumed. He led one of the point companies until it was reduced to 6 ORs and when the advance was held up made his way back to Battn. H.Q over 600 yards of open country exposed to snipers, MG fire and shelling bringing a valuable report. The coolness, bravery and determination of this officer throughout the two days of operations was an example to all.[xiv]

Although the recommendation was once again for a DSO, he was awarded the second bar to his MC, thereby becoming one of only 168 servicemen to receive this distinction in the First World War. Pa made no mention of it himself, but Ian Campbell records that a bullet passed through Pa's water bottle during this action.[xv]

Reflecting on this period of very intense fighting in the last months of the war, Ian Campbell went on to say: "In the end, I came to look on my time with the 93rd as the best of the whole war, for there were lots of efficient people to do my work, and all I had to do was to direct and encourage. The morale was very good indeed… When it came to fighting, they expected to be in the hottest place; for who but the 93rd could be expected to do the job properly?"[xvi]

Shortly after the engagement at Le Cateau and the crossing of the Selle, Pa went back to Britain on leave.

"Although the rest of 1918 was spent in the big advance to victory, we had heavy fighting, rather reminiscent of Arras, at Villers Guislain, Montay and Englefontaine. The battle of the Selle was adjacent to the battle field of Le Cateau, where the 93rd had its first big battle in 1914.

"My final bit of good fortune came at this time. As I had been for 2 years continuously with an infantry battalion, I had qualified after the battle of the Selle for a month's home leave. I took the leave and was at home with my parents when the Armistice took place. Jack Watson, my Assistant Adjutant, who answered for me while I was away, was badly wounded during the final advance through the Foret de Mormal. It might well have been me."

The final 60 mile advance that began on 18th September and ended with the Armistice on 11th November cost the Battalion 25 Officers and 650 Other Ranks killed or wounded, the same number of casualties as during its earlier period on the Somme.

The war ended as the advance continued beyond the Canal d'Escault, which runs between Dunkirk and Cambrai in North East France. After a short time the Battalion moved to Le Havre where it was responsible for local security, and prepared to send drafts home on demobilisation. The Military Band was called forward from Ireland to rejoin the Battalion to provide entertainment, perform in ceremonial events and take their share in the many duties that fell to the war-weary soldiers. Among them were a number of Band Boys, and Pa insisted that they should have a full programme of sports as well as their other duties. When he found that the Bandmaster was ignoring his direction that they should play football or some other sport every afternoon, he had him placed in close arrest. This was Kenneth Ricketts, who was better known by his nom-de-plume Kenneth Alford, the composer of Colonel Bogey, later made famous as the theme tune for *The Bridge over the River Kwai*. Pa was always well known for his appreciation of music!

A&SH Pipes and Drums, Le Havre 1919. Pa third from left, centre row

Normality was beginning to be resumed with the ceremonial arrival of the Colours which had been laid up in Stirling Castle for the duration of the War. A full battalion parade was mounted to receive them on 21st December.

The change in tempo must have caught up with him, since he is recorded as being admitted to hospital on 29th March 1919, but was back in the saddle at some time in April. There is nothing to say what the reason was, but this was the period when flu swept through Europe. It cannot have been a serious outbreak or many more admissions would be in the record, so it may have been a sports injury. This was the only mention of him being away from duty, though he was in England at one time during the War to receive his MC.

By this time the original Battalion was being scattered to different corners of Europe, many going home on demobilisation, and a number moving to Germany as members of the occupying force. Lieutenant Colonel Campbell left to command 5th Battalion A&SH and Lieutenant Colonel R.C.B. Anderson took over. Meanwhile the Battalion received reinforcements both from trainees from Scotland and from other battalions which were disbanding. Finally it was their turn to move, first to Colchester, where they arrived on 15th May, then to Stirling for a civic reception, and thence on leave on 22nd May 1919.

Pa summed up the war briefly in a tribute to all who served in the 93rd: "I would say that I was fortunate to belong to the best battalion in the Army, with an unbreakable spirit. You can see this from the record of their operations – and then look at the casualty list: 63 officers and 1175 men killed, and ready for anything at the end of it all."

Postscript

On the Work of an Adjutant in World War I

When asked about the Adjutant's working day, Pa was quite clear in his explanations to Peter Liddle:

"First thing and probably the most important was not so much in action, but when you got your orders to go and fight somewhere or to move, the Adjutant had to write up the orders for the Battalion. I used to write the order to the 4 Companies and Battalion HQ on a message pad with 5 bits of carbon paper underneath. That having been written by me in my own hand with a hard pencil, it would then be sent out by runner to each Company Commander and that was probably the beginning of the Adjutant's working day prior to action."

Did the CO sign them before they went out?

"Oh no. I signed them. The CO would just tell me roughly what was required and I would interpret his instructions, when I wrote the orders in ordinary form."

But was there no check on your interpretation?

"No. The CO trusted his Adjutant. If there was any point of doubt, I would have asked him and then, of course, after that it was really a question of making quite sure that one kept in close touch with the Companies by runner or telephone wire."

Reverting to his day, once orders had been sent out, the Commanding Officer and the Adjutant would separately visit the Companies to see if all was going well. This would not preclude a certain amount of private venture work, as when he described a reconnaissance that he was carrying out with *Peter* Pinckney. The two of them were observing the enemy lines from a hop field when they were spotted and German machine guns opened up on them. Not only did they have to dodge the bullets as they made a hasty retreat, but also the hop poles which were flying about.[xvii]

There was a bit more to the Adjutant's role than his comments might suggest. Although Pa seldom spoke of his time in the Great War, by piecing together snippets of information one can get a glimpse of what life must have been like for him. Being at the hub of the Battalion he would have been involved with constantly transforming plans made by Brigade and Division, as well as by his Commanding Officer, into orders to the Company Commanders and any supporting forces. During the periods from a week to 10 days when the Battalion might occupy the front line but were not caught up in major actions, his duties would be less onerous as the Companies fought their own engagements. Orders for relief, either going forward or when returning to support, training or labouring tasks, would be complex, ensuring that the handover went without attracting the attention of the enemy who would know that it was a moment when they were most vulnerable. Timings and check points for the move would have to be worked out, and arrangements for transport, to ensure the minimum of hanging about in vulnerable locations, would have to be meticulously planned. Reliable communications to adjust the plans when enemy action or even worse weather than usual threw the calculations out would have to be in place.

Usually, when returning behind the lines, a long trek in the dark through the muddy crumbling trenches would be followed by a further march for a considerable distance before being picked up by road transport, or in some cases by light railway. Having worked out the details, he then had to ensure that the orders reached all concerned in time for their action. It is noticeable that on rare occasions the War Diary thinks it worth recording that a relief went smoothly. Disrupted changeovers do not merit a mention!

During major engagements the Adjutant would be trying to follow the battle, which was frequently made almost impossible because the telephone cables, reeled out behind the companies while they were advancing, were continually being cut by shellfire, and communications often had to rely on runners who might get lost or killed between the forward positions and Battalion Headquarters, which itself would move forward as soon as ground was taken. Add to this the problems the companies themselves found in recognising landmarks and therefore being able to give accurate reports, and by the constant noise and disruption caused by shelling coming from both sides, and one can picture a scene in which a degree of divination was needed to make any accurate plot of the situation.

Things became more complex when flanking units failed to show up where they were expected, and when the artillery refused to alter the targets they were engaging when told repeatedly that they were landing their shells in the middle of our own troops. This was a criticism that Pa voiced with feeling many years later, blaming the Gunners' inability to co-ordinate their barrages with the advancing troops on a failure to synchronise watches beforehand. This may have been a little simplistic, but it reflected the frustration felt by so many when casualties had been caused by so-called friendly fire. Communications were always a problem but the War Diary reports one occasion when Brigade tried to overcome it by sending a basket of pigeons so that the Battalion could send back information. They failed to include the carriers to clip on to the pigeons' legs, and so, until these were found, the pigeons ran a serious risk of supplementing the rations.

Since the Intelligence Officer's post is not mentioned until late in the war, it is likely that the few officers in Battalion Headquarters shared this important role, co-ordinating patrols, and keeping both the Companies and Brigade informed of any new information on the enemy. The Battalion's ability to capture prisoners both by patrolling during quiet periods and by rounding up large numbers of enemy during their offensives must have made handling and quick interrogation of prisoners an important part of the job. The saddest, but unfortunately very onerous, part of the Battalion HQ's task will have been recording the casualties. Even in quiet periods in the line it was exceptional to escape with no deaths.

When out of the line, the Adjutant's life could become even busier. Drafts would arrive to replace casualties, and would need to be allocated to the rifle companies or to specialist tasks if they had the necessary skills. Where gaps had occurred in the structure of the Battalion, the more experienced officers and men would be moved to fill the vacancies, while the newcomers took their places in the rifle platoons. No doubt the Chief Clerk bore the brunt of keeping the record of who was where, but a great deal of the decision making would rest with the Commanding Officer, advised by the Adjutant and the Company Commanders. An illuminating point in this regard comes in an answer to Liddle's request about what happened if the performance of companies was being affected by the quality of the company level leadership. "You soon got to know where possibly officers were wanting in some of the more desirable qualities. You changed them. It was done by the CO. Find some other use for them"

The 93rd were conscious of the need to avoid unnecessary casualties through sickness, and discipline was one more aspect of the Adjutant's responsibilities. Pa records: "We wintered 1916/17 on the right flank of the Somme area, where the wet trenches made trench foot liable to occur. We exerted very strict discipline in regard to changing socks and had very few cases."

During the longer periods out of the line there was a transformation in the way of life. Nearly always there would be visiting officers, for whom a parade would be mounted. This was the traditional peace time responsibility of the Adjutant, supported by the Regimental Sergeant Major, and no doubt the Quartermaster's staff would earn their pay by ensuring that worn out equipment and clothes were replaced and laundered fit for the next deployment.

When the time out of the line permitted anything more than cleaning up, regrouping and preparation for a resumption of duty in the trenches, a programme of training and sports would take place, the training often being specific to the next anticipated battle. Such training involved introduction to tanks before the battle of Cambrai, and co-operation with aircraft at a later rest period when the Battalion was manning coastal defences near Dunkirk. The operation for which this was preparation did not take place, however, as the Battalion was urgently needed to plug a gap in the line.

Football was the main sport played, whenever there was a moment. Rifle competitions were also run, as well as athletics meetings. During one period there were mounted games involving the officers, and mounted wrestling and a number of mounted paper chases, and boxing matches took place, with a separate competition for the officers. Apart from a mention that a number of the officers' chargers had been hit by shellfire and a report that the Commanding Officer attended a Staff Ride with the senior divisional officers, this is the only mention in the Diary that the horses had come to France at all. I doubt if Pa would have missed them!

When time allowed, the talent in the Battalion was put to good use by performing in concert parties, and of course the Pipes and Drums were assembled from the companies to which they deployed for operations, to beat Retreat or lead the parades. The Military Band was in Kinsale. (There is no explanation of why they were there, as the Battalion had set off for the war from Fort George.)

During one such period of rest and training in August 1918, an entry in the War Diary shows Pa's touch. It reads "The Inspector General of Training gave a short demonstration of platoon training. A number of new ideas, some of debatable character, were introduced." I wonder if people at the sharp end were equally sceptical of the doctrine he produced after the Second World War, entitled *The Conduct of War*?

The billeting arrangements for units out of the line would often be the same as on previous periods of respite. Among Pa's papers is a dog-eared postcard with a picture of Chateau Belloy Saint Léonard, near Amiens and close to the Somme, dating from 1919. It has a brief message to *le Baby*, signed by Madeleine, Yvonne, Collette and Philippe de Hauteclocque whose family owned the chateau and may have provided billets for British officers. Philippe, who was 5 years younger than Pa, joined the French Army in 1922.

The fact that Pa had clearly treasured this tattered postcard, probably keeping it in his uniform pocket during the war, and had then retained it amongst his papers had led us to speculate that Madeleine, who was of the same age, had been a rather special friend. However, her great nephew, Jean de Hautecloque, the current owner of Chateau Belloy, tells us that in 1917 Madeleine was engaged to marry Renaud, a young French officer who failed to return from the front after the end of the war in November 1918. As his body had not been found, he was reported missing, presumed dead. In her desperation, Madeleine became seriously ill. Renaud reappeared at the end of 1919, having spent a year in hospital, unidentified because, as a result of brain damage he had lost his memory and carried no form of identification. In the end, his memory returned and he remembered who he was and his fiancée, and returned to Belloy. He and Madeleine were married, but she never recovered from her illness and died in 1920.

Many years later, Pa was asked by David Thomson, then Colonel of the Regiment, what the Adjutant did when the big engagements took place. He replied that the Adjutant and the Regimental Sergeant Major followed the advance with a revolver in each hand, and it was their duty to shoot anyone who ran away before desertion became a rout. He didn't add whether he had ever had to do this. The record of the 93rd's success in offensive operations shows that they either didn't need this threat behind them, or it was a very effective deterrent. He stated to Liddle that he had never had to sit on a Court Martial, which suggests that desertion was not a problem.

Château Belloy Saint Léonard: Message from de Hauteclocque family, July 1917

CHAPTER 3

Between the Wars (1919-1939)

by
George

After a civic reception in Stirling, the 2nd Battalion of the Argyll and Sutherland Highlanders dispersed on 22nd May 1919, some six months after the Armistice, for some well-earned leave.

Of the next decade of his life (till his marriage on 10th August 1929), we know nothing outside his regimental activities – not even the date of his parents' migration from Ealing to Farnham. That is likely to have occurred when his father decided that under-writing at Lloyds was not for him. We know that his older brother *Judy* stayed with Lloyds and kept a generous eye on him.

I have only one memory of our grandfather – collecting eggs from his chickens. The house and garden – now built over – seemed large.

After its post-war leave, the Battalion 're-formed' on 1st September 1919 at Duddingston in Edinburgh under the command of Lieutenant Colonel W.J.B. Tweedy. A note from 'David' specially acknowledges Pa's help in this process. After a week-long excursion to Glasgow to cope with a rail strike that never materialised, the Battalion moved to Aldershot in October. As Adjutant, Pa would inevitably have been involved in organising some ceremonial events – a parade and inspection for the Shah of Iran, lining the streets of London for the President of France (being entertained by the Lord Mayor of London, because mere Presidents didn't consort with royalty); and the funeral of the Empress Eugenie. There were also visits to Aldershot from Churchill and the King and Queen to thank the army for its war service.

In March 1920 some serious soldiering interrupted the social round: he spent two weeks at the Hythe small arms' school on a 'short course for adjutants on rifles, light guns, light mortars and bombing'. After two years as war-time Adjutant in France, one might have thought….. But he was now qualified according to the book to instruct in such matters as a Platoon Commander.

The Battalion was warmly congratulated on its efficiency in running the Bisley ranges for the Imperial meeting that summer.

Meanwhile, the 'Bad Times' or 'Troubles' were coming to a head in Ireland. So in July they sailed to Belfast. After spending a week there keeping angry Protestants and Catholics apart, they moved to Claremorris in County Galway. The railwaymen were sympathetic to the IRA and refused to carry troops, so they marched the 170 miles over five days, but sent the baggage by train. Perhaps it wasn't too surprising that, when the train reached Claremorris, one of the wagons had been looted. Though it's hard to imagine how else they could have proceeded, I hope that sending the baggage by rail wasn't the Adjutant's decision. This experience may have given an edge to their searches – often successful – for IRA weapons caches. Generally, though, things were fairly quiet till mid-November 1920, when sixteen British officers and known British sympathisers were murdered in Dublin, so triggering the 'Croke Park Massacre' on 21st November. Two days later the Battalion received orders to round up all known IRA members. They turned in fifty soon afterwards, and seem to have made life difficult for their colleagues, who were staging ambushes and murdering policemen.

On 3rd December 1920, still a mere Lieutenant doing a Captain's job, Pa handed the adjutancy over to a Brevet-Major. Appreciative notes from Hugh B. Spens, Lieutenant Colonel Ian Campbell and 'David' (whom I can't identify) speak enthusiastically of his competence and particularly of his *'esprit de corps'* – something Pa himself felt to be at the heart of any successful unit. During the four momentous years of his adjutancy, nine COs came and went. So this 'pivot' must indeed have seemed like a fixed point in a turning world.

Looking back on Pa's service as Adjutant, Judy's son-in-law, David Harrison, wrote: "My observation, as someone who spent 16 months as Adjutant on operations of a completely different nature in Northern Ireland, is that it is remarkable how much of the day-to-day direction of the Battalion should have devolved to such a young and inexperienced officer. The turmoil caused by casualties and the constant change of CO, meant everyone would have looked to him for direction and guidance. The Battalion's distinguished record in my view is a direct reflection of his remarkable courage and leadership under fire."

He was appointed acting OC 'C' Company (a Captain's job). Jim Cunningham, who was later to be his best man, was nominally the company commander; but he seems to have been away a lot. They were just getting into their stride with 'flushing out' the IRA, when operations were halted in July 1921, following a reconciliatory speech by King George V which opened the way for peace negotiations. In retrospect, Pa felt that, given that the IRA had been so weakened and their forces were so concentrated in just one small area, a military victory would have been possible had truce discussions not been opened up at this time.

Pa used to say that he found the 'Troubles' hard to handle: in the trenches one at least knew where the enemy was; but in Ireland one never knew who he was. Nevertheless, the Battalion was warmly congratulated on its work (achieved without loss) and returned to Aldershot in January 1922, following the signing of the Anglo-Irish Agreement the previous month.

Peace at last! Active warfare gave place to gentler pursuits – training courses, athletic competitions and exams. The pen being at least as mighty as the sword, Pa capitalised on his Distinction in Higher Certificate English by becoming the first editor of a resuscitated 2nd Battalion A & S.H. Magazine, the *'Thin Red Line'*.

The *'Thin Red Line'* refers to Sir Colin Campbell's defence of the port and vital base at Balaklava during the Crimean War when commanding the 93rd Highlanders at the mature age of sixty-five. With a large area to defend, he told his men to spread themselves thinly, conceal themselves behind the small ridge (in the undergrowth) and, when the Russians approached, to jump up and fire a volley. The plan worked. Colin Campbell, son of a Sauchiehall Street joiner, it's said, had joined the 93rd Highlanders in the Napoleonic wars, the cost of his commission being defrayed by an uncle. He was badly wounded under Wellington in the Peninsular War, but soldiered on, and eventually commanded the Regiment in the Crimea. When the Indian Mutiny erupted, he was dispatched to sort it out. He was noted for his careful preparation, which saved many lives, but didn't appeal to young officers, who dubbed him Sir Crawling Camel. On his return from India he was ennobled as Lord Clyde. The government considered buying Finlaystone to give to him as a token of gratitude; but before they could do so, he died. His statue is in George Square in Glasgow, quite near the City Chambers.

In the spring of 1922 Pa had a serious accident, when a motor-cyclist came through the windscreen of his car and left a lasting dent in his forehead. He was not passed 'fit for general duty' until 12th September 1922.

In May 1923 he received plaudits for gaining a rare distinction in an education course at Shorncliffe. A senior officer wrote "… I have never seen a better report, and I'm sure you deserved every word of it…" This qualification could well have influenced his subsequent peace-time appointments, several of which involved running courses.

He remained with C Company for the next three or four years, either in command or second in command to Jim Cunningham, sometimes running battalion courses, sometimes running races or representing the Battalion at cricket and hockey.

When Princess Louise (the Colonel-in-Chief) visited the Battalion in July 1923, he came second to *Prof* Grant (as usual, it seems) in the 'mile' in the highland games that followed the parade.

It may have been about this time that he 'incurred the displeasure of the GOC 2 Infantry Division for not wearing a waterproof when ordered to do so' (alluded to by Dick O'Connor in a letter in 1954).

In October the Battalion moved to Parkhurst on the Isle of Wight. Pa's batting average rose to a respectable 23. We know he won a three-mile race. Was *Prof* Grant away? Or did he prefer a shorter distance? Unfortunately, there's no record of the victory in the annals – possibly due to the editor's modesty, though the fine silver cup later held a place of honour while he was living at Gogar Bank, the residence of the General Officer Commanding, Scotland.

The Battalion sometimes crossed to the mainland for exercises. On one occasion (a Brigade exercise at Lavington Park) Pa, while still a Lieutenant, was seconded from C Company to act as Brigade Major.

From 1924 to 1927 his spare time must have been spent, at least in part, preparing for exams – Promotion Exam for Captain in 1924, and three shots at the Staff College Exam in the succeeding years. His results in the Promotion Exam look impressive. His marks for Organisation and Regimental Duties in Peace; Administration of Discipline and Military Law; Imperial Military Geography; Military History; and Tactics, Administration of Troops in the Field, Map-reading and Field Works were uniformly 80% or above (the pass mark being 50%). While still commanding 'C' Company (Jim Cunningham being away, perhaps in Kenya) he was at last made Captain in August 1924.

1925 was a busy year. He took his first and most successful shot at the Staff College exam, with a total of 5704 out of a possible 10000 marks – enough to qualify for the Staff College, subject to his being nominated. Apparently, very few candidates obtained unconditional entry. Compulsory subjects were: Training for War (4 papers), Organisation and Administration (2 papers) and Imperial Organisation (2 papers). This year, he took optional papers on Movements and Political Economy.

He joined Cluny Macpherson, Robin Macalpine-Downie and *Prof* Grant in a Battalion athletics team that reached the Army finals. He made thirteen catches when representing the Battalion and in one match he took two wickets for three runs. C Company won the Battalion athletics (though he himself could manage only third place in the mile). C Company also helped to run Bisley again, and won high praise from the responsible General – "the most efficient since the war".

There's a somewhat cryptic entry in this year's *Thin Red Line* under 'Things we'd like to know' – 'Why the Captain rode uphill seated on the horse's tail?' – a clear allusion to Pa's well-known antipathy to horses. But what was the occasion?

The year of the General Strike (1926) found the 93rd still based on the Isle of Wight. As Jim Cunningham left for Kenya in April, Pa was again OC C Company when a large detachment of the 93rd relieved the Duke of Wellington's Regiment in their Portsmouth barracks. Boarding the three small transports, which were moored side-by-side, proved a scramble for the kit-laden soldiers – and not least, it seems, for Pa: the Company correspondent reported (under the headline 'Boarding Sir Evelyn Wood') that "It was here that a regrettable incident occurred. The officer commanding C Company, doubtless distraught by the dangers of embarkation, omitted to salute the quarter-deck (if any) and a few moments later was discovered shivering his timbers by numbers on the after-poop". The voyage was further complicated by their being landed in Gosport and having to take a commercial ferry across the harbour to Portsmouth itself. Once there, they had a lovely time, playing every kind of sport. C Company was again Battalion Champion, with the highest aggregate for tug-of-war, hockey, cross-country and soccer (in which Pa is noted as having participated, presumably in addition to hockey and running). In a cricket match he took four wickets for six runs; and his batting average was 14.67 (4th highest in the Battalion).

In July Princess Louise, as Colonel-in-Chief, presented the Battalion with new colours, featuring battle honours of the Great War. Pa, being her Orderly Officer, and therefore in full dress uniform, seems not to have taken part in the three days of sports that marked the occasion.

All this activity may explain his poor showing in his 1926 Staff College exam – a mere 4995 marks, with zero in both French and Political Economy (anyone gaining less than 300 marks out of a possible 1000 in these optional subjects received a zero).

In 1927 Jim Cunningham resumed command of C Company. When Pa was preparing for his third shot at the Staff College exam, the Battalion was told that it would be going to the West Indies later in the year and actually sailed in August. It looks as if he was counting on getting nominated for the course that began in January 1928, which would have made his West Indian posting ridiculously brief. So he gladly accepted the idea, put to him by *Lightning* Speirs (an officer in the 1st Battalion, which was to be based in the UK) that they should swap places – only to discover that Speirs' reason for wanting to go abroad was that he intended to ditch his wife. Pa confessed to some guilt at being an unwitting accessory to this ungentlemanly manoeuvre.

He received his exam results on 21st July. His French was even worse than in the previous year; but he redeemed his reputation on Political Economics. He did respectably on 'Movements by land sea and air'; but the subject was clearly losing its shine, because he lost as many marks on this paper as he gained on Political Economy. His total this time was 5446. It must have been with some relief that he reported to the Depot in Stirling pending joining the 1928 Staff College course.

Of his time in Camberley we know surprisingly little. It was expected that officers should take part in the Staff College Drag Hunt – something that Pa would not have welcomed. But he was lucky enough to hire a horse that preferred 'terra firma' to jumping: it was known, appropriately enough, as *The Tank*.

Princess Louise presents Colours to 2A&SH, Parkhurst. Pa in Full Dress

I'm almost certain that it was here that he first met Dick O'Connor, who was on the Directing Staff. In his letter enclosing the money for Pa's portrait in 1954, Dick refers to the fact that Pa was always 'driving west' to see his future bride. Since Marian Blakiston-Houston had a MacAlpine-Downie aunt (the redoubtable Aunt Eff) who lived at Appin, Argyll, there could have been a northern element in his navigation.

It's said that at one point Ma said she had had enough letters and told him not to write any more. His response was to send a telegram.

At all events, on 10th August 1929, they were married in Holy Trinity Church, Ballywalter, Co. Down by the Primate of All Ireland (the Anglican Archbishop of Armagh). 'Our Lady Correspondent' of the *Belfast Newsletter* had a field day reporting on the wedding.[xviii] Apart from Miss Marian Blakiston-Houston's "numerous relations", very few were named unless they had some sort of title. But that still meant that twenty-five people got a mention, along with notes on their attire. Though the catering was done by a Belfast firm, the cake was baked by Mrs. Parker (cook at Roddens and Finlaystone) who later showed me how to make scones and porridge.

Wedding Photograph, 10th August 1929

After dining at Orangefield, the couple took the ferry to Heysham and thence to the Austrian Tyrol for their honeymoon.

By the time of their marriage, Pa must have got to know his future father-in-law, Richard Bailey Blakiston-Houston, known as "Flath", if only through having to ask him for his daughter's hand. He was a large land owner in Northern Ireland who had married Ma's mother, Lilian Kidston, whose father owned Finlaystone, in 1897. He was obviously quite a character and provided a lot of amusement. David recalls how Ma always smiled when she told stories about him, often recounting his many sayings about life:

'Flath'

Flath's Sayings

About a know-all. "He would teach you how to build a clock".

About a mean man. "He would skin a flea for its hide".

About a woman. "She had shins like a Mullingar heifer".

Deep pile carpets in a hotel. "Carpets like snipe bogs".

A notice which he put up on the silo at Roddens, his farm in Co. Down. "If you have nothing to do, don't do it round here".

"Carry a man on your back for a mile, and he will be the first to kick you when you put him down."

"Time, patience and perseverance will drive a snail to Jerusalem."

"I would rather be pecked to death by ducks than talked to death by women."

About this time they also stayed at Appin, where Ma served a kind of apprenticeship to her beloved Aunt Eff. They were put to work cutting stobs and building *fanks* (sheep pens) on the island of Shuna, just off-shore. One gets the impression that it was quite hard work, not rewarded with gushing gratitude. While at Appin, they went fishing on the Sabbath – presumably, the only day they weren't working. As they packed their car with the gear, they were watched disapprovingly by an old man leaning on a gate. Inexplicably, the car burst into flames.

Meeting his bride's numerous aunts must have seemed like a lifetime's task; but it can seldom have been dull. I am grateful to David for the following documentary evidence:

Aunt Eff

Aunt Eff was the youngest of Ma's Blakiston-Houston uncles and aunts. She was married first to James Macalpine-Downie of Appin who died from wounds towards the end of the 1st World War. She later married Arthur Maclintock who died very soon after. Twice bereaved, she continued to farm around Appin in Argyll and also had the island of Shuna as summer grazing. She made the cattle swim across to Shuna in the spring and back again in the autumn.

The story goes that she was having a Sunday lunch party for a lot of relations. At the end of lunch they all remarked what delicious beef she had given them. Aunt Eff replied that she had been lucky as, when she was looking around the cattle on Shuna, she had come across a dead calf and had taken the back leg off it for their lunch.

We went to see her in the mid-1960s when Alastair was still in a basket. She was probably in her 80's and kept herself busy looking after ponies for a grand-daughter. Liv asked her if she could change Alastair: the answer was "Yes, I am afraid that the bath is full of horse food, but the loo works." At lunch we were given a very slippery pudding made in a shape. She told us we had to finish it as a neighbour had given it to her when she heard that she was having guests. Aunt Eff said "She always does it so we must not disappoint her."

After lunch we went with her in her battered old car which she drove in the middle of the road, to check on a dead ewe which she thought she might not have buried deep enough. She was still making hay by hand well into her 80s and would always be watching the weather whenever she came to Finlaystone for anniversary celebrations and the like. One summer she was asked to be a "Granny" in a television film about the massacre of Glencoe. She was meant to sit and knit as an extra. After the first day, before everybody went home, a smooth television executive came round and apologised that nothing had happened. He turned to Aunt Eff and said "Come back in the morning, dear." "No, you had better find yourself another Granny, I have got hay to make tomorrow."

She lived to be just short of 100. Not long before she died she lost an eye from a splinter while splitting firewood. She did not get a glass eye, just saying that at her age she could not be bothered with one.

On another visit to meet her relations Ma took Pa to an aunt on her mother's side. One can imagine how he must have wondered what he was letting himself in for when the aunt came to the front door to welcome the happy couple on all fours, barking like a dog.

The aunt was well known for being eccentric. There is a story that she was very suspicious of a house maid who she was sure was stealing the silver. She told the maid that she was sacked, and that she would be confined to her room until the next morning when she would be taken to the train by the chauffeur. Having done this, she felt sorry for the maid and climbed up a ladder and handed her a bunch of flowers through the bedroom window.

They probably returned to Camberley for the final term of the Staff College course. Ma didn't take easily to the life of an army wife: she talked scornfully of the 'Mandarin wives' – those who congregated at the Mandarin Café for want of something more productive to do.

The plan had been for Pa to rejoin the 91st on leaving the Staff College; but, in fact, he was put on the strength of the Depot in Stirling till his War Office job started on 1st March 1930. That seems to have been a good chance to do some shooting.

He held two consecutive jobs in the War Office – first (possibly under Dick O'Connor) as a Staff Captain, doing a kind of apprenticeship in the Military Secretary's Branch (which deals mainly with appointments), and then, from 19th February 1932, as a G.S.O. 3 doing a proper job in the Military Operations Branch.

No. 11 Ashley Gardens was a convenient base from which a bowler-hatted officer could walk to work. My only recollection of it was that, because it was a flat with another below it, I was constantly being warned not to tread too heavily, because "Mrs. Swain's underneath". I never met the lady in question. The parents were much amused by the care-taker/lift-operator, Mr. Cricket, who remarked of his wife that "Her legs ain't much to look at; but what a top on her!"

The Game Book

One of Pa's favourite leisure activities was shooting; and this provided a good excuse to visit friends in various parts of the country. On the evening after a shoot he recorded the results meticulously in his game book, which, as a result, provides a useful record of his whereabouts throughout much of his life. It also shows how Ma gradually took up the sport – unusually for a woman in those days – and eventually became a good shot.

Pa's game book records plenty of shooting tours between 1929 and 1934. The general pattern consisted of Scottish tours in September and early October and around Christmas, and the occasional excursion from the War Office to various parts of England. Scotland offered lots of informal shooting at Finlaystone, with visits to Appin and (more extended) to Fyvie Castle, the home of the Forbes-Leith family. There was also some stalking, notably with Ian Campbell (his CO in 1918) at Benula, near Inverness.

Entries trace Ma's progress in the field. At first it is "Marian walked all day"; then "Marian carried the game bag". Then, on 4th October 1930, at Fyvie, alone with the Forbes-Leiths, Ma had a "not very successful" go with a 20-bore gun.

Huge bags of rabbits are sometimes recorded:

"Sutton Valance (with the Wheatleys) on 13th December 1930, 96 rabbits and slightly fewer pheasants."

"Fyvie on 30th September 1931 – 2 duck, 1 woodcock, 1 pigeon and 86 rabbits (ferreting)."

Carrying the game bag could have been quite taxing.

Over the next decade Ma made steady progress:

"26th October 1933 - Touch. Copper Buchanan and I shot in morning and part of afternoon. When I left, Marian took my gun and killed a hare" – quite a feat, because Pa's gun was off-set, to allow him to use his left eye.

"20th December 1939 Finlaystone. Fog early and birds wouldn't fly; bad shooting later – except for Marian, who killed nine pheasants (out of 34)."

At the end of June 1932 Pa received this letter: "Sir, I am directed to inform you that you have been selected for promotion to the brevet rank of Major. Such promotion, however, will only be made on the definite understanding that you will not be granted the increment of pay laid down in article 285 or half pay laid down in article 501, Pay Warrant 1931. You will, however, be eligible for all other advantages attaching to Brevet rank – e.g. the higher age limit for compulsory retirement and the counting of brevet rank for the purpose of widow's pension". So he was still on a Captain's pay.

On 27th February 1933 Pa was passed 'Fit' in Glasgow. I suspect this followed a serious accident in the Finlaystone sawmill, when a log hit his head.

'Flath' died on 21st May 1933. His Ulster properties (Roddens and the Orangefield estate) went to his surviving son, Johnny. His widow, Lilian, lived on at Finlaystone.

Pa re-joined the 91st, now in Edinburgh, on 19th December 1933. We lived in 2 successive houses, left temporarily empty by their owners – Abden House (later to be the residence of the Principal of Edinburgh University, until the building of nearby students' residences made it intolerably noisy) and a house in Belgrave Crescent, beside the Dean Bridge.

There was a potentially embarrassing incident at this time. Ma, having ascertained that the GOC would not be using his box for the military tattoo, occupied it with John and me. To her surprise, the General and his entourage turned up; and one of them sat in the chair under which Ma had put the picnic box. She sat tight in the front row – until John needed to visit a loo. Then there was nothing for it but to climb past the assembled multitude. I'm not sure how the picnic box (a three-tier affair) was recovered.

The big event of 1934 was Pa's command of the Guard for the Royal Family at Balmoral between 21st August and 2nd October. The 91st provided three officers and fifty men. The officers, at least, were accompanied by their wives. Their duty was to turn out at Ballater station for the arrival and departure of royalty. The Prince of Wales (later Edward VIII), the Duke of York (Bertie, later George VI), his Duchess, and daughter Elizabeth (our present Queen) and George Duke of Kent and his bride, Princess Marina, arrived at various times. But most of their time was spent attending parties and shooting and fishing both on Balmoral and in the neighbourhood. As the husbands were fully occupied with shooting, it fell to the wives to do the fishing. Ma and a friend caught six of a total of ten salmon.

HM King George V inspects the Guard on arrival, Ballater, 1934

The *Aberdeen Press & Journal* gave minute descriptions of who met the royal train and where, and what the royals were wearing – highland dress or bowler hat. As she left Ballater station the Queen had a word or two with Ma, wearing a toque 'in a new shade of brown', while the King, in a bowler, talked animatedly with Pa as he inspected the guard. The main topic of conversation at all times seems to have been the suitability of the weather for shooting.

The King was described as looking 'very fit'. He died less than two years later (20th January 1936).

Distinguished visitors came and went. One of these was Sister Agnes (Foundress of the King Edward VII Hospital for Officers and a long-time mistress of Edward VII). This formidable lady gave Pa some amusement at a party, when a conjurer asked for a £1 note. No one admitted to having such a thing, except Sister Agnes. To retrieve it she had to expose herself to public view by standing up and raising her skirt to extract her purse from her knickers. When the note was returned unharmed, the process was repeated. Pa had had a previous encounter with Sister Agnes when, shortly after the end of WW1, he went to visit Jack Watson who was recovering from serious wounds in her hospital. Pa was sitting talking to Jack when she came into the ward and spotted his bowler hat lying on the white sheets of his bed. According to Pa, the fearsome lady gave him a monumental rocket for parking his filthy hat on the bed!

At some point in late 1934, Pa ran a course at Redford Barracks for Staff College candidates. A Colonel on the General Staff, in a note dated 14th December, passed on a message of appreciation to Major G.H.A. MacMillan MC from the General Officer Commanding in Chief congratulating him on the 'zealous and efficient way in which he carried out the programme'. Clearly, the incident at the tattoo was now forgotten.

Earlier in 1934 (12th June) Dick O'Connor wrote to tell Pa that he would be leaving next March to be a G.S.O.2 at the Royal Military College (RMC), Kingston, Canada to prepare Canadian officers who had been selected for the Camberley Staff College. He even outlined possibilities for the remoter future – perhaps teaching at the Staff College itself – which didn't happen. He notes in passing that the 91st looked like moving to Tidworth in January 1935. Pa did not go with them. Indeed, he can't have been with them much in December, which was devoted to shooting, mainly at Finlaystone.

In mid-March Pa and Ma left Glasgow on the Anchor liner *SS Caledonia*. John and I lit a chain of minute bonfires along the woodland walk, which would have been invisible from the ship; but the Captain was persuaded to hoot several times as he passed Finlaystone. *The Glasgow Evening News*[xix] noted that they were more important passengers than even they thought:

"Ships that pass … our modest stars … to and from the Clyde.

What do you think of this? Major MacMillan's name was marked on the passenger list as follows: Bt. Major and so on – Bt. Standing for "Brevet", of course.

I asked the bell-boy the way to his cabin, showing him the name on the list. "Oh!", said the small boy smartly: "It's the Baronet's room you want"."

The grounds of the RMC were spacious and beautiful, occupying a peninsula. On one side, across the mouth of the Rideau River, lay Kingston, and on the other, high on a promontory, across a bay, stood the huge ruin of Fort Henry (built to protect the naval dockyards of Kingston from the Americans). But to people accustomed to Balmoral, or even Finlaystone, the officers' married quarters might have been disappointing. They consisted of two parallel rows of flat-roofed, red-brick, two-storey houses, whose back doors faced each other across a dirt track called 'Hogan's Alley' after a neighbour's dog. Each row had once consisted of eight dwellings; but, by now, the houses had been doubled in size and halved in number, so that each had two of everything. There was a small garden front and back – with railings at the back and open (as is normal in North America) in the front –

something that must be rectified forthwith. When John and I and our resourceful nanny arrived in early May, there were wooden boxes everywhere. When smashed, they revealed the ingredients of a hedge for the front garden.

With their base secured, the new arrivals lost no time in getting to know the neighbours – notably the Russells, at the other end of our block. At the end of May the *Whig Standard* reported on a "Very jolly and unique party – a 'treasure hunt' arranged by Mrs. G.H.A. MacMillan and Mrs. C.N. Russell (RMC)." It must have involved huge preparations: "Much of its success was due to the splendid co-operation of shop-keepers and other inhabitants of various communities through which the trail led." It ended with delicious ice-cream in the newly-enclosed garden.[xx]

A fortnight later, the *Montreal Gazette* reported that Major and Mrs. G.H.A. MacMillan had been invited to luncheon at Government House.[xxi] Meanwhile, John and I rode our trike and bike in the RMC's grounds, swam in the lake from the flat rocks below Fort Henry or lay in our wigwam – John chewing the parsley that grew below the kitchen window.

It must have been about now that a gang of labourers, organised under a government scheme for the unemployed, laid a gas or water main along the far side of the road that ran past our house. Ma, who was shorlty to give birth to Judy in August, thought little of their efforts at re-instatement. So she hired a barrow and tools from two 11-year-old entrepreneurs (John Agnew, son of the Deputy Commandant and Jimmy Waite, son of a Squadron Leader colleague of Pa's) and, with a little help from her children, landscaped the whole length of pipe opposite the row of houses. It became known as 'Hogan's Park'.

Between Hogan's Park and the bay lay quite a wide stretch of swampy land, an ideal home for snipe. It's not clear whether Pa obtained, or even sought, permission to do so; but he organised numerous – often fruitless – shoots throughout October 1935 and 1936, though fully aware that the Commandant of the RMC, Brigadier Matthews, disapproved. He did so, it's said, because his house overlooked the shore, and his wife normally enjoyed an afternoon nap.

When Sir Ian (*Beery*) Forbes-Leith came up from New York for a week-end in October 1935, Pa took a rare chance to repay him for his boundless hospitality at Fyvie. The two of them plodded through the marsh, but to little effect. Preparations for this visit had exercised the parental minds for some time beforehand. He was a very tall man (about 6 feet 7 inches) and the metal-framed beds (of a type found in hospitals of the time) were about 6 by 3 feet. Rather than follow Procrustes and amputate his extremities, they decided to lay two beds side-by-side and put the mattresses across them, in the hope that he could sleep on a diagonal. It wouldn't have taken a princess to detect the iron-work under the hospital mattresses. Let's hope that a day's marsh-bashing was an effective anaesthetic.

The Game Book entry for 22/23 October 1935 records an unforgettable shoot on Pelee Island in Lake Erie. The ten guns (Pa, four Colonels and five civilians) shot ninety-six pheasants. The strategy was for the guns to line up along the island's shore and advance to the centre. The game book's comment is brief – 'Dangerous and exhausting'.

While we were in Canada, death struck Pa's family twice – first his father (8th April 1935) and then his Uncle Gordon, killed while hunting on his 71st birthday on 3rd April 1936 (*Judy* had played rugger for Scotland twenty-one times in the late nineteenth century). It must have been frustrating not to be with either his mother or his aunt at the time of their bereavement. Unfortunately, though Amy Johnson and Amelia Earhart were busy flying around at the time, they weren't taking passengers. So sea travel was the only option.

1936 was notable for three extended journeys.

Early in August our intrepid nanny Cowap took John, Judy and me across Canada by train to spend a month at Banff, Alberta. Judy had her first birthday at Winnipeg. We had a lovely holiday, going to the station to see the gigantic engines, which paused for quite a while before continuing their long climb over the Rockies. The drivers would clamber all over them with oil cans and check the stock of sand in boxes for helping the wheels to grip the track. But we spent most of our time in the sulphurous swimming baths of the Banff Springs Hotel. Towards the end of our time there we were joined by our parents, who had driven west by car – a journey complicated by the fact that there was no trunk road right across Canada. That necessitated dipping into the U.S.A. by taking a ferry from Sault Ste Marie to Duluth and re-entering Canada south of Winnipeg. While they were with us, we went on an 'all-day picnic' in the Rockies. I'm sure the scenery was spectacular. But for me the trip was memorable mainly for the fact that we lit a small fire on the shores of the Lake on the Mountain and put potatoes to cook in the ashes – and then drove off, leaving the potatoes snug but unconsumed. We also spent an evening in the car parked on the local rubbish dump, hoping to see bears. I recall the rubbish; but I must have nodded off at the crucial moment, when, according to John, our nanny was so busy watching one bear that she failed to spot another that was sneaking up behind her. She was a very nice nanny; so I'm glad to say she survived.

The parental visit to Banff was incidental to a more ambitious journey, taking in Calgary, where Pa ran a course for militia officers from western Canada at Sarcee Camp, and Vancouver, where he delivered a lecture and they both did some fishing. The Calgary course closed with a memorable party, where one of the students, Jim Dunwoody, OC Fort Garry Horse, 'paid me the compliment of impersonating me – considerably better than I could have done it myself'; and another colonel decided not to go to bed at all.

Vancouver was somewhat more relaxed. Pa was pleased with his catch on the first evening – an eight-pound Blue Back, a Cohoe of 14.5lbs and a Spring of 11.5lbs; but his achievement was eclipsed by Ma's 37.5 pound Tyee – followed next morning by two more of 38.5 and 42 pounds – all landed after a vigorous fight, not made easier by her right wrist, sprained while changing a wheel on a solo drive from Calgary to Banff.

Ma's catch in Vancouver, 1936

While on Vancouver Island, they were taken to see the Butchart gardens and a home at Cowichen where under-nourished British children were being given a healthy re-launch. (In 2008 I too visited Cowichen; but my purpose was less lofty – to sample wine at one of the Island's many burgeoning wineries).

After an extensive tour of the Californian coast as far as San Francisco (where the Golden Gate Bridge was still under construction and Al Capone was behind bars on St. Quentin island), they returned to Kingston by Yosemite, Salt Lake City and a string of mid-western towns which impressed them as little as they did Bill Bryson.

About this time the huge task of restoring Fort Henry was undertaken. For us the main item of interest was a large steam-powered caterpillar-mounted crane which crept snail-like up the road on the far side of the bay. Even with the aid of this giant (whose name was Bucyrus), progress on the restoration was barely perceptible. Yet by 1940 it was judged fit to house German prisoners of war. It's now a thriving visitor attraction. I know, because I visited both Fort Henry and the RMC when participating in a Clan Gathering in Kingston in 2010. At first I missed our house altogether, even though I was fairly sure I must be near its site. On closer inspection I found that the two parallel rows of houses in Hogan's Alley had been enveloped in a glass-roofed structure. The facades of the houses formed the lower part of its outer walls. I assumed that they were now the offices for some kind of storage depot. The view of Fort Henry is now obscured by a colony of students' residences built on the snipe bog of old. The word is that these buildings are notoriously damp. The garden and its hedge have disappeared. But at least it was a comfort to know that, though grotesquely transformed, the house where Judy was born on 7th August 1935 still existed. Perhaps there's wisdom in the maxim 'never go back'.

After giving John and me an exciting Christmas present – a pair of skis each – the parents took trains to New Orleans. Why? It's a long story, and a tragic one from the British point of view.

Not content with fighting Napoleon, Britain was also involved in the so-called 'War of 1812', in which the U.S.A. gave Canada some trouble, and the British managed to burn the Congress building in Washington D.C.. Peace was signed in Ghent on 24th December 1814; but the news didn't reach General Pakenham, who was cruising in the Caribbean, intent on capturing New Orleans. His force of about thirteen thousand men landed about eighty swampy miles from their target. Their slow advance gave Andrew Jackson just enough time to improvise defences, including a rampart and shallow ditch, no more than five or six feet deep, before the British attacked on 8th January 1815.

Their plan was to fill the ditch with fascines (bundles of sticks, as in 'Fascist') and storm the rampart. Unfortunately, the unit that had been given that job 'forgot' the fascines: some say that its commanding officer, Colonel Mullen, thought it too dangerous a task for his men. During the consequent lull, Jackson's men showered their enemy with grape shot and (as Jane and I were told when we visited the field in 2001) with accurate rifle fire, which took out many British officers, including General Pakenham himself. The 93rd Highlanders were particularly hard hit, losing 526 (killed and wounded) out of eight hundred men, including their commanding officer, Colonel Creagh.[xxii] By the time someone eventually ordered a retreat, the British had lost 3000 men and the Americans nineteen. Colonel Creagh was wrapped in the colours of the 93rd, which, after his burial, were brought home and presented to his family.

In the early 1920s, Colonel Creagh's descendant, a Miss Creagh, gave the colours to the 91st & 93rd to hang in Stirling Castle. Although we have no record of that presentation, it clearly caught the imagination of the young Acting Captain MacMillan, who "thought it would be interesting to visit the battlefield if he was ever in North America". That's his side of the story.

Various local newspaper reporters saw it differently. Here are some excerpts from their articles, based loosely on a 'polite' interview in their hotel room soon after they arrived by train from Kingston.

From the *Times-Picayune*: "There will be none of the bare-kneed marching of highland clans to the pibroch's skirling of 'The Campbells are coming' and 'Hielan Laddie' at Chalmette field today as a Scottish officer reviews his regiment.

"It will be a unique review, born of the promise made fifteen years ago by Major G.H.A. MacMillan MC of men dead more than a century under the aim of Andrew Jackson's Tennessee riflemen at the battle of New Orleans... (At the presentation of the colours) Major MacMillan made a silent vow to his comrades in colours of a century and a quarter ago that, if he should ever reach this continent, he would pay a tribute to their valour and a visit to their graves.... Major MacMillan, accompanied by his Scots-Irish wife, is ready to keep that pledge....

"The annual observance of the Battle of New Orleans will take place on January 10th with bands playing. But today a Scottish tribute will be paid to gallant dead and Major MacMillan will whistle the bars of 'The Campbells are coming' at the review of the dead; for that is not only his battalion's battle air, but his clan's cry as well. His grandmother was a Campbell."[xxiii]

From *The New Orleans States*: "A tall handsome officer of one of General Pakenham's highland regiments surveyed the Chalmette battlefield again today. But no plans for assault upon

New Orleans were in the mind of Major G.H.A. MacMillan of the Argyll & Sutherland Highlanders. His most dangerous weapon was a folding camera in the hands of his bonnie wife, who took pictures of interesting points on the field."

From the *New Orleans Item*: "Because he made a solemn vow to the memory of clansmen dead more than a century, a British army officer climbed, pants splattered with mud, to the levee behind the Chalmette battlefield and stood a moment silently watching the heavy mist rise over the river.... Major MacMillan, blond with short-clipped moustache, plans to report his tour to the Regimental quarterly magazine, using the snapshots taken by his wife, brown-haired, blue-eyed, fair skinned."

Pa's article in the *Thin Red Line* opened with an expression of "considerable shock" at the "author's inventions including a statement that I had made a solemn vow at Stirling Castle fifteen years ago that one day I would "honour the dead" at New Orleans…and "would whistle the tune of "The Campbells are coming"…!!" But from his account of their visit, it's clear that they were given a very warm welcome as a result of this publicity and shown sites of interest, including the levees, which featured in the recent events surrounding Hurricane Katrina. We're also given a glimpse of New Orleans social life to which they were invited.

"Fortunately for us we had an introduction to some kind residents in New Orleans, who entertained us most hospitably in our spare time. Part of this entertainment included taking us to the "Harlequins Ball", a costly, exclusive entertainment, half pantomime and half masked ball, at which debutantes were "presented" to a "Queen". After this serious ceremony was over, the "youth" (masked and disguised as beetles) danced with the "beauty" who were not masked but seated in the stalls in the huge auditorium where the entertainment took place, anxiously awaiting a summons to take the floor. These lavish entertainments, we were informed, take place almost weekly during the New Orleans season, culminating in the Mardi Gras Festival. No supper is served and the whole show is over by about midnight, but much money is expended on the band, the scenery and the dresses of the participants, not to mention favours for the fortunate ladies, and it is probable that no such spectacle of its kind could be seen anywhere else in the world."

The winter of 1936/7 proved unusually snow-free. On their return from New Orleans, the parents took us to try skiing on a thin veneer of slush on a golf course – a good try, but a disappointment for us all.

In the spring of 1937 we returned to Britain by separate ships and were soon re-united in the Old Rectory, Fittleton, adjacent to Netheravon on the edge of Salisbury Plain. As from 13th April, Pa was back with the 91st, based at Tidworth. It was a glorious summer. We crossed the plain in a baby Austin to attend a nice little school. The trip was sometimes enlivened by the sight of a red flag – a sign that live ammunition was being fired. Once at school, John and I did mental arithmetic; I read a simplified version of the Pilgrim's Progress; we sang hymns like 'Holy, holy, holy…' and our dear head-mistress explained the doctrine of the Trinity. The big event of the year was the coronation of George VI on 12th May.

Our chief occupation was walking in the local lanes with Ma looking for wild flowers to press. She amassed a formidable collection.

While growing up in Ireland she had been a keen horsewoman, training polo ponies on the shore near Roddens. Our summer on Salisbury Plain must have seemed a good chance to introduce John and me to the horse. After church parades we occasionally mounted the regimental mascot, a minute Shetland pony called (traditionally) Cruachan. One day I found myself on a larger beast with some such name as 'Toots', but not for long: it stopped rather suddenly, projecting me over its head. My reluctance to remount must have been a disappointment to Ma, but easily understood by Pa.

At some point there was a big parade. As Pa marched past us, drawn sword in hand, at the head of his company, they suddenly broke into a 'yomp' (as it might now be called) in perfect formation, with a detachment of tanks rumbling close behind them. That was our only sight of Pa 'in action'.

It must have been about this time that Ma and Pa became increasingly aware that my sight was deteriorating rapidly. In those days the group of diseases known now as *Retinitis Pigmentosa* was unnamed and mysterious. Their own sight was excellent, and no other known member of either of their families had shown signs of poor sight on this scale. It must have been distressing for them but they handled it with characteristic care, efficiency and lack of fuss – so much so that I, for one, was hardly aware that there was a problem. I was immediately taught Braille and touch-typing. I spent a day having pictures painted of the backs of both eyes to aid consultation with an Austrian specialist. We regularly visited eminent Glasgow oculists, and even a faith-healer.

Like me, Judy and David eventually also developed similar symptoms from about the age of seven. Our parents recognised that our sight at that time, with a few aids, would allow us to cope with life in a sighted school and the schools generally responded well to their challenge. Apart from taking us to various specialists, our parents treated all of us in the same way, without becoming over-protective, nor ever making our impaired sight an issue that demanded that we be given special treatment. This great sensitivity on their part helped to make life easier for us, so that we have never felt different or excluded from being involved in anything.

Towards the summer's end Pa drove us to Euston to catch the Coronation Scot for Glasgow – a non-stop journey of six and a half hours (about two hours quicker than normal). As we flashed under bridges and over level crossings, we occasionally consulted *The Track of the Coronation Scot*, a booklet that documented every one. We were on our way to stay at Finlaystone while the parents moved to 47 Chester Square so that Pa could take up the post of G.S.O.2 Staff Duties Branch 3 in the War Office.

His job, for part of this period at least, was concerned with Officer Training Corps, mainly, if not exclusively, in public schools. It gave him an opportunity to assess the schools, as well as their O.T.C.s. He put Eton and Ampleforth at the top of his list, largely because boys were given more responsibility than elsewhere.

Meanwhile, we lived in some style, supported by a Captain's pay supplemented by fees for marking promotion exams, and, very probably, by Ma's investments. The square was spacious and lent itself to children's games – unless Miss Webster (the resident of number 60) took exception. Like Mrs Swain in Ashley Gardens, she never seemed to appear in person; but the mere mention of her name could quell a riot. I remember Pa trying to teach John and me to play cricket. We must have been disappointing pupils: I recall only one session.

On week-days John and I attended Eaton House, just short of Sloane Square. We all spent almost every Sunday at Hillingdon House, Harlow, where our kind aunt Emily gave us lunch before we all settled down to work on our 'allotments' in her garden. John and I did very well on tulips, which were sold for us in a flower shop round the corner from Chester Square by Margaret Swanson (a step-daughter of the conductor Sir Adrian Boult). She and her friend Grace Dove were to re-emerge in the early 1950s, when Ma was beginning to arrange flowers as a business around Edinburgh.

On 1st August 1938 Pa was at last made up to a substantive Major. The consequent pay rise would have helped to pay for the house, the car, the cook and the nanny. Although Pa was not responsible for his pay, it was here that Mault, the batman, began an association that lasted well beyond the end of the Second World War. Perhaps the rise in income allowed Pa to take time off to read to us of an evening – A.A.

Milne, Kipling's Just So Stories and articles from Blackwood's Magazine, as I remember. Meanwhile, Ma made patchwork bedspreads, knitted at high speed or worked on her set of twelve dining-room chair-seat covers. Of these, all but the last (which was still in the making) were burnt along with almost all their possessions when Hitler's people dropped an incendiary bomb on a warehouse in Pimlico during the 1940 Blitz.

Ma's masterpiece in needlework also had a lucky escape. Though we think it dates from Chester Square days, it was not put into storage when war broke out. This was a pipe banner with the MacMillan two-handed sword in gold and silver on one side and the Regimental Crest (the Cat and the Boar's Head) on the other – all done in the minutest of stitching. On his promotion to Major, Pa became entitled to have his banner flown from the drone of a member of the Regimental Pipe Band. Since the cost of having it made professionally was well beyond his pocket, Ma volunteered her services. Having no experience of fine needlework, she attended classes at the Royal School of Needlework and applied her newly-acquired skills to the banner while they were still fresh in her mind.

The biggest social event of this period was the wedding of Neil (later Gen. Sir Neil) Ritchie to Sunny Minnis in St. Columba's Church in Pont Street. The reception was held in 47 Chester Square – a very tight fit. John and I (perhaps assisted by the staff of the Mayfair Catering Company) were given things to hand round. Such was the throng that our only recourse was to crawl round people's feet, occasionally emerging to offer a dish to surprised – even, perhaps, embarrassed – guests. During the war Sunny (who was Canadian) spent some time at Finlaystone, while she packed Red Cross parcels in Glasgow for prisoners of war, while Neil briefly commanded the 8th Army in the Western Desert.

When not at Hillingdon, we sometimes visited Hurlingham Club, of which Pa seemed to be a member. We saw the occasional polo match or glanced at men in white kit, fencing. But the main source of interest was the tiger lilies, whose bulbils we collected and propagated – a long-term project, as it took at least two years to produce a flower.

For a year, perhaps, we had a German au pair girl, Gretel. Looking back, it's possible that Hitler had sent her, among many others, to see what was going on in Britain. If so, I doubt if she justified his investment: perhaps she told him where the chair covers went.

David was born on 15th January 1939. Not long afterwards, Hyde Park was desecrated by the excavation of air raid shelters. After the summer term, John, Judy, David and I, with Nanny Fortescue, were despatched to Finlaystone. The parents stayed on for some time in London. Pa's work took him to H.Q. Eastern Command at Hounslow. I think Ma started working for the Victoria League (whose purpose was to strengthen ties between the nations of the British Empire) – work for which she later received an OBE.

School holidays were now invariably spent at Finlaystone.

War was declared on 3rd September; and about a fortnight later John (aged seven and a half) and I (nine) took the train for Aysgarth. Tommy Thompson, the headmaster, met us at Darlington. As he drove us to the school, he pointed to a speck in the bright sky and said "That's a Spitfire".

CHAPTER 4

The Second World War (1939-1945)

by
John

Synopsis

In contrast to Pa's earlier military career, which had seen his acknowledged excellence rewarded with a promotion rate that would seem snail-like in the modern day, World War 2 brought a rapid rise through the ranks. It had taken 23 years from his commissioning for him to reach the substantive rank of Major in 1938. Between April 1940 and May 1943 he went from Major to Major General!

At the beginning of the war he was on his third staff appointment as a Major at Eastern Command, where he spent a year until he was posted to HQ 55th Division in April 1940 as Lieutenant Colonel. In May 1941 he took command of 199 (Lancastrian) Brigade, and became a Brigadier. He held this appointment until December, when he was chosen to be the Brigadier General Staff in the Headquarters of 9 Corps, preparing for the invasion of North Africa. As the battle for Tunisia ended, he began a series of rapid moves, all in his rank of Brigadier.

From 5th to 27th May 1943 he was Brigadier General Staff 1st Army. He then commanded 12 Infantry Brigade for a month, and was finally moved to command 152 Infantry Brigade, which he prepared for the invasion of Sicily. When victory in Sicily had been achieved, he was brought back to England and given command of 15th (Scottish) Division, being promoted to Major General in August 1943. He remained a Major General until the end of the war.

All the ranks mentioned were 'temporary' or 'acting', and, as was the case for most officers in the British army at the time, his substantive rank took a long time to catch up with the reality of the posts he was filling. For example, having filled Brigadiers' posts since 1941 and been a Major General since 1943, the War Office gazetted him as a Colonel in November 1944!

His periods in command of 152 Brigade and 15th (Scottish) Division were probably the most exciting and satisfying of his wartime career. After being wounded in Normandy while commanding 15th (Scottish) Division, he returned to command 49th (West Riding) Division during the winter of 1944, and was then transferred to command of 51st (Highland) Division immediately after the Rhine crossing. Both the latter phases of the conflict involved battles at Brigade and Battalion level, and the scope for command at Divisional level was largely in maintaining the support of these lower formations rather than conducting major engagements.

When the War ended, 51st (Scottish) Division was at Bremerhaven, and his war concluded with the co-ordination of the victory parade in that part of Germany. Shortly afterwards he was posted to the War Office in London as Director of Weapons and Development.[xxiv]

On the Home Front (1939-1942)

When war was declared on 3rd September 1939, Pa was nine months into his time as a Major on the staff of HQ Eastern Command at Hounslow, having completed two years in a similar appointment in the Training Branch of the War Office. He had been able to commute to Hounslow from our beautiful rented house in Chester Square, though he must have found it less attractive than walking through St James' Park to get to his office in the War Office. From the family point of view, the change in his work made no difference and George and I continued to go as day-boys to Eaton House School in Eaton Gate. George was due to start boarding at Aysgarth School in north Yorkshire in late September, and, as Eaton House had decided to leave London and become a boarding school somewhere in the south of England, it was more sensible for me to go to Aysgarth at the same time as George, although I was still six months younger than the usual age for boarders.

We were at Finlaystone for the summer holidays when war was declared and I remember hearing Chamberlain's broadcast. Being just 7 years old, it didn't mean a lot to me, but Granny and Ma were pretty gloomy, having seen it all before and being under no illusions about the horrors of war. Everyone had been indoctrinated with the idea that any future war would be dominated by bombing, and the sirens sounded that afternoon just to rub it in.

Pa must have then moved into a mess or a club, as the house was packed up, and all but the most essential items were put into store in Pimlico; a few, including some photograph albums came up to Finlaystone, which became our home until we moved to Gogar Bank, near Edinburgh, in 1948 when Pa was appointed GOC Scotland.

It is hard to find any detail of Pa's work in Eastern District, though the Headquarters as a whole must have been concerned in the mobilization of troops and units for the defence of the Eastern seaboard of England as far north as its junction with Northern Command at The Wash. Either in this appointment or in his next one, as the senior Staff Officer at Headquarters 55th Division in 1941, it is alleged that he and Neil Ritchie, who was later to command the 8th Army, were involved in experiments to provide night illumination by shining searchlights against the clouds. If this is so it would have been the precursor to what later became known as *Monty's Moonlight* which was used extensively in Normandy and in the subsequent battles in France and the Low Countries. The *Great Showman* would have been glad to have a real success linked with his name!

The move to 55th Division took place in April 1940. At this time the defensive structure consisted of coastal forces and the Home Guard being largely responsible for watching the coast for signs of an invasion. There were also formations, mainly comprising Territorial battalions, grouped strategically to engage any airborne landings, or to move swiftly to any coastal areas where the enemy was attempting to establish a foothold. Support for these battalions was very limited, as most of the armour and artillery had gone to France where much was abandoned at Dunkirk: transport consisted of a motley collection of requisitioned cars and buses.

55th Division conducted many exercises to practice the control of movement from the deployment areas to those points on the coast or in the interior where enemy landings were anticipated. At divisional level, these were largely skeleton exercises, but the brigades practised the moves as complete formations, often ending in the recognised training areas around Catterick and Thetford where more exercises would take place over periods of several weeks. The 1942 War Diaries show 55th Division and 199 Brigade being in Northern Command, though it is possible that while Pa was in the Division it was part of Eastern District and its role in home defence covered East Anglia. Formation moves were not uncommon, and at the end of 1942 the records show that the Division was transferred once more, to the South West of England.

Whatever the locations, Pa was General Staff Officer (Grade 1) (GSO1) of 55th Division from April 1940 until May 1941. At that time he became the commander of 199 (Lancastrian) Brigade, comprising 2nd/8th Lancashire Fusiliers, and 6th and 7th Battalions the Manchester Regiment. These were all Territorial battalions, and the Brigade Headquarters would have initially been largely staffed by territorials, reinforced by an increasing proportion of regulars on mobilisation. Whether Pa imported him in his time or he arrived subsequently, it is interesting to see that the Brigade Major in 1942 was Leslie Neilson, who later commanded the Argylls. Judging by Pa's comments in his 1977 interview with Peter Liddle, about dealing with less than satisfactory officers in the First World War,[xxv] one suspects that he may have eased the previous Brigade Major on his way and found someone on whom he could rely to replace him. Indeed, rumour has it that he was given command of the Brigade because he persuaded the Divisional Commander that the previous commander should be eased out, and was told that he ought to go and try to run it better!

One document written by Pa remains from this time. It consists of the Foreword and first chapter of a training directive. The Foreword is concerned with a comparison with the efforts that top class athletes and sportsmen put into training in the techniques of their sports, and the attitude to military training which considers people should know the principles, but not take them to the next stage which is to translate them into rules of conduct.

He stresses that "a soldier on the battlefield, beset by fear and doubt, is far more in need of a guide to action than any games player at Lords or Wimbledon. Better to know instinctively some orthodox line of conduct than to be paralysed by the uncertainty of what to do. Let us, therefore, study and draw up some lines of conduct – simple guides for the simple soldier – so that we may ensure that our soldiers, when faced with problems on the battlefield, will have an answer to them."

In the chapter on 'The Attack', he stresses the need for very swift reaction to any enemy landing, so that he may be thrown off balance before he can get properly established. No doubt he had seen the pedestrian reaction of many British and French formations during the Blitzkrieg, and learnt that the German approach often put speed before security, and therefore left them vulnerable to a swift and determined counter-attack. To enable the Brigade to achieve this, he insisted on a study of the many options that could face his troops in their wide-spread area of operations, and the drawing up of contingency plans so that there was no dithering about what to do next if an airborne or seaborne landing should take place. Luckily this was never put to the test, and he was faced with another range of problems when the Government began to consider how to take the war to the enemy.

He left 199 Brigade on 27th December 1941 to become the Chief Staff Officer in Headquarters 9 Corps. The Corps had been responsible for the defence of England north of The Wash, both as a fighting formation and as the co-ordinating HQ for all activity involving the Police, Home Guard, Coast Guard, and strategic industry. A paper, signed by an old friend of Pa's (General Gregson Ellis, known to us as *The Mousey Man*) in the War Office, recommended the formation of two Corps Headquarters capable of taking any two, three or four divisions under command for operations. 8 and 9 Corps HQs were hived off from their respective area commands, and botched together from any ingredients that they could persuade the War Office to pass their way. Pa's responsibility was to bring this motley collection together, to provide the basic rules by which it would operate, in the shape of Standing Orders, and then to implement the Corps Commander's orders to train and exercise it. General Francis Nosworthy was his first Corps Commander, and at some later date he was succeeded by General John Crocker.

Initially the task of the two new corps was to strengthen the command of the operational formations involved in the defence of the UK. 9 Corps was given command of 3rd Division, 53rd Division and 9th Armoured Division and, over the period immediately after it became effective, it was supporting Eastern Command. The Main Headquarters moved to Cockley Cley in Norfolk, close to the Stanford training area.

In December 1942 the Corps Commander went to visit the Chief of the Imperial General Staff (CIGS). I assume that this was for the start of the planning for the Corps' deployment as part of the invasion force for North Africa. By this time the Signal Squadron had at last acquired the necessary sets to provide a very limited communication system. In the summer of 1942 they had designed the vehicles which would provide the offices and radio stations but were still getting delivery of them late into the autumn. This meant that there were only two fully equipped exercises before they went to the Clyde to embark for North Africa in February 1943. By this time some troops, such as Transport Units, Military Police and Medical and Supply Units had been added to the Corps' structure. These elements now had a race against time to acquire all they needed to operate far from home, and to carry out exercises to prove that the systems worked before they were used in earnest. One of the papers deposited in the Imperial War Museum gives the Staff Table for the allocation of vehicles and the groupings for movement of the elements of the Headquarters and the Corps troops. No doubt Pa had taken a close personal interest in drawing this up, and in ensuring that the vehicles were stowed in an appropriate order when they set sail from the Tail of the Bank.

North Africa
Map 2. **9 Corps Operations in Tunisia** (March to May 1943)

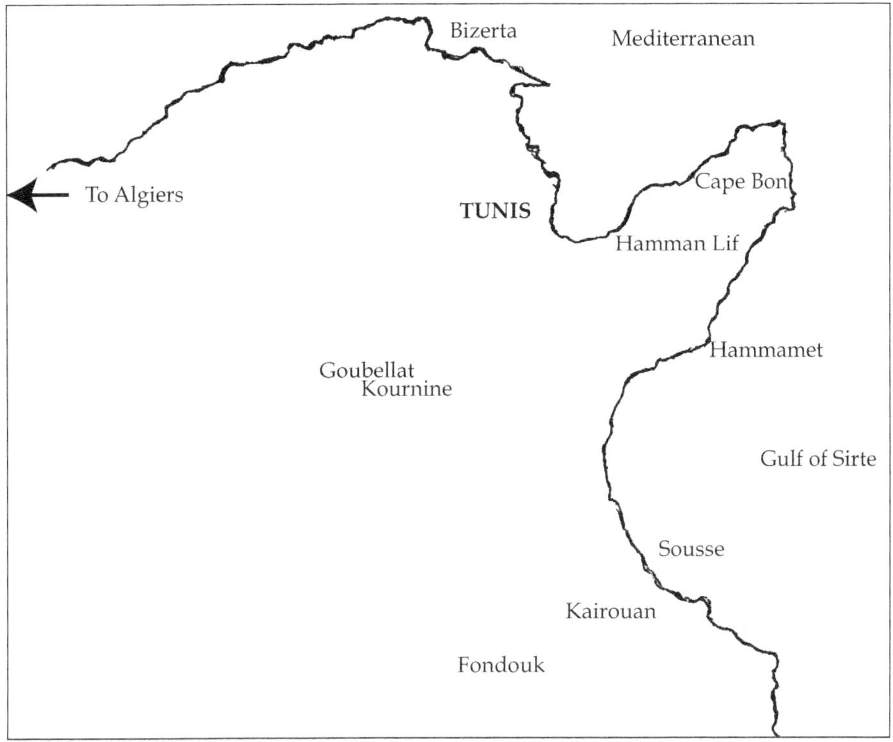

9 Corps Headquarters was at last established and ready for operations by 23rd March, with all vehicles and troops concentrated at El Kasr, not far from Algiers where disembarkation had taken place. 6th Armoured Division was placed under the Corps' command, and was the only formation which would be a constant element of the Corps during the eventful two months of this fast moving campaign. In outline, the Corps was to fight three major battles and travel 470 miles, involving fifteen Headquarters moves in six weeks. For each battle the infantry divisions were always different, providing a challenging problem of co-ordination at the level of Corps Headquarters. The fact that flanking formations were as likely to be United States or Free French forces as British added an extra dimension.

Fondouk

The first battle took place near Fondouk, and led on to the junction of forces of the First Army with leading elements of the Eighth Army, advancing north to Kairouan. The battle was not a simple one, as it depended on the French advancing on the northern flank of 9 Corps, and the US Army securing objectives south of Fondouk. The British elements of 9 Corps were positioned between the French and the US forces, and the US 34th Infantry Division was placed under command of General Crocker. His plan was for British forces to take the high ground on the north-east side of the Fondouk pass, and for the Americans to do likewise on the south western side. The armour would then pass through the gap and race on to cut off any enemy withdrawing in the face of the Eighth Army's northward advance parallel to the coast.

34th Infantry Division had already made two unsuccessful attempts to take their objectives, but their failure had been attributed to sending too small a force to take on a difficult task. With a more substantial effort, working in parallel with the assault by the leading elements of 9 Corps on their left, General Crocker believed they would be successful this time. General Ryder, commanding 34th Infantry Division, pointed out the difficulty he anticipated but was overridden.

The battle was meant to open on 7th April with a heavy aerial bombardment, but the Americans asked for a postponement of H-hour as they were snarled up in traffic jams on their approach to the start line. The Air Force was unable to provide the bombardment at the later time, so the opposition was insufficiently softened to allow the Americans to make the progress intended.

In the event, the advance on the British front also went less speedily than had been hoped, and the key feature of Djebel Ain el Rhorab was not taken until late on 8th April, thus exposing the Americans to a degree of fire from their left flank that caused them casualties and a serious delay. The outcome was that by 9th April the ground between the British and American forces, over which the armoured breakout was to take place, was still exposed to enemy fire, and sappers working on their feet were unable to clear the minefields to permit the tanks to pass through. 17/21st Lancers were told to break through at any cost, and between 9 and 11am they tried many lines of approach, only to lose large numbers of tanks to mines or gunfire. They did, however, identify a possible route, where the dry *wadi* gave a degree of cover, and 16/5th Lancers succeeded in forcing this gap, albeit after further considerable losses to their tanks. The features on either side of the pass were at last in allied hands by the evening of 9th April. 6 Armoured Brigade then took up the battle and were able to make contact with elements of the Eighth Army at Kairouan during 10th April.

The delay unfortunately permitted more Axis forces to withdraw safely to the north, and thus prolonged the campaign in North Africa. The fact that the German commander had had to divert a number of units and artillery and anti-tank weapons to contain the Corps thrust through the Fondouk Pass meant that the resistance elsewhere was weakened, and, once the break-out was achieved, withdrawal was the only option left to him.

The ultimate success of the battle was unfortunately marred by recriminations on the part of both the British and the Americans. In the official US military history, *The US Army in World War 2, North West Africa*, Pa is quoted as having made a statement to the author in 1950. General Crocker had stated that the US 34th Division was not fit for offensive operations and required retraining (rather tactlessly it was suggested that the British should do this training).The Americans maintained that the plan was flawed in the first place and that General Crocker and his Chief of Staff, Brigadier Gordon MacMillan, had both underestimated the strength of the force holding Djebel Ain el Rohrab and the key role that this feature held as a point from which to control fire on to the flanks of the American advance.

Subsequent operations of 34th Infantry Division were confined to tasks which were well within their capability, and, once confidence born of minor victories had been built up, they had a most successful campaign in Italy. This is reminiscent of the experience of 93rd Highlanders in World War 1 when they were tasked with introducing newly arrived US troops to the realities of operations. Perhaps Pa and General Crocker appreciated how much the British had already learnt since 1939, and genuinely felt that the Americans could benefit from such instruction.

It is likely that this was the occasion that Pa came into contact with General Patton, who had come to carry out a post-mortem on the action, and to inject new life into 34th Division. He is reputed to have said that too many casualties were being inflicted on US troops who were not wearing helmets. They were to be worn at all times, and anyone found disobeying this order would be shot.

The first person arrested and marched in to him was a Brigadier General. "Well, General, you know the penalty?" "Yessir" was the reply. "Right! That'll be 20 bucks."

The excellent report of the battle by Alan Moorehead in *The End in Africa* describes the electric effect this battle had on the morale of the First Army, who could now scent final victory, after a long slogging match. He also says that the American formations who failed here learnt quickly and were superb in the final stages in Tunisia.

Goubellat and Kournine

Once the two Armies had linked up, the final phases of the campaign were fought as a single operation. While Montgomery pushed northwards along the coast of the Gulf of Sirte, the First Army attempted to drive further wedges into the flank of the retreating enemy, cutting their escape routes to Tunis and Cape Bon. Formations were moved rapidly from the Eighth Army to join in these operations alongside the First Army. For the next battle, some forty miles north of Kairouan, 9 Corps comprised its old friends from 6th Armoured Division plus 1st Armoured Division and 46th Infantry Division, which included the tanks of 5th Battalion The Royal Tank Regiment. In conjunction with 8 Corps' assault on Longstop Hill to the north, 9 Corps was to make a breach in the defences before Mount Kournine and press on once more to cut the coast road.

This did not go altogether as planned. The start was thrown by a fierce German counter-attack on the left where the infantry of 46th Division were forming up to make the initial assault, while 138 Brigade on the right were initially successful, but were driven off their first objectives by another counter-attack. The battle swung once more and the infantry on the left managed to breach the positions and allow 6th Armoured Division to pass through. Trying to exploit this success, a hook by 1st Armoured Division even further to the left to encircle the troops delaying 6th Armoured Division's advance, unfortunately came to a halt, necessitating yet another change of plan. Instead of outflanking the enemy, 1st Armoured Division was ordered to come in behind the weary forces of 6th Armoured Division and pass through them to renew the attack. This enabled the Corps to reach Kournine but the opposition was too strong for them to press on all the way to the coast. Despite failing to attain their objective, the Corps had diverted large numbers of the enemy from other areas of the battlefield, and helped make the successes elsewhere possible.

A battle of this complexity must have been a nightmare for the staff at Corps Headquarters, where the many changes in plan would have had enormous repercussions on all the forms of support which the Corps had to co-ordinate. These would include rescheduling the artillery and air support, controlling the few routes up which supplies and fighting vehicles had to travel, arranging for transferring responsibilities and boundaries between the divisions and feeding the fighting formations with the latest intelligence on the enemy in a very fluid situation. All this would be the responsibility of the Brigadier General Staff, while the Corps Commander visited every critical point on the battlefield and made the overall decisions. This activity was all taking place with the threat of a small but effective enemy air force ready to cause havoc if the Headquarters could be located, and with communications to the forward troops strained to the limit. The fact that such a complex battle took place with the degree of success that was achieved reflects credit not only on the front line troops but also on those who were juggling with these problems and creating order out of what was potentially chaos.

By 26th April a stable situation had been achieved and 9 Corps once more moved northwards and took new formations under command for the final phase of the Tunisian campaign.

Tunis and Cape Bon

For the assault on Tunis and the destruction of the Axis forces before they could escape at Cape Bon, 9 Corps was allotted 4th Indian Division and 4th British Division (both infantry divisions), 7th Armoured Division and their old faithfuls, 6th Armoured Division. While the northern coast line was to be cleared by other formations, 9 Corps was to approach Tunis with a frontal assault from the South West. The two infantry divisions led the attack, following close on the heels of an aerial and artillery bombardment. Progress was slow to start with, and the opposition determined, but, once a breakthrough had been achieved late on 6th May, the defence crumbled and troops entered the suburbs on 7th May. The final phase of the campaign succeeded because of the dash and determination of 6th Armoured Division who drove relentlessly for the coast. In a night attack on Hamman Lif they destroyed the last strongpoint that the Germans tried seriously to defend, and continued their assault till they had secured Hammamet. This effectively cut the Axis formations in two, with those south of Hammamet unable to escape the Eighth Army driving northwards, and those already in the pocket of Cape Bon disoriented, and unable to flee in boats which were promised but never came, and out of contact with their command structure which had been torn apart by the rapid advances. A vivid description of the procession of Axis vehicles, overflowing with troops who had discarded their weapons and were seeking the security of prisoner of war status, can be found in *The End in Africa*.

By 13th May the operation, and the Tunisian Campaign, were complete. The following day Pa was transferred to be Brigadier General Staff at the Headquarters of First Army.

He would not have known it at the time, but Lt. Gen. John Crocker wrote the citation covering Pa's contribution to the success of this campaign on 17th May. He said:

In just over 40 days 9 Corps has carried out 15 operational moves over a distance of 450 miles and conducted three major operations.

It is largely due to Brig. MacMillan, in his capacity as BGS, that the HQ has met the demands made upon it with such success. His knowledge, drive and ability have produced a smooth-working efficient organisation which has created a feeling of confidence in the constantly changing formations under its control and thus made a considerable contribution to the successful outcome of the operations in which it has taken part.

I consider his service during this campaign to have been of a very high order and worthy of recognition.

The recommendation was for the DSO. He was awarded the CBE, gazetted on 5th August 1943.

The Sicilian Campaign

Few appointments can have been so high-profile or so brief as Pa's time at First Army Headquarters.

9 Corps was no longer required in theatre and prepared to go back to UK.

Pa joined First Army Headquarters for an extraordinarily brief yet high profile appointment as Brigadier General Staff.

While the main tasks of the Headquarters fell to the administrative staff, establishing prison camps, securing enemy weapons, and re-equipping the formations for the next phase of the war, the General Staff was immersed in the plans for the Victory Parade.

Within five days of the end of hostilities, arrangements were made for representatives of the French, US and British armies and Air Forces to move into staging camps close to Tunis, to rehearse and to parade, and finally to disperse to the many camps where their parent units were regrouping for the next phase of the war. Regiments which had been immersed in the battles in the desert, and in the more luxuriant plains and hills of Tunisia, had to find respectable uniforms, and where possible, the musical instruments of the pipe, fife, bugle and military bands. Forming up areas for this mass of troops were identified, and the Air Forces of the allied nations were tasked to present a fly-past to round off the parade. Pa kept the schedule of participating formations among his papers, clearly appreciating that this was a monumental endeavour, with 26,000 troops marching past the saluting base, which went off without a hitch. I remember him saying that some American General was immensely impressed by the way the British formations marched past with their hobnailed boots ringing on the cobble stones. The US infantry, with rubber soled boots, could not match them in any way. The British army now has rubber soles!

An interesting coincidence for Pa was that Montgomery decided to honour the French "L-Force", headed by General Philippe Leclerc, for its contribution to the North African campaign by designating it as the lead formation in the victory parade.[xxvi] Leclerc had been the young Philippe de Hauteclocque who, together with his sisters, had signed the treasured postcard in 1917: he had changed his name when he joined de Gaulle and the Free French in London in 1940, to reduce the risk that the Germans then occupying France might take reprisals on his family. Deeply scathing of former Vichy commanders in North Africa, he had refused to be part of the main French contingent in the Tunis parade. Pa and Philippe must have met again then, but whether they recognised each other after 26 years and a change of name, we do not know. Leclerc subsequently held very important commands during World War II, and was awarded both a KCB and a DSO by the British. He led the first French division to enter Paris in 1944 and subsequently signed the Armistice with the Japanese, on behalf of the French Government. By then known as General Philippe Leclerc de Hautecloque, he died in an air crash in Algeria in 1947, and was posthumously appointed Marshal of France in 1952.

Meanwhile the Eighth Army, which had fought through the desert, took command of all the troops who were to land somewhere on 'the soft under-belly of Europe'. Much speculation took place over the scene of the invasion, with confusion being spread in Axis minds through many different means of which the most complex, and probably the most effective, was the launching of *The Man Who Never Was* close to the Spanish shore, with documents relating to the forthcoming landing in Greece.[xxvii]

In this period of reorganisation and training for an amphibious and airborne invasion, Pa was first posted to command 12 Infantry Brigade to which he reported immediately after the Victory Parade, only to move some 4 weeks later on 22nd June to command 152 Infantry Brigade.

This command was highly appropriate, as it was one of the three brigades in 51st Highland Division, with 2nd and 5th Seaforths and 5th Camerons forming the battalions of the brigade. The Headquarters was also largely staffed by officers and men from these regiments. Among those who became lifelong friends was the Brigade Major, Ian Robertson who, in the 1960's, as Major General, commanded the 51st Highland Division.

The Brigade was undergoing amphibious training with the Royal Navy at Djebilli, a delightful spot of cliffs and comparatively green hinterland that contrasted with the desert which had been all that most of the men had known for the past two years. Shortly afterwards they moved to a dustier training area near Souse, to prepare for the engagements they expected to meet when they landed at what was still an unknown destination. Bathing in the blue Mediterranean made up for the energetic training that took place further inland. The presence of a Greek interpreter added to the belief that the destination could be Greece or Crete.

Map 3. **152 Brigade Operations in Sicily** (July to August 1943)

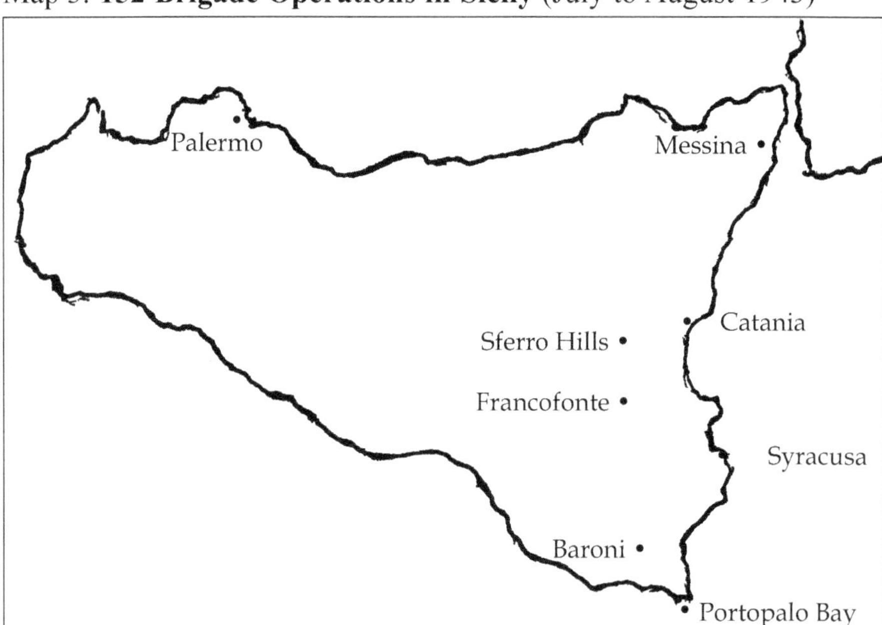

It was only 19 days after he took over its command that the Brigade landed in the South East corner of Sicily, at Portopalo Bay on 10th July. The beach head had been secured by the other two brigades in the Division. 152 Brigade were able to move off inland at 2300hrs, having first hit the beach only ten hours earlier. They moved without transport, and their supporting artillery was still disembarking during the night, so that they were not available to support the infantry until 0900hrs on 11th July. A reconnaissance carried out at first light that day showed the layout of the defences near Baroni, and a copy-book engagement followed. Two companies of 5th Camerons moved round the left of the defended location and totally outflanked it, having been concealed by the low hills between their line of march and the objective, while the troop of tanks in support of the Brigade moved under cover of artillery smoke to shoot them in from the right flank. Fifty prisoners and 12 guns were captured for the loss of no casualties to 152 Brigade. Reinforcements which came forward to assist the enemy were broken up by artillery fire. By mid-day the advance continued, led by one of the other battalions of the Brigade.

The rapid advance continued to Scorda and Vizzini. By now a limited number of trucks had joined them, and, by dumping the stores, they were able to ferry forward the marching troops, and then return to pick up their loads once more. Unfortunately there were no scout cars or other reconnaissance troops allocated to the Brigade, and the advance guard had limited capability to probe far ahead of the main body. This resulted in an unfortunate episode when the advance guard was checked, as it approached Francofonte. The main body closed up behind them in a place where the hills were precipitous, and movement off the narrow track, high above a ravine, was extremely limited even for men on foot. The other side of the valley was occupied by the enemy, and they were able to pour a considerable weight of small arms fire into the column before they were reduced by fire returned by the units caught in the ambush, and by the artillery and mortars from further back. The situation was not resolved until a night attack along the ridge overlooking the ambush area had driven the enemy off their positions. By the time the battle was over the Brigade had captured a thousand Italian prisoners, including a general. Once again, the co-operation of tanks, infantry, artillery, mortars and machine gunners had achieved success, albeit with appreciable casualties to the units involved. Despite this setback, the Brigade had advanced 20 miles since the previous dawn, opening the way for the other brigades of the Highland Division to take up the advance.

This continued against fairly light opposition until 153 Brigade came up against determined resistance as they tried to move round the eastern side of Gerbini airfield, and take the town of Gerbini. Once again the Division's favoured tactic of a night attack was tried, but the units became bogged down and had to repel a number of determined counter-attacks. Meanwhile, 154 Brigade secured the high ground on the south west side of the Dittaino river upstream of the Gerbini battle, and held a small bridgehead over the river.

152 Brigade was warned that its next operation was to break out of this bridgehead and take the high ground beyond. The objective was the Sferro Hills, a ridge about 1000 feet high, rising steeply out of the Dittaino valley. The ridge was well prepared for defence, but the main strong point was at the eastern end, overlooking the Gerbini plain. Unusually, the Brigade was given time to prepare, and patrols over the five days preceding the assault gave them a very clear picture of the defences.

The plan was to launch two battalions, 2nd Seaforth and 5th Camerons, on a narrow front close to the centre of the ridge, with 2nd Seaforth swinging left, once the centre of the ridge was secured. The third battalion, 5th Seaforth, was then to follow up and swing right along the ridgeline to catch the strong enemy position at the eastern end in the rear. To avoid detection while they were at their greatest vulnerability coming down the face of the hills held by 154 Brigade, the attack was to be launched at last light.

Surprise was achieved until they were close to the enemy positions, but then resistance became severe. Casualties were heavy in the leading battalions and reinforcements from 5th Seaforth were needed to enable the leaders to secure their objectives. After a bloody engagement the ridge was taken, and 5th Seaforth were able to move on to the eastern end, effectively destroying the enemy in that area.

The plan had been to pursue the enemy over the far side of the ridge, and then withdraw to positions just behind the ridge line, out of observed artillery and mortar fire. Determined counter-attacks, supported by artillery and armour were anticipated. Despite the failure to reach out far beyond the ridge line, the positions were made secure as dawn broke, and the anti-tank guns and supporting tanks were close behind the infantry in preparation to repel the expected counter-attacks. This part of the battle went exactly as planned. The enemy made determined efforts to regain the ridge, but were beaten off with heavy casualties, and no penetration was made into the hard-won positions. With this strategic position in allied hands, the advance of the formations further east was able to go ahead.

The main thrust of the advance now shifted to the divisions on the left of the Highland Division, who were to swing right-handed round the northern side of the island, until they trapped the defenders in the area of Messina. Securing the Sferro Hills had enabled the artillery to move up close behind 152 Brigade, and take up positions from which they could support this manoeuvre. The result was the rapid withdrawal of the Axis forces, who managed to evacuate a considerable part of their army across the Straits to the Italian mainland. The campaign in Sicily ended thirty nine days after the landing.

The Brigade moved forward close to Messina to await instructions for its next operation. To the relief of men who had not seen Britain for more than two years, and in some cases three or more, the word came that the Highland Division was to move back to the UK to train for another landing in Europe. Pa said goodbye to them on 23rd August, knowing that his journey would take him on promotion to command 15th (Scottish) Division.

On his return to Britain he would hear that he had been awarded the DSO for his time in command of 152 Brigade. The citation reads:

Brigadier MacMillan commanded his Brigade on 14th July 1943, when they met stiff resistance from German parachutists at Francofonte. He personally assisted in the mounting of the 2 Seaforth attack which finally cleared the village and led to the withdrawal of those of the enemy which remained.

Again on the 31st July his Brigade played a major part in the Battle of the Sferro Hills, when all of his three battalions were engaged, which again led to the Germans' immediate withdrawal over the River Dittaino on the Divisional front.

Early on the morning of the 1st August, he visited his forward troops, and found the situation still confused and heavy fighting still in progress. Under his personal direction, he partially reformed his Brigade by the skilful redistribution of his reserve battalion, and so supervised the general distribution of these and the tanks under his command that all enemy counter-attacks put in that day were successfully beaten off, to such an extent that on his Brigade front alone over 100 enemy dead were subsequently buried.

In both these actions he rendered distinguished services to his Division and to the Army.

The recommendation for an immediate DSO was upheld by General Montgomery, commanding the 8th Army, and General Alexander, the C-in-C Army Group. It was gazetted on 18th November 1943.

15th (Scottish) Division

Probably the command that Pa felt closest to was that of the 15th (Scottish) Division.

As soon as the campaign in Sicily was over he came back to Britain to take command, being posted on 23rd August 1943.

He had time to come to Finlaystone, and, after he had unpacked some of his belongings, he came into the drawing room where Ma was sitting in her usual seat on the sofa and tossed his Tam-O-Shanter into her lap, saying "Would you mend that?" It had a neat hole in it. He then explained that near the end of the time in Sicily he had been in his jeep with his driver when they heard or saw an enemy fighter coming at them, and dived under the vehicle. One of the bullets that the plane loosed in their direction went through his bonnet. I never heard if it was still on his head, or if he had dropped it when he took cover, but it was an incredibly near miss.

15th (Scottish) Division had existed in the First War, but had then been disbanded, to be resuscitated in 1939. It comprised three Brigades, 46 Highland, 44 Lowland and 227 Highland. It had not been deployed overseas when Pa took command but it was now destined to be part of the invasion force which was to land somewhere on the coast of mainland Europe.

The various units comprising the Division were in camps around North Yorkshire, centred on Catterick. Since it seemed likely that Pa would be in that part of the country for some time, his mother moved from her hotel in London to Yorkshire, spending some time close to us at Aysgarth in the Green Tree Inn at Patrick Brompton, as well as in Richmond.

Much of the Division's training was in the high ground at the head of the Yorkshire Dales, and every now and then Pa would appear at Aysgarth in uniform as he returned from exercises with the Division. He usually only stayed for a short time but it was a very nice bonus, and gave us a bit of extra cred!

HM The Queen visits 15 Scottish Division before D-Day, 1944

Reports by the units under his command show that the training was hard and the weather throughout the winter generally as testing as the physical side of the exercises, but the techniques of working with tanks and artillery were brought to a high state of refinement. In particular, an excellent rapport was built up with 6 Guards Armoured Brigade. It was unfortunate that this affiliation was broken for the first battle in Normandy, as the tanks were still disembarking. Later they were able to fight together.

In late May the Division moved to a concentration area in Sussex, where all movement out of the camps was sealed, so that the true destination of the invasion force would be hidden from the Germans. A very comprehensive deception plan, which included indications by radio traffic and dummy equipment of an additional army in the South East of England and a high level of air activity over the Pas de Calais, convinced the Germans that this was the destination for the invasion force, and that, even when the landings took place in Normandy, they were only a diversion.

Gen. Dick O'Connor and Pa at 15th Scottish Division Highland Games, Hove, 1944

During the period in these quarantined camps the final orders for the invasion were given out.

15th (Scottish) Division was to be in one of the early waves following up the original landings, scheduled to start coming ashore on D+1 (7th June) and to build up over the next four days. Storms in the Channel forced a delay of 6 days on this plan and leading elements only got ashore on 13th June, with the main body complete on 17th June.

This delay provided us with a memorable surprise. I was at Eton taking the scholarship exam, and Ma and I were staying with Mrs

Vaughan at Willowbrook. We heard the incredible rumble of the thousands of aircraft that were going over to support the invasion during the morning of 6th June, but certainly didn't expect Pa to turn up one evening. The need for secrecy had passed, and the delay meant that there was no further work that could be done until they got the signal to embark.

Much of the Division had a most unpleasant crossing, spending a great deal of time tossing about in small craft in the Channel, waiting for conditions to allow them to land. The Mulberry Harbour was badly damaged, and stores and ammunition for the troops already ashore had priority. The relief at getting ashore must have counteracted the anxiety about the imminent battles that were to take place.

The delay had allowed the enemy to bring some reinforcements into the area of the landings and to improve the defences around Caen, where the initial landing forces had been halted. Fortunately, Hitler would not release the Panzer Divisions grouped around Calais, being still totally convinced that the Normandy landings were only a diversion. The Division was, therefore, able to concentrate with comparatively little interference from either air or ground forces.

Monty's Generals, France, 22nd June 1944: Pa is on the left of the back row

On 26th June the Division was launched into a major battle which was to continue with scarcely a pause until 2nd July.

Map 4. **Operation Epsom** (End of June 1944)

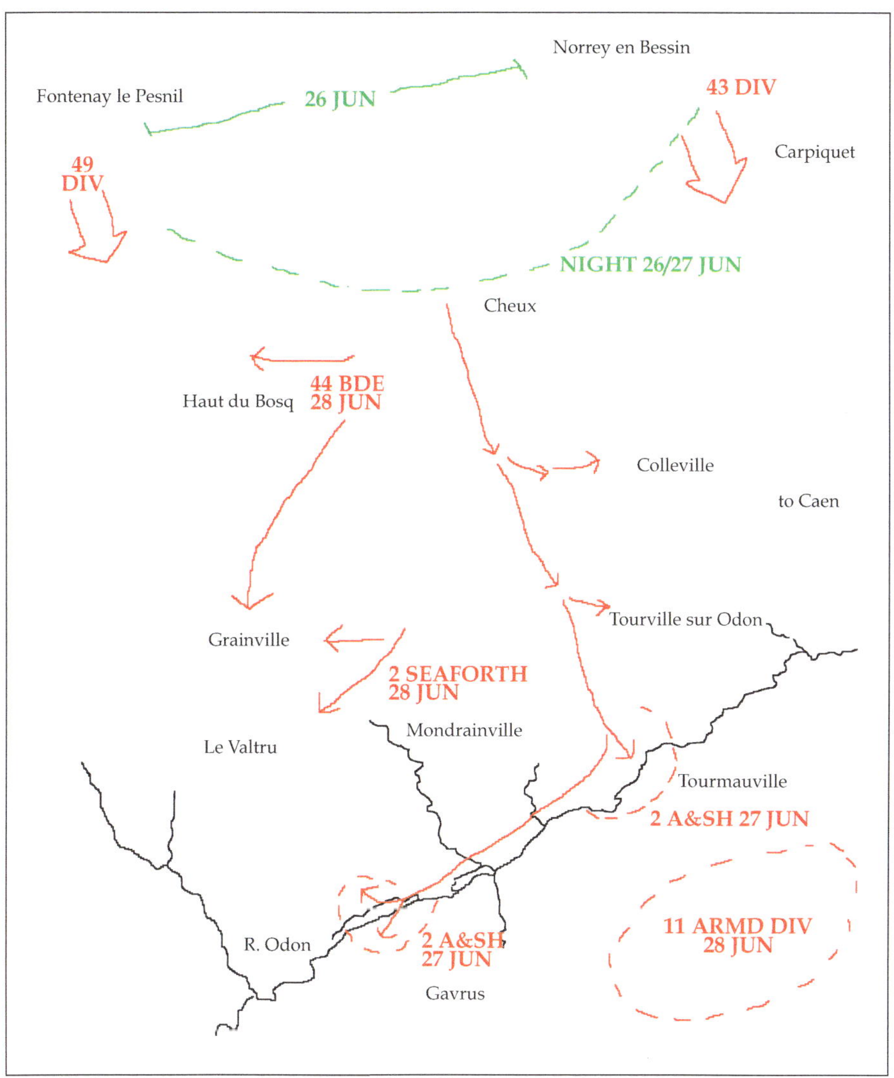

The German forces had held Caen, and the area protecting Carpiquet airfield since the initial landings. A number of attempts to dislodge them on the northern side of Caen had resulted in small advances at great cost in tanks and men. An attempt to move into Caen itself was thwarted, partly because of the well prepared defences, and partly because the preliminary bombing of the enemy positions missed the targets and caused very heavy casualties among the Canadian forces and 51st (Highland) Division as they were preparing to launch their attack. With stalemate on the left and centre of the British front, it was essential that success was obtained on the right.

Operation Epsom was the name given to the attack by 15th (Scottish) Division. This was a battle involving the three Divisions of 8 Corps: 15th (Scottish) Division was flanked by 43rd Division on the left, and 49th (West Riding) Division on the right.

15th (Scottish) Division's line of advance was through the small town of Cheux, and the hamlets of Colleville, Tourville and Tourmauville. The other divisions were to move in parallel. The left was strongly defended because it overlooked Carpiquet airfield and the southern approach to Caen which was still firmly held. On the right, 49th Division was exposed to the German divisions attempting to prevent a unified front developing between the British and the Americans. Perhaps not surprisingly both these divisions had great difficulty in making progress to match 15th (Scottish) Division in the centre, though no witness would deny that the opposition in the centre was very determined at least until Cheux was in allied hands.

An intense artillery barrage, including naval guns from the battleships lying offshore, preceded the attack which was launched south-eastwards through the allied front line between Norrey-en-Bessin on the left, and Fontenay-le-Pesnil, about 16 km to the west of Caen, on the right. Because of weather conditions the planned air support was cancelled. This may have been the cause of the first changes of plan, since the advance was slower than anticipated, and the battle to take Cheux extended till evening. It had been hoped that the whole operation might have been achieved in a single day. Cheux became the scene of heavy fighting, followed by continuous shelling once it was in Allied hands, early on the morning of 27th June. The destruction of the buildings caused yet another bottleneck, delaying artillery and maintenance vehicles which had already been held up negotiating the narrow gap in the minefield as they left the start line. Extremely heavy rain on the evening and night of 26th June had left all these choke points a sea of mud, hampering all movement even more.

June 27th was a day of great success for the Division, with 227 Brigade, which had been in reserve on the first day, sweeping all opposition aside. The leading battalion, bearing the name of Pa's first unit, the 2nd Battalion of the Argylls, cleared Colleville, and cut the road through Tourville and Mondrainville and then dashed down to the Odon crossing at Tourmauville, securing the bridge intact. This was an advance of four miles since dawn, and the small bridgehead was established, allowing the tanks and mounted infantry of 11th Armoured Division to pass through the following morning.

It was an anxious time for all in the forward positions, as this narrow corridor stretched far ahead of the divisions on either side. The infantry of 11th Armoured Division were not able to take over the bridgehead from the Argylls until first light, but the Battalion wasted no time and during the night were able to secure the bridges at Gavrus in addition to the valuable Tourmauville crossing. The Armoured Division, supported by their riflemen mounted in carriers, then moved up to the high ground beyond the river. Spasmodic fire from small arms kept the Argylls on their toes, but this was just a prelude to the major battles that soon developed.

The Germans, who had been concentrating on the two divisions on the flanks of the 15th, now realised that they had been by-passed, and brought forward any armoured divisions that they could bring to bear to cut off this dangerous salient. They recognised the threat to their own rear areas if 11th Armoured Division was able to exploit the gap created by 15th (Scottish) Division. The rest of 227 Brigade had closed up behind the Argylls, and were now fighting off determined counter-attacks coming in from the south-west on to the villages of Valtru and Grainville which had proved hard to capture. 44 Lowland Brigade had to be moved from the left flank of the attack to complete the capture of Grainville and the clearance of the Haut du Bosq which dominated the road from Cheux down which 227 Brigade had advanced so successfully.

The company of the Argylls at Gavrus was also under pressure with heavy mortar and artillery fire causing almost total destruction of the vehicles that had been brought forward with ammunition, rations and radios, and the road down which supplies had to come was under accurate small arms fire as well as artillery and mortar attack. Carriers were unable to take the wounded back from the forward positions until darkness fell. One platoon was cut off by the enemy counterattack, but the survivors were eventually led back to their company after all their ammunition had been expended. Anti-tank guns, incidentally from another Argyll Battalion, the 5th, which had been converted to an anti-tank regiment at the outbreak of the war, combined with excellent support from the artillery, enabled them to inflict heavy casualties on the assaulting German forces. Control, however, became difficult when the radio to Brigade HQ as well as other links within the Battalion were knocked out and the Commanding Officer became separated from his HQ when he got pinned down by enemy fire while visiting the beleaguered company near Gavrus. Enemy infantry succeeded in infiltrating between two of the companies, and heavy mortar and artillery fire caused a number of casualties to the Argylls holding the Gavrus bridgehead. It had been decided to withdraw them but the message only reached the forward troops when a troop of tanks was sent to make contact and cover their withdrawal. They eventually withdrew to a reserve position behind 7th Seaforth who were fighting off similar counter-attacks near Valtru. (The

Commanding Officer of 2A&SH was surprised to find the position deserted when he returned to his headquarters, but was able to sneak past the German occupants while they were enjoying their breakfast).

Behind the Argylls, on the left of the corridor, the battle swayed to and fro in the area of Colleville, which was a critical point on the route to the forward battalion and to the Armoured Division, already across the Odon. The 2nd Battalion of the Gordons eventually repelled this counter-attack and secured the left of this narrow salient.

The Germans on the southern flank put in further spirited counter-attacks, coming close to achieving success in their attempt to regain the high ground at Haut du Bosq before 44 Brigade drove them off once more. These were reinforcements from a number of Panzer divisions, including 9 SS Panzer Division, brought from the Russian front to join in the massive effort to throw the Allied forces back into the sea. It was later stated that, had they not been thrown piecemeal into the battle, but been better co-ordinated, they would have succeeded in cutting the salient and making life very difficult for the infantry of 15th (Scottish) Division in the forward areas and for 11th Armoured Division who still held their ground across the river. The successful repulsing of the German counter-attacks inflicted a great many casualties on their infantry soldiers and their supporting tanks. German snipers continued to cause trouble even in areas which the infantry had already passed through, but those who had strapped themselves in trees to pick off the unwary were summarily dealt with by the *Crocodile* flame-thrower tanks.

By 2nd July the 15th (Scottish) Division had been relieved in the front line, and concentrated once more in comparatively peaceful surroundings to re-equip and absorb reinforcements sent up to replace the casualties.

Unfortunately some of the ground that had been gained by their gallant and successful advance was later relinquished. 11th Armoured Division was withdrawn once more behind the Odon river. But the success of the Scots in driving forward to the river had produced such a threat to the German defenders that, at the height of the battle they were reported to have elements of six Panzer divisions trying desperately to drive them back or cut them off, and to prevent any more serious threat developing in the rear of their formations.

This achievement was recognised by the Corps and Army Commanders who sent messages expressing their highest praise for this first successful move to break out of the Normandy beachhead. Although it had not proved possible to follow it through with a rapid armoured advance, it shook up the defences so that the Division's next major battle would achieve a similar outcome, disrupting the German plans to counter the American breakout.

Monty sent a congratulatory message on 3rd July, immediately after the Division had been relieved, saying "I would like to congratulate you personally, and the 15th Division as a whole on the very fine performance put up during the past week's fighting. The Division went into battle for the first time in this war, but it fought with great gallantry and displayed a fine offensive spirit. Scotland can feel great pride in the 15th (Scottish) Division and the whole Division can be proud of itself. I am sending a present of 180,000 cigarettes, and I hope the men will enjoy them." (In those days smoking was considered less of a health risk than facing the Germans.)

Bimbo Dempsey, who features in so much of Pa's war story, also sent a handwritten letter saying how much he admired the splendid way in which the Division had fought.

Dick O'Connor, the Corps Commander, added his own congratulations to those that he forwarded from his superiors.

The period in reserve was short-lived, and little of it could have seemed peaceful. The biggest task was to receive reinforcements to replace those who had become casualties, and to integrate them into the Division. Although a number of them came from the elements of each unit that had been left out of battle, the others coming forward from reinforcement units included a fair proportion of English soldiers. Pa later gave great credit to these men, who quickly took their places in a formation which was entirely formed from units from Scotland, in which hardly a soldier at the outset was from south of the Border. In a talk in Langbank immediately after VE Day he told his audience how much he admired the spirit of the Jocks, but took care to include these press-ganged 'Scotsmen' in his tribute.

There had also been a large number of vehicle casualties. The repair organisation worked tirelessly to make those which were damaged fit for further combat. However, the storms which had delayed the landing of the Division, had also played havoc with the supply of replacement vehicles, so every Quartermaster's ingenuity was challenged to bring their units back up to scale. Captured German vehicles were pressed into service, and, when the call came to take part in their next major battle, re-equipping had been successfully achieved. There were also a number of lessons to be learnt from the experience of this battle, and all units were pushed through a series of exercises to bring this home. A few lucky folk were able to get away to the seaside for a short break. I very much doubt if Pa was one of them!

The Division's next battle was part of a thrust southwards to take the pressure off the American forces preparing to break out of the Cotentin peninsula. It consisted of two British Corps and one US Division (the

5th). 8 Corps, consisted of 15th (Scottish) Division, 11th Armoured Division and the Guards Armoured Division. On 8 Corps' left was 30 Corps, and on their right 5 US Corps. 15th (Scottish) Division was delighted that their close armoured support now came from 6 Guards Brigade with whom they had trained so hard in Yorkshire.

Map 5. **Operation Bluecoat** (End of July to early August 1944)

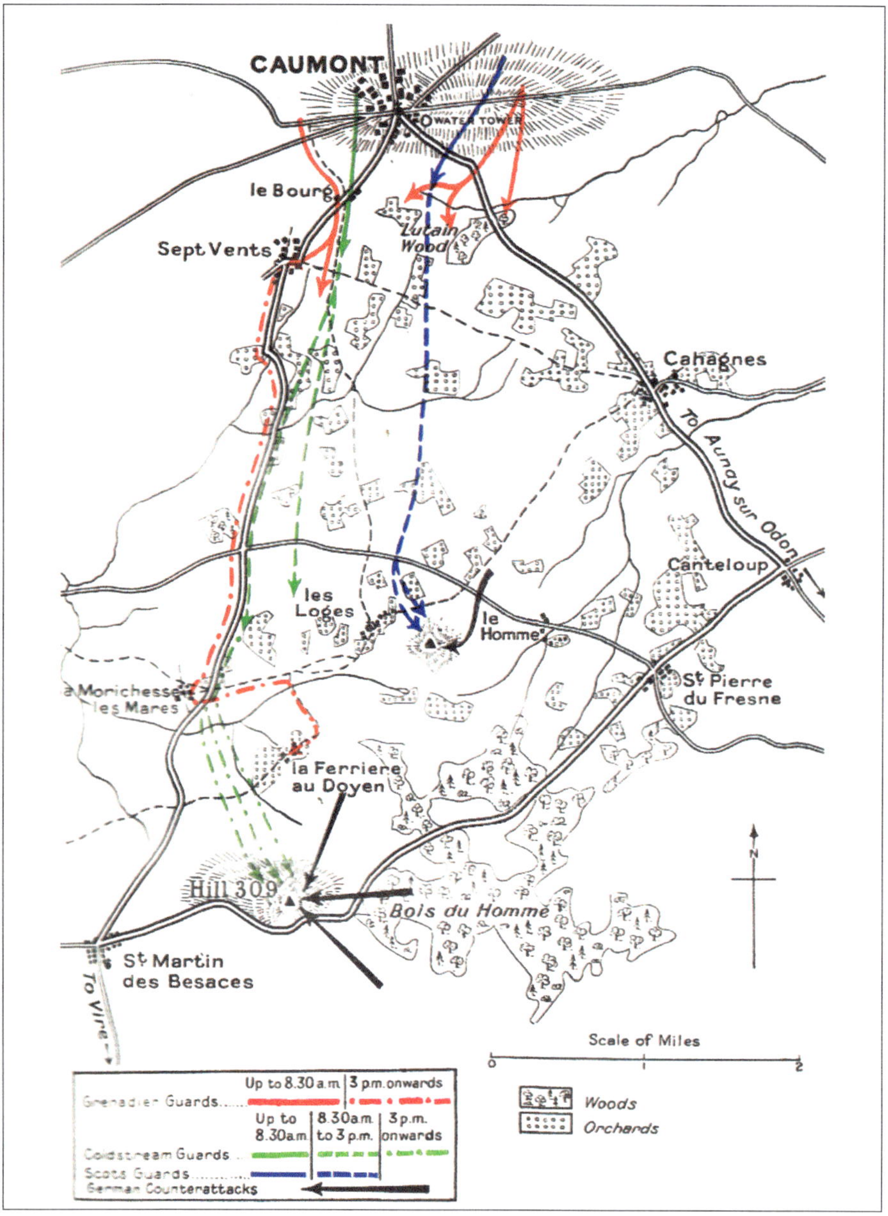

(*History of the 6th Guards Armoured Brigade*)

The Army Commander's plan for *Operation Bluecoat* was to take over part of the front held by the US forces, so that more of their resources could be released for the major offensive through Avranches and St. Lo which would then swing North East to encircle the German forces in what was to become the Falaise pocket. 8 Corps and 30 Corps were therefore moved secretly under cover of darkness to conduct this relief in the area of Caumont.

The relief went remarkably smoothly, despite the huge number of vehicles moving through roads and across country over which a good deal of fighting had already taken place. The British troops were pleasantly surprised to find the devastation far less than had been the case around the *Epsom* battlefield. There were even live cows in the tiny fields of this area of mixed woodlands and pastures, known as *bocage*, in contrast to the stinking corpses of their earlier battlefield.

They were not, however, allowed to enjoy this pastoral interlude for long, as *Monty* realised that the more pressure he could exert on this part of the front, the less the Germans would be able to devote to facing the American advance in the South West. He also hoped to be able to go far enough to create a backstop to prevent the Germans retreating in front of the Americans from escaping from this pocket. He therefore decided to mount an offensive using the two British Corps and the 5th US Corps to strike south from Caumont towards Evrecy and Vire.

Believing that this part of the front was very lightly held, *Monty* planned for the attack to start on 30th July, giving just a single clear day for the preparation of an operation involving three corps, supported by a very heavy air assault. For 15th (Scottish) Division, the time was even shorter as a considerable depth of enemy-held territory had to be secured before the main assault, which was due to follow immediately after the aerial bombardment at 9 o'clock on the 30th. This meant night moves forward, and a dawn attack on two features, which indeed proved lightly held, but covered with effective minefields which delayed the advance. Meanwhile the formations to take part in the main attack moved forward to the southern edge of Caumont and awaited their turn to advance.

The air assault on the German positions for once was able to go according to plan and had a devastating effect on the defenders. The advance was, however, much slower than planned, with the armour finding the dense hedges and deep banks of this *bocage* country extremely difficult to negotiate, and the minefields causing many casualties and imposing delays while clearance operations were carried out. Despite this, 15th (Scottish) Division made better headway than their flanking formations, with 43rd Division on their left scarcely getting beyond their start line before they were literally bogged down in the marshes on either side of a small river. History seemed to be repeating itself, with the effective operations of the infantry, and the excellent co-operation of 6th Guards Armoured Brigade allowing 15th (Scottish) Division to reach two key features overlooking the large wooded area of the Bois du Homme where considerable German forces were still entrenched.

The success of the armoured formation and their speed of advance meant that their infantry support fell behind. Their transport was given a lower priority than the armoured vehicles, and the single road providing the artery for the advancing division was subject to a number of choke points. They also had to clear pockets of resistance, by-passed by the armour. This led to the only serious setback of the day when two *Jagdpanthers* (or German tank destroyers), which had been well concealed near the Scots Guards' objective, made their presence known and destroyed twelve Churchill tanks in as many minutes. The infantry, who might have been able to clear the surrounding area, arrived shortly afterwards, but this was a dire warning of the vulnerability of armour on its own in this dense country.

An effort was made to bring up infantry to provide security on the other key objective before nightfall, by sending back tanks to ferry men forward, but the congestion was so severe that eventually the infantry dismounted and made their approach more quickly on foot. Their own transport was still locked in the traffic jam, which had been made more severe by elements of 11th Armoured Division on the right straying into 15th (Scottish) Division's area and adding to the traffic chaos. The most serious effect on the forward positions was the lack of the infantry's anti-tank guns, which necessitated the armour staying on the objectives, instead of withdrawing to replenish, ready for the next day's advance.

Order must have begun to return overnight, but the enemy had also taken advantage of the comparative quiet to bring the Division's old adversaries, 21 Panzer Division, into the line opposite the 15th. The success of the previous day had left them in the now familiar position of being the spear-point of a narrow salient, with forward positions lightly held, and the left flank, in particular, dangerously exposed.

11th Armoured Division on the right had made progress and was close behind 15th, but 43rd Division were still on the start line, some six miles behind. The two key features which the 15th held on either side of the Bois du Homme were vulnerable to infiltration between them, besides the threat from the flanks. The second day of the battle was therefore spent in furious defence against counterattacks on these positions, and in consolidating the line so that the gap between these features, and the ground behind them, which should have been secured by 43rd Division, was filled. The forward positions were attacked again and again, but their own valiant fighting, and the enormous weight of artillery fire which they were able to direct on to the counter-attacks meant that they were able to hold on, and cause heavy casualties to the enemy. By making space for 43rd Division to come forward within the 15th's boundaries, they were at last able to move up on the left, bypassing the bottleneck on the river which had foiled their earlier operations.

Meanwhile the balance on the German side was altering. The long-expected invasion of the Pas de Calais was now considered unlikely, and at last formations were being redeployed to join the battle in Normandy. Infantry formations were being thrown into the line on the Caen front, and armour was being transferred to face the developing American thrust. The formations heading South West suddenly realised that the *Bluecoat* forces were threatening their flank, and diverted to face this new development.

August 1st was spent by 15th (Scottish) Division strengthening their position with minor tactical advances to produce a more coherent line, while continuing to fight off the determined counter attacks being launched against them. Preparations were also being made for the next phase which was to see 15th (Scottish) Division providing a firm base from which Guards Armoured Division and 11th Armoured Division could resume the advance in parallel with the American Corps.

The Bois du Homme was successfully secured, and elements of 15th moved to their right to take over the ground won by the Guards Armoured Division near Le Beny Bocage. This was less simple than had been expected, since the enemy were still active in the area, and two hard-fought engagements round St. Pierre Tarantaine and Catheolles were reminders that the front still had a number of holes which the Germans were ready to exploit. The two Armoured Divisions were still pushing ahead, but progress was more difficult as elements of 9 and 10 SS Panzer Divisions had arrived to stiffen the resistance.

3rd August was spent in preparations for the next phase of the attack with a series of conferences taking place in the Headquarters of the Guards Armoured Division. A number of senior officers pointed out to General Alan Adair that his HQ was in a particularly vulnerable position, and that the coming and going of senior officers, including the Corps Commander, would be under the eye of German artillery observers. He is reported, however, to have said that the disruption caused by moving, now that his telephone lines gave him communications to all his units, would be too serious to risk while the situation was so fluid. Pa attended the conference at 5pm, and, as he was leaving, a heavier stonk(1) than usual caught him in his jeep, and he was brought back into the Headquarters with a shrapnel wound to his knee.

Dick O'Connor wrote to his wife that evening *"Babe* is slightly wounded. It is a tragedy as he has been the mainstay of this party, and stands out head and shoulders above everyone else. He is one of the best, if not <u>the</u> best, and commands the best lot out here. This is beyond dispute. I shall miss him as a friend, collaborator and adviser. Most of the success out here has been the result of his initial efforts."[xxviii]

In 2011, I spoke to Alastair Ritchie, who was a Staff Captain in Adair's HQ, and he said he had seldom seen anyone so angry as Pa when he came in to be patched up. At that time Pa didn't know the severity of the wound, and even when he was taken to his own Aid Post, he was hoping it could be sorted out there, and he would be able to continue in command, but the decision was made to evacuate him. Brigadier *Tiny* Barber therefore took over the Division and remained in command for the rest of the War.

Pa was eventually evacuated back to England.

David recalls Pa telling him in later years that, after he and his driver had been wounded, he was taken to a first aid post and was given penicillin, which was very new and precious. A matron in charge of it took an open dish of liquid out of a fridge and a syringe fitted with a large needle which she pushed into him. When he was asked what hospital he would like to go to, he said Broadstone Hospital, Port Glasgow. He was told there was no such place, but eventually convinced someone that he knew best, and he arrived in an ambulance at Finlaystone on his way to the hospital on Judy's birthday, 7th August. Half an hour after he had left, the Langbank policeman came puffing up on his bike with a long, serious face, and told Ma he had some very bad news about Pa being seriously wounded, to which Ma replied that she had just been talking to him a few minutes ago!

Pa was well cared for in Broadstone, and we were able to bicycle in and see him most days of the holidays. He taught George and me to play three handed bridge, and wrote out a report about the battles in Normandy, which I read to George and he typed so that Pa could send a copy to the War Office.

The Division was once more singled out for lavish praise by Generals Dempsey and O'Connor. It had been key to the success of *Bluecoat* by securing the points overlooking the Bois du Homme and the wood itself, and this enabled the armoured divisions to continue the

---

(1) World War 2 British slang for a massed artillery bombardment.

advance. Once again the success was not absolute, as the pocket was never totally closed, because of the diversion of the German Panzer divisions to face this thrust. It did, however, mean that these German divisions were not able to move to face the American advance, which had been their objective, and therefore made the successful break-out of the US forces more certain. The casualties inflicted on the German forces during the many counterattacks they mounted against the Division also weakened them for future operations.

Sadly, the days following Pa's evacuation didn't go so well for the Division. Although they acquitted themselves creditably, the price they had paid in almost continuous contact with the enemy since late June had begun to take its toll, with many leaders killed or wounded and a tiredness among the front line troops. Estry proved a hard nut to crack as the Germans fought desperately to keep open the jaws of the trap into which they had fallen, and successive battalions struggled to seize control of the village, only to become bogged down under constant mortar and shellfire, until the German forces facing the American break-out decided they must pull back or be lost. The British armoured thrust which had been the reason for opening up the *Bluecoat* front made slight gains ahead of 15th Division's 'firm base', but they were insufficient to close the trap at that stage on the Germans. That had to wait for greater success at Falaise.

By the end of *Bluecoat*, when it was withdrawn to rest and re-equip, 15th (Scottish) Division had been in Normandy for 50 days, of which 37 had been in close contact with the enemy. It went on to fight with distinction through France and the Low Countries, and Pa once more came across it when he took command of 51st (Highland) Division. The two divisions had been the leading forces crossing the Rhine by boat and ferry in conjunction with the airborne landings, and fought alongside each other to expand the bridgehead.

Pa would not have been aware when he was hospitalised that he had once more been singled out for an award. The citation reads:

Major-General G H A MacMillan assumed command 15(S) Division in August 1943.

During the months preceding the invasion of Europe he was indefatigable in training his Division and in seeing to the welfare and comfort of his troops. He never spared himself in his efforts to bring his formation to the highest pitch of efficiency and morale by D Day.

That he succeeded in this has been amply proved during the recent operations in France. In the savage and bitter fighting during the advance to the Odon his Division worked magnificently. Despite heavy losses it retained its morale and yielded no ground in face of heavy and constant counter attacks.

Again in the British thrust through Caumont 15(S) Division performed magnificently. In fact, through six weeks of intensive fighting and in spite of heavy losses the Division has never lost its form.

I attribute this in very great part to the excellent example and untiring efforts of General MacMillan.

Not only did he work for long stretches without rest at planning his operations but he was constantly in the forefront of the battle under shell and mortar fire.

He was eventually wounded.

I cannot praise General MacMillan's work too highly and I unhesitatingly recommend that he should be made a Companion of the Order of the Bath.

The citation was initiated by Lieutenant General O'Connor, the Corps Commander, and endorsed by Field Marshal Montgomery. The award of CB was gazetted on 1st Feb 1945.

The Final Phase of the War in Europe

A very frustrated general followed the fortunes of the war while he lay in his hospital bed in Port Glasgow, and afterwards while he rebuilt his strength at Finlaystone. The wound had embedded a number of pieces of metal in his knee, and surgery was unable to remove them all, which left him for the rest of his life with a periodic infection but no other problem to reduce his long-term fitness.

He had not long to wonder what the future held for him. On 28th November he found himself once more on the Continent, taking command of 49th (West Riding) Division, known as *The Polar Bears* because of the flash they wore on their shoulders. His predecessor, General *Bubbles* Barker had been promoted to command a Corps. Pa was later to take over from him, once again, in Palestine, and he once commented that he was a great person to succeed as "he never let any of his subordinates as much as undo their fly buttons without having to supervise the operation". Pa's style was based on trusting his subordinates, and getting rid of the ones who didn't deserve to be trusted, and they found the change in attitude very refreshing.

He arrived at a moment when a great many other changes were taking place in the Division. They had been fighting close to the Dutch coast, but were in the process of moving further inland, to take over an area known as The Island. This lay between Nijmegen, which had been successfully taken during *Operation Market Garden*, and Arnhem which was in German hands. The bridge at Nijmegen was the only major supply route to support the forces in The Island, and the low lying land between the rivers Nederrijn and Waal was waterlogged, severely restricting anything but infantry operations. Mines added to the hazards of movement. The front line was ill-defined, with villages and clusters of farmhouses changing hands in patrol actions and skirmishes. The waterlogged fields made it impossible to dig trenches, so every farmhouse or hamlet became a strong point, only to become in consequence a target for artillery and mortar bombardment. Besides the change in location, there were also changes in a number of senior appointments, including Brigade and Battalion commanders, and a reorganisation of some of the supporting arms.

No doubt Pa would have liked to have forced his way across the river, but this was not a priority area and the resources needed were to be used elsewhere. It therefore became a winter of stalemate, broken only by the need to redeploy part of the formation and to fight two engagements larger than battalion size.

Map 6. **North West Europe** (November 1944 to May 1945)

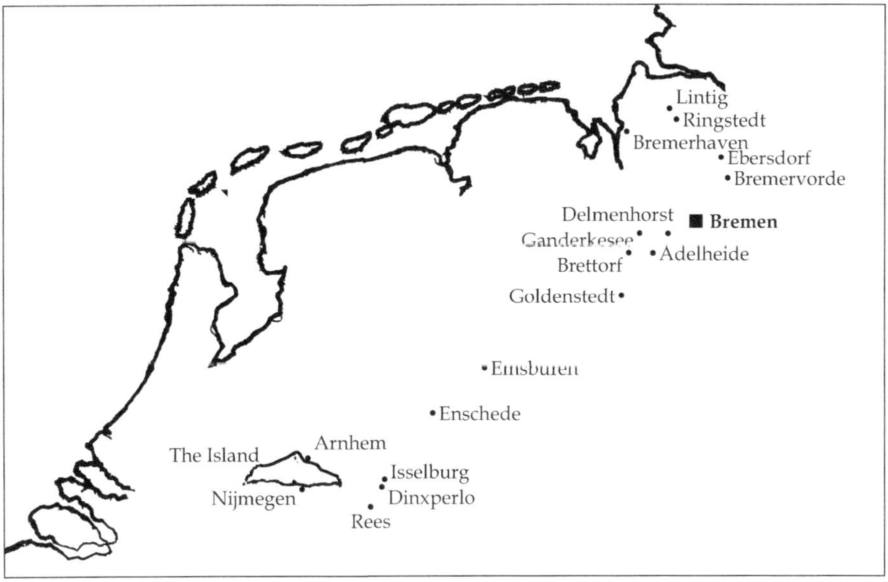

The first engagement followed the breaching of the Waal dykes by the Germans on 2nd December. Two days later they launched a determined assault on to positions held by the Duke of Wellington's Regiment, but were driven back with considerable loss by the efforts of the defenders and heavy artillery fire.

The second engagement occurred in mid-January. The importance of the Nijmegen bridge was not lost on either side and a number of attempts were made by the Germans to destroy it, including through the use of midget submarines. On this occasion, they attached a number of mines to rafts of logs which they floated down the river. One exploded against the wreckage of the original bridge, but a number of others failed to go off, but would not explode when engaged by firing weapons at them. The gallant bomb disposal teams had to dismantle them by hand, an unattractive prospect in the swirling icy waters of the river in January.

Following this attempt to reduce the Division's ability to reinforce the forward positions, the German 7 Parachute Regiment launched an attack on the part of the village of Zetten which had been held by the British. 156 Brigade was deployed to support the defenders, and in an engagement characterised by exceptionally heavy use of mortar bombs, in addition to comparable support from the heavier guns of the artillery, the Germans were driven out of their half of the village and its formidable castle.

49th Division had had to double the frontage it covered, since its neighbour, 51st (Highland) Division, had been drawn away to join the formations facing the unexpected German offensive in the Ardennes. Patrolling was intensified, using foot patrols wading in the icy fields, and sometimes using boats or the amphibious *Dukws*, with the aim of keeping the German formations tied down and therefore unable to reinforce the troops further east where the crossing of the Rhine was to take place.

While sympathising with the troops manning the forward positions, and enduring a particularly wet and bitter winter, with the added distraction of a by-no-means dormant enemy facing them, it is hard to reconcile this with the comparative luxury enjoyed behind the front line. Christmas provisions brought forward by NAAFI not only allowed the allied forces to enjoy the occasion, but they also shared them with the less fortunate civilians who had spent the previous years close to starvation. A leave programme enabled people to go as far afield as Paris. By rotating the formations through the front line the opportunities to clean up, re-equip and perhaps enjoy the leave facilities were not confined to the 'base wallahs'.

While he commanded 49th Division, a story is told that Pa had given his battalion and brigade commanders a rocket for exposing themselves unnecessarily in dangerous places, saying that it was their job to command their formations and not act as section commanders. They were too valuable to lose for little purpose. Not long afterwards he was spotted in a place that was generally considered highly dangerous, and some bold subordinate made a gentle reference to stones and glass houses. Pa's immediate reply was that "good Lieutenant Colonels and Brigadiers are like gold dust, but Generals are two-a-penny".

For Pa this assignment, that was reminiscent of the First War, came to a sudden end.

He had just launched an offensive to clear the Germans out of their remaining positions south of the Waal when the assault crossing of the Rhine took place near Rees to the east. The Allies were at last on German soil, but on the day of the crossing (23rd March), 51st (Highland) Division lost its commander when his jeep received a direct hit from a mortar bomb. Pa was immediately required to go and take over command of the Division.

His time in command of 49th West Riding Division was recognised much later, when he was gazetted in August 1945 for a Mention in Despatches 'In Recognition of Gallant and Distinguished Service in North-West Europe'. Much later, in 1947, he was to receive a further award from the Queen of the Netherlands.

51st (Highland) Division

Thomas Rennie had been a long-standing friend of Pa, so it must have been with mixed feelings that he arrived to take command of one of the divisions that had had the highest profile of any, since it had been in the forefront of the fighting from Alamein onwards. It was the division in which he had commanded 152 Brigade in Sicily eighteen months earlier, but few of the people he knew then would still have been serving after so many had been killed or wounded during the advance from Normandy. He was immediately plunged into one of the most important operations performed by the British army since the breakout from the beachhead.

The crossing of the Rhine had been achieved the previous day with an airborne operation by parachute and glider-borne forces, and an assault river crossing by the two Scottish Divisions, 15th and 51st. This had secured the initial objectives, but there was still heavy fighting to carry out to enlarge the bridgehead and permit the following formations to break out into the German hinterland.

The next 24 hours after Pa's arrival saw a slogging match as they drove out determined resistance from the area of Rees, on the north bank of the river. The Division had already had a long, bitter and expensive campaign in Rees on the southern side to secure the ground from which the crossing was launched. 152 Brigade led the advance through the broken streets and buildings during a day and night battle which culminated in D Company of 1st Seaforth suffering heavy casualties as they took the final strongpoint known as the Holland Hof.

The Division then turned northwards, leaving the crossing points in the hands of 3rd Division. The momentum was sufficient for them to capture the bridge over the Issel at Isselburg intact, and the only resistance they met was heavy artillery fire as they secured the town, which appeared to have been evacuated by the German ground forces. Support from Typhoon aircraft subdued the enemy artillery and the advance continued, securing crossings over the Astrang. 5th Seaforth were surprised as they arrived on the north bank of the river by a force escaping from Astrang, to their west, and their battalion headquarters were captured. Fortunately they were freed soon afterwards when the tanks were able to cross the river, and 206 of their captors became prisoners themselves.

As each brigade secured its objectives, the advance was taken up by the next brigade, crossing the series of rivers which intersected the low land in their path. The *Buffaloes* which had carried many of them across the Rhine came into their own again where swollen rivers had burst far beyond their banks. With the capture of Dinxperlo, the Division was at last permitted to relax while the Guards Armoured Division took over the lead.

51st (Highland) Division's achievements were generously acknowledged by General *Bimbo* Dempsey who sent a congratulatory message saying: "Now that the battle of the Rhine has been won and the break-out from your bridgehead is under way, I would like to give you and your magnificent Division my very sincere congratulations. You were one of the two divisions which carried out the assault crossing of the river, defeated the enemy on the other side and paved the way for all that followed. A great achievement and I am sure you will all be very proud of it."

The contrast of the next few days must have seemed magical. After a short rest in the remains of Isselburg, they were moved to a small Dutch town called Enschede. It seems to have escaped the destruction that had marked so many of the places they had seen and the cleanliness and the warmth of the reception from the Dutch people made a wonderful contrast to what they had just endured. The routine of replacing men and equipment lost or damaged in battle was taken up once more and they were ready for the last advance, as part of 30 Corps, now under command of the Canadian Army. The Corps was tasked to clear North Holland and advance to the Elbe. 51st (Highland) Division's line of advance was to take them north eastwards from Enschede to Bremen.

The resistance varied in determination, and while it may have looked quick and easy as part of the larger picture, a number of hard-fought engagements marked their advance.

The brigades leap-frogged on a narrow front. Progress was rapid and 5th Seaforth were delighted to capture 100 German troops in bed at Goldenstedt. The first serious resistance was encountered at Emsburen on 6th April, but it fell on 7th, and the advance was resumed on 12th. A number of the towns that lay in their path were evacuated after the Burgurmeister had been contacted by telephone, which surprisingly continued to work. An ultimatum that the place would be flattened by artillery and bombing frequently had the desired effect. This did not always work, however, and at Brettorf and Hockensburg the 5th/7th Gordons met considerable resistance on 14th and 15th April, and a few days later 5th Camerons had a hard fight to capture the two bridges and the airfield at Adelheide after a night attack. The success of this attack discouraged the Germans from putting up any resistance in the larger town of Delmenhorst, but on 20th and 21st April, the fanatical defence of Ganderkesee by young soldiers of the parachute forces required a major effort. The artillery and the flame throwers on the *Crocodiles* put an end to this last fling of the dice.

There may have been no further major engagements but the war was not yet over. Mines continued to inflict casualties in areas which had been over-run, and Pa would have been particularly sorry when the senior artillery commander in the Division, Brigadier Gerry Shiel, was killed by one on 29th April, having survived all the battles since Alamein.

By 2nd May, after capturing or replacing two bridges, 5th Seaforth found the Germans in Bremervorde ready to surrender without a fight, but beyond that town they met stiff resistance from their old enemies of 15 Panzer Division at Orel. 5th/7th Gordons had to fight for every house in Ebersdorf. German artillery still shelled the advancing forces, despite the Red Cross asking the Division to avoid shelling, since it was endangering a hospital near Lintig.

At last on 4th May, the beginning of the end occurred. The Derbyshire Yeomanry had provided an invaluable reconnaissance force for the Division, and it was one of their leading squadrons which demanded the surrender of Ringstedt. The German Major said that he could not surrender, but, if a truce was arranged, contact could be made with the German Divisional Commander. Brigadier Oliver agreed to this, and both sides agreed that Ringstedt should become a neutral area while negotiations took place.

General Roth and the senior staff officers of 15 Panzer Division maintained a dialogue for some time, stressing that their's was the only formation retaining any structure in that part of the front, and, rather in the manner of the losing team in a closely fought football match, suggesting that their long history of direct opposition to 51st (Highland) Division gave them a special status. They agreed to surrender, but tried to negotiate terms that would allow them to receive a degree of honour in the operation. This hinged on the officers wishing to retain their revolvers, in the way that German officers of a previous era would have been permitted to retain their swords, and requesting that they should be permitted to march into captivity as a formed body.

Eventually it was agreed that the officers would parade ceremonially, and the senior ones would lay their revolvers with due deference on a table in front of the GOC. Meanwhile the remainder would drop theirs into sandbags held out by NCOs marching down their ranks.

With honour satisfied, General Roth was told that he was in charge of disarming all the other members of the forces in the Jutland peninsula, and he was to appoint officers to supervise the mapping, marking and eventually lifting of all minefields. With due German efficiency, these duties were carried out in accordance with the instructions from the Army Commander.

The German surrender had been finalised on 8th May. There remained one further ceremonial function with which Pa was becoming a bit of an expert: the Victory Parade. As in Tunis, it was done with speed and efficiency. Despite orders that kilts should not be taken overseas, the massed pipe bands of the Division somehow found themselves equipped like the Highlanders they were, and there were other contingents in the parade who were also properly dressed.

On 12th May, Pa led the parade in Bremerhaven and, after passing the saluting base, joined the Corps Commander, Lieutenant General Brian Horrocks and the Commander of the 29th US Division on the dais. The four Brigades who formed the Division marched past, followed by the supporting armoured formations together with representatives of the Royal Navy and a fly-past by the Royal Air Force. It must have been a moment of great pride to him and all those who participated, and marked the moment that Nazi power was destroyed.

Pa was soon to leave Germany for a post at the War Office, as Assistant Chief of the Imperial General Staff, later renamed Director of Weapons and Development. Before his transfer to England he had to redirect the energies of the Division to sort out the chaos in their area of a Germany that had been beaten into submission, where roads, bridges and power stations had been destroyed, and where the buildings which were habitable were required for the allied troops as well as the surviving German population and the hordes of displaced persons who had either been bombed out of their homes or had fled from the Russian armies driving into Germany from the East.

The disciplined nature of the Germans, and especially the structure which still existed in 15 Panzer Division, made this a great deal less difficult than the shambles that many years later followed the fall of Saddam Hussein in Iraq when the victorious forces immediately dissolved the national army. From their prisoner of war compounds, General Roth and his officers were required to disarm all the service personnel in the area, and then to use them to clear the mines which lay over much of the countryside. They also had to provide guards for the dumps where weapons and military equipment were being gathered in. There were plans for civil administration to be taken over by the Control Commission, but in the early days the only formed bodies of men able to act to a coherent plan were the allied servicemen. Gradually the Control Commission were able to take over, and the slow process of demobilisation and repatriation to Britain of the war-weary troops began.

Victory Parade Bremerhaven

Before the Highland Division left Germany Pa was able to circulate the messages of congratulations that flooded in from *Monty*, *Bimbo* Dempsey and Brian Horrocks, and added his own personal thanks and congratulations to all who had fought in the Division. As he had said after the crossing of the Rhine, it was the co-operation of all Arms that had made the Division's operations so successful. At the Rhine, he talked of the specialists who had been involved in the unusual duties of controlling the crossing points, driving the *Buffalo* amphibious vehicles, the sappers building and maintaining pontoon bridges under constant artillery fire, the medical personnel evacuating the wounded from the front line, and stabilising them in the field hospitals. One sub-unit that got a special mention was the team of signallers who were laying a vital cable across the river, when their boat was sunk. They swam ashore, took up the task successfully the second time, and kept the link operating despite the damage from shellfire and from the constant churning by the tracks of armoured vehicles on both side of the river. "Never since Alamein had there been such an interlocked unity of purpose". This same unity of purpose had carried them through the 250 or 300 miles that they had travelled in the 41 days that he commanded them.

Pa was to receive notification of a Mention in Despatches for this phase of the war, when it was published in April 1946. His last award for service in Europe came in July 1947, when he was made a Knight Grand Officer of the Order of Orange Nassau with Swords by the Queen of the Netherlands for his part in the liberation of her country. This related to his time in command of 49th Division. The citation says the decoration was for:

Exceptional valour, leadership, loyalty, and outstanding devotion to duty and great perseverance, displayed in action against the enemy during the operations for the liberation of Netherlands enemy-occupied territory, thereby setting, in every respect, a highly praiseworthy example to everyone in those glorious days.

CHAPTER 5

With Granny at Finlaystone (1939-1949)

By
David and Judy

David's Memories

Throughout the war we lived at Finlaystone with Granny Houston. Finlaystone was down to a skeleton staff as any younger able-bodied people had been called up to serve in the forces. There was Crowe, the head gardener who was helped by several land girls, including Jenny Duncan; Willie Ross, the chauffeur; Willie Love, the carter, who worked *Captain*, the Clydesdale horse which was the only means of moving stuff about the place as petrol was strictly rationed. I think there was an elderly carpenter, and Armstrong, the gamekeeper.

With so few people and all the buildings around Finlaystone and 16 or so farms to be maintained, it was not surprising that the place was pretty run down by the end of the war. Soon after the war, the estate also became smaller, with the result that the income from rents that helped to pay for maintenance shrank. Five or more farms were compulsorily purchased for a pittance for building at the top of Port Glasgow. I recall Granny Houston being very upset about it. When the local councillors came to discuss the land grab, I remember them not being allowed into the house and being given chairs to sit on outside the back-yard. In order to prevent building development between Finlaystone and the Clyde, Granny gave Parklea Farm to The National Trust for playing fields for Port Glasgow.

Two bombs fell near the house in 1942, one only about ten yards from the south end of the building and one in the rose garden. Many of the windows were blown out but there was little structural damage. When the bombs fell, Ma, who was an Air Raid Precautions warden, had just come down off the roof (presumably wearing her black steel helmet). I was in my cot on the ground floor and only about three years old, and was said to have asked Ma if it was Armstrong shooting rabbits.

Soon after that, I can just remember Andrew having to be christened by the Langbank minister, the Rev. Gilfillan, in the library because he was not expected to survive as he was so sickly.

Rationing was strictly enforced by government inspectors. They must have got wind of Granny having more than the legal number of hens. They arrived in an Austin 7 and parked outside the front door. When they returned from a fruitless search for the surplus hens, mysteriously the Austin 7 was lodged in the branches of the cedar tree down the slope from the house. We were all worried that Granny was going to be put in jail for having too many hens.

I do not remember seeing Pa much during the war, apart from the time before he embarked at the Tail of the Bank for the 1st Army landings in North Africa, when he was at Finlaystone with about 6 generals and brigadiers, sitting around the breakfast table before departure.

Even during the war, many visitors came to Finlaystone. One of the most regular was Bill Logan, a cousin of Ma's on the Kidston side. As children we swung from being in stitches from laughing at him to finding him a bit frightening. He managed the Clyde Shipping Company, the family business started by George Jardine Kidston which ran tugs on the Clyde and ships trading with Ireland. While he was living at Finlaystone, Ma asked him one day if he was going to be back late. He said he probably would be as he was going to have dinner on a BP tanker and he would be trying to get a towing contract from the Chairman. The next day Ma asked him how he had got on. "I got the contract. I gave him quite a bit to drink and when it got late I banged his head on the floor until he said 'Yes'."

Judy and I had a governess and nanny. I do not think that our education reached any great heights, in my case due to me rather than to *Nut* Cracknell, the governess. When I was about 6, I used to escape up to the home farm, Burnside, run by Margaret and Johnnie Dunn. There I helped with milking by hand and drove the cart horses bringing in the hay and the harvest. Much to the alarm of Nanny and *Nut*, I picked up a fairly varied vocabulary, to say the least. The crunch came one day when Dolly, the land girl, had been winding me up, and I chased after her shouting "Dolly is a bugger". This was relayed to Margaret Dunn who took to the moral high ground, and told me she would never let her son, John, near Finlaystone in case he picked up such dreadful language.

Things were so different in those days: the pace of life was very slow compared with now. It would take Willie Love all day to take *Captain* to Kilmacolm to be shod. There were no chain saws and so we were taught from an early age by Ma how to cut up large trees that fell with a cross-cut saw, axing the smaller branches, and splitting the bigger bits with hammer and wedges. Nowadays the *Health and Safety* would have had a fit.

Ma, probably at her engagement

As well as all her other work at Finlaystone, Ma took on the job of running the Savings Scheme in the district. This involved her visiting many of the farms and workers' cottages to collect money from the residents and, in return, she would give them a stamp to match the value of the money which would be licked and put into a savings book. The stamps could be cashed or converted into savings certificates by Mr Templeton in the Langbank shop-cum-Post Office. In those days few people had bank accounts, so this was a government-run scheme to encourage saving with which to finance the war effort. Ma spent much of Sunday night doing the paper-work, filling in the full names of the certificate-holders – Sandy Brown, for instance, being 'Alexander Cranston Brown'. He was a big saver with a long name. When there was a special Savings Week, paper-work soared. We might take as much as £500 (enough to finance a Spitfire) to the shop that Sunday. Because of petrol rationing, her round would be done on foot or bicycle.

As children, we would go with her to the nearer farms. The kitchen-cum-dining room of the farm houses would have a flag stone floor which would be regularly scrubbed and would be kept spotlessly clean.

Each time the floor was scrubbed, when it had dried the farmer's wife would make a pattern of continuous circles out from the skirting board around the room for decoration as there were no carpets. One of the farms on Finlaystone was Lepardstone, tenanted by the Campbell family. There was the father who had been gassed badly in the 1st World War and sat in the kitchen all day and coughed a lot. There was the mother who did everything on the farm, possibly with some help, and their super-active son Colin, now a successful businessman in Kilmacolm, who was yelled at every few minutes "Sit down there, Colin!"

When Nanny used to take us for a walk down to the signal box at Parklea, I would be allowed to help the signal man pull the levers for the signals and wind the wheel to open and shut the level-crossing gates.

In those days, Finlaystone's electric power was an on-and-off affair, generated by a Pelton wheel, which ran when there was enough water coming down the burn. Granny somehow managed to get enough materials to rewire everything and put the place on the mains in 1947, despite the rationing.

SS Fastnet, Cruise Liner 1940s style

Soon after the end of the war the whole family as well as Mary and Ann Forbes-Leith and their parents went on a Clyde Shipping Company cargo-passenger ship, the *Fastnet*, for a week or so, sailing from Glasgow to Dublin, Waterford and Cork. This was our first and only ever family holiday, and was presumably planned by Ma as a chance for us all to relax and enjoy ourselves. I enjoyed it because, whenever we arrived in a port I would spend all day helping the man on the crane loading and unloading the ship. Pa, however, seemed to have a very short fuse at this time, which, in retrospect, is not very surprising as he had just come back from 6 years of war only to be shut up in a boat for a week with too many children and a nanny he disliked, in rough weather!

Judy's Recollections

We could hardly have found a better place to spend the war than at Finlaystone with our maternal Grandmother. When we arrived, I was about four years old and David was not yet one.

Granny had a good twinkle and was easy to tease. Always neatly dressed in a coat and skirt made of pretty tweed, jerseys that were tied in a droopy bow at the neck, slightly frilled blouses and hats made of stitched tweed, either in plum reds or purply blues, the whole effect feminine and elegant. Her hair was snowy white and a little unruly but controlled a bit by many hair pins. Her legs remained shapely even when she became a bit bent with age.

Granny was in charge of the house-keeping while Ma spent most of her time gardening and working in the woods. In spite of all the other challenges, she was intent on improving the garden, and laid out the herbaceous border during the early years of the war. Such tasks, however, did not fit with having small children in tow and we usually only saw her after tea for about an hour before going to bed.

Ma would devote this time entirely to us, reading and playing games and showing us how to make lavender bags, or to knit simple scarves on a peg machine, and stick cuttings into brown paper scrap books. Granny was usually there too and would join in card games and hunt-the-thimble. If we got over-excited, she had her own solution. Taking a few of her hair pins out, she would make us each sit down on them, explaining that, if we sat quietly enough for long enough, the hair pin would turn into a penny. She would periodically come round and check on progress and in due course we would be told we could stand up and see for ourselves if the pin was now a penny.

As I grew older, in term-time my mornings were taken up with lessons with *Nut*, but in the holidays Granny kindly put up with my company while Nanny hand-washed our clothes and David had his morning rest. Granny spent time after breakfast in the kitchen with the cook, first Mrs. Parker and, when she retired, Mrs. Petrie. The menu for each meal was carefully written on a slate and they would discuss what needed to be ordered from Coopers the grocer, Ingalls the fishmonger or Irvine the butcher, all of whom brought things out in a delivery van. Granny would then head for the store room and unlock it. It was a small room in the back passage, beautifully fitted out with wooden shelves, cupboards and drawers and large metal bins. It was like a little shop and I loved helping Granny scoop up rice and sugar out of the bins into containers to be taken to the cook. She had blocks of washing soap, bins of soap flakes which tickled your nose, cupboards holding candles, loo paper, dusters, clothes pegs, brush heads and shoe polish. On the shelves were tins of fruit, spam, sardines, mouse traps, dried fruit and suet. Bella White, the house-maid, would arrive to replace cleaning materials and, when all was sorted, we would brush the floor and leave, locking the door behind us. Granny was very methodical and orderly and nothing was out of place: the drawers and cupboards were all labeled, saying what they contained.

She was very kind and delighted to have her grandchildren around, provided they behaved and helped. Already in her seventies, she never moved that rapidly but worked away steadily on her various chores. She looked after the hens, feeding, cleaning them out, collecting the eggs and checking on their state of health. She had a high-wheeled cart, made from a tea chest, with two handles which she took wherever she went outside. David and I much enjoyed collecting the eggs and we had a favourite white feathered hen, called Isobel – after a white-haired great aunt – who did not object to being picked up and pushed about in Granny's cart.

Granny also looked after the low rose garden, now the sunken garden. It had ten beds, all planted with different varieties of roses, and, thanks to regular care, flowered well for much of the summer. They were disbudded, dead headed and no suckers were ever permitted. One of the German bombs landed right in the middle, destroying one of the beds and a rather nice stone urn with a lid resembling a large sugar sifter. It took a bit of time to fill the crater, sow grass and remake the bed, but, in due course, new roses were planted. Granny would gather all the full blown roses and withering petals and spread them out on the grass to the left of the front door. As we went to bed at dusk on a summer evening we would look out of the landing window and see rows of rabbits tucking into these discarded flowers and clearly enjoying them. The garden itself was supposed to be rabbit proof but they were not discouraged from the front of the house where they helped to keep the grass down. We ate rabbit at least once a week but I don't recall that the meat was rose flavoured!

Granny was extremely kind and considerate to everybody and generous with her time. Due to rationing, presents had to be home made and she was very clever with her hands and imaginative about what she created. Before Christmas she would spend the evenings at a table near the fire covering coat hangers with scraps of material and binding the handles with ribbon tied in a bow. She bunched up dried helichrysum and gypsophila flowers and wrapped them in green tissue which she took to all the farmer's wives, along with a year-at-view calendar. The Minister's family was always given a brace of pheasants, taken to church around Christmas and handed to his wife in the pew behind. I'm pretty certain she did not relish the plucking and cleaning of them and might have preferred the dried flowers in green tissue. Hen's eggs were rationed but Granny used goose eggs to dress up as babies, complete with bonnet and long nightie. They would be laid in a bed made from a Price's candle box and sent away to friends as "Wilton Babies". She showed us how to make pen wipers out of wish-bones. The bone had a sealing wax head and feet and then was enveloped in layers of absorbent material and stuck onto a base made of more material. A little verse accompanied the creation which went:

Once I was a wishbone growing on a hen.
Now I am a Merrythought, made to wipe your pen.

Despite the war, lots of people came and went. Canadian army friends of our parents who were unable to spend leave at home with their families, young WRNS who Granny had been asked to befriend while serving ashore on the Clyde, wives whose husbands were in ships briefly at the Tail of the Bank as well as overseas servicemen, sent to spend their leave with us by the Victoria League.

Food was rationed, but there was a steady supply of home-grown fruit and vegetables, as well as brambles and game. Eggs were stored in *waterglass* to help them keep and beans were layered in salt for winter use, as there were then no deep freezes. Surplus fruit was bottled in *kilner* jars, so that black currants, gooseberries, raspberries and plums could be enjoyed with milk pudding throughout the winter.

When Mrs. Petrie went on holiday, Ma who had spent her young days surrounded by household help, had to take over the cooking. On one occasion she used so many eggs in making custard that it became so hard that it had to be passed through a potato-wormer to make it edible. Pa's concern over Ma's limited culinary abilities must have prompted him so send her on a *Cordon Bleu* cookery training course when they lived in London after the war. Each day she brought the results of her lessons home and they were eaten for supper.

Ma discovered that sea-boot stocking wool could be bought without clothes coupons. She bought it in large oily skeins, washed the oil out, dyed it and turned it into kilt stockings, jerseys, gloves and mittens. A lichen that grew on the dykes made an orange coloured dye called crottle, and we spent a lot of time scraping it off stone all over the place. For years we must have looked conspicuous in our unusually coloured woollens.

From a young age, we were kept well employed in the school holidays. Besides working in the garden and the woods, we would pick and bunch large quantities of daffodils which were packed and sent to market during the Easter holidays. We each had a small garden, where the compost heaps now are in the framing yard. John specialised in growing fine gladioli which he sold to Urquhart, the flower shop in Port Glasgow. George had a lot of herbs including a large angelica plant which blew over and was so thick it had to be chopped with an axe. All of us grew vegetables which Granny kindly bought from us.

Besides producing hydro-power, the dam provided a lot of entertainment for us all. Some of us would fish for trout of an evening to provide a fishy breakfast for those who wanted one. The canoe that our Uncle George had made at Eton was originally the only craft on the dam and we all jostled to have a paddle. Soon after the war, after much saving of pocket money, we bought an air-sea rescue rubber dinghy to add to the fleet. Battles raged with much flicking of slimy weed off the tips of paddles and a lot of capsizing. I think it must have been in 1947 that all public swimming baths were closed due to a bad outbreak of polio. It happened to be a hot summer and, despite the mud and the marsh gas, the dam became our swimming pool: we even rigged up a diving board and cheerfully dived in through the thick patches of water-weed.

Remembering those far off days as seen through a child's eyes, I see a familiar backdrop which is outdoors at Finlaystone. Centre stage is Granny, head down, pushing her special cart and oblivious that she is the leading lady. Her supporting cast are the various members of staff who worked at Finlaystone throughout our ten years' stay and are so connected with the place in my mind they are almost part of the scenery.

Surprisingly, as I look back on these days, I realise that Ma was rather a remote figure at that stage of my life. David and I were looked after by Nanny and *Nut*, and were in many ways much closer to Granny than to Ma. Without Pa being around, her responsibilities of bringing up 5 children, combined with the constant worries over his exposure to danger, must have been overwhelming. On top of this, she was working hard physically in the garden and the woods for long hours, and in the evenings never sat idle but would knit or sew, making lovely little dresses for me and romper suits for David and Andrew. She had to spend a lot of time on the Savings Scheme, and her service as an ARP warden required her to patrol the area at night to ensure that all houses observed the blackout. It is hardly surprising that she found small children hindered her activities and dreaded it when Nanny went on holiday and she had to look after us for a couple of weeks!

In those ten years we saw very little of Pa but, when he was around, he tried hard to get to know us. He chose and read lots of good books beautifully to me which I always enjoyed. His homecomings also provided rare opportunities for travelling by car out of Renfrewshire. In the time of petrol rationing, he was allocated extra coupons to enable him to carry out his duties as Colonel of the Argylls. I have vivid memories of when George, John and I accompanied Ma and Pa on an all-day expedition to Stirlingshire, where many of their regimental friends lived. During the day, we met many families whose members were to remain friends to this day. We visited John and Betty Watson where I was mortified to watch my cairn terrier, Fyvie, lift his leg on their drawing room curtain. Betty teased me about the mishap in a kindly jokey way and we departed after a really happy visit. We then went on to the Connal Rowans at Meiklewood for lunch, and ended up having tea with *Copper* and Doreen Buchanan and family at Seaton Lodge: Neil, Patrick and Nigel – then known as the *Pink Scone* – were there.

Before tea, Pa had to drop in on the Regimental Depot at Stirling Castle. Having recently become Colonel of the Argylls he thought he would make his number with the officer who was in command at the Castle. We drove up to the gates and were not unsurprisingly stopped by the sentry who predictably wanted to know the purpose of Pa's visit. Pa became incandescent and, glaring at the luckless sentry, demanded "Don't you realise who I am?" Pa, though normally very calm, was known throughout the army for his sudden bursts of fiery temper but this was the first time I had witnessed it in action. I think we all subconsciously dreaded being the recipient of a lash of his tongue!

When we were very small, Ian Campbell came to stay and told me and David, his godson, that you could always tell if a general was angry by looking at the back of his neck and seeing if it was turning red. The episode at the Castle gate was definitely a moment when Pa's neck was vermilion! It always blew over rapidly but was probably never forgotten by the recipient of the blast.

Pa and Ma 1947 (de Walden Street)

CHAPTER 6

The Post-War Years in Uniform
(1945-47 and beyond)

by
John

With the outbreak of peace, Pa's life began to take on a different rhythm – at least for the first two years, during which he worked in the War Office. This chapter covers that period but it also traces his role as Colonel of the Argyll and Sutherland Highlanders in the years beyond, both while he served in Palestine, Scotland and Gibraltar as well as after his retirement.

As soon as the war ended, Pa was transferred from Germany to an important desk in the War Office as Assistant Chief of the Imperial General Staff (Weapons), later designated Director of Weapons and Development. This meant living in London, where the war had destroyed so many buildings that accommodation was very hard to find. By chance, he and Ma were visiting us at Eton and decided to look in the antique shop in the High Street, probably with an eye to finding the odd bit of furniture to start replacing all their belongings that had been destroyed in store in the first raids of the Blitz. They were chatting to the owner when he said that he had a flat to let in London. They immediately said they were interested, and shortly afterwards were able to move in. This suited for some months but then they had to move again, and were able to find a much nicer maisonette on two floors of a building in de Walden Street. The snag was that it was filled with furniture which the owner insisted on selling to them. This was helpful for the time being, but it was not exactly to their taste, and, when they eventually came to live at Finlaystone, some of the pieces they picked up then were a little incongruous. That didn't matter so much as the feeling that they had been to some extent ripped off by having to pay a lot for a load of fairly rubbishy odds and ends in order to get the flat. Anyhow they agreed on the terms and lived there until the job in London ended.

Ma spent most of the time at Finlaystone but was able to get away now and then to stay with Pa, and George and I spent some of our long leaves from Eton with them both in London, but the family base was still definitely Finlaystone.

On one of our London visits we went to Pa's office, and he showed us pictures of all the guns and armoured vehicles that were part of his responsibility under his Weapons hat. He was also responsible for drawing up a pamphlet based on the lessons learnt in the War. It was called *The Conduct of War* and became the "Bible" on which all the more detailed pamphlets in the series that trained the Army were based. The only record we have of its gestation is a note in a file that commented that it was too long. Whether he completed the task before he moved on to Palestine is not clear.

Among his duties was the chairmanship of a committee which made recommendations on how the soldier's life in the Army could be improved. Many of the recommendations were later adopted, though no doubt the Treasury would have ensured that funding was released so slowly that they took many years to come to fruition. One of the major reforms was that each soldier in a barrack room should have control of his personal light switch!

At this time he must have been persuaded by Ma to address the Langbank Savings group. In his speech he sought to convince them that savings were just as important to help rebuild Britain as they had been to pay for the ships, aircraft and munitions that were needed to fight the war. He looked forward to the years to come, pointing out that the world had changed dramatically with the jet engine shrinking distance, and the atom bomb transforming the shape of future wars. He stressed the need for strong ties with our wartime allies, and especially with the nations of the Commonwealth.

He also took the salute at a Victory parade in Port Glasgow, after the defeat of the Japanese. This included a march-past of the very large number of service and civilian organisations that had played their part in the war, either abroad or on the home front. It was, fortunately, a lovely summer day and Port Glasgow was looking its best.

Much more is known about his involvement in the affairs of the Argyll and Sutherland Highlanders than about his work in the War Office.

He was appointed Colonel of the Regiment in October 1945. This is a job which comes in addition to any paid appointment and has to be fitted in around one's other duties. When he took over, the 1st Battalion had just returned from Italy and was training in Lincolnshire. The 2nd was moving from one station to another around Germany, assisting with the control of displaced persons, keeping order, and protecting weapons and munitions, while a degree of civil government was restored. The 7th was shedding its members either at the termination of their war service or on transfer to other regiments or corps in the neighbourhood of Bremerhaven, where he had left them in 51st (Highland) Division, and the 8th Battalion was doing much the same in Austria. The two Royal Artillery Regiments which had been formed at the outbreak of war from the 6th and 9th Battalions still owed a strong allegiance to the Regiment, and he personified this tie by becoming Honorary Colonel of 554 Light Anti-Aircraft Regiment (TA), formerly the 9th Battalion. He did not have the same formal link to 402 Anti-Tank Regiment (RA), the former 6th Battalion, but, when he was unable to attend their "house-warming" in Greenock in June 1947, Ma was invited to take his place.

Besides his concern for all of these units which had borne the brunt of the fighting, he had contingents in training establishments in Stirling and at Elgin, as well as the new peacetime Territorial Army structure and the cadets to watch over.

When the Regimental magazine, the *Thin Red Line*, was resuscitated in 1947, he wrote the Foreword. It had previously served only the 2nd Battalion, but was now to embrace the whole regimental family, cadets, territorials, the depot and the regular battalions, as well as the affiliated units.

One of these affiliations was with the Royal Marines. During the war there had been two notable occasions when the Regiment and the Royal Marines were thrown together. For two years after the rump of the 8th Argylls had been retrieved from the disaster at St Valery in 1940, the reconstituted Battalion formed part of the Royal Marines Division, based on Plymouth. They trained for many amphibious operations, only to find that they were cancelled, or the operation was reduced in scale and they were left behind. In 1942, the Battalion rejoined the more conventional forces destined for North Africa. The compliment was returned when the Royal Marine detachments that had been saved when HMS *Prince of Wales* and HMS *Repulse* were sunk off the Malayan coast, were posted to reinforce the 93rd in the last days of the campaign before the fall of Singapore. The bonds forged in those last days of the fighting were reinforced by the long years they spent as prisoners of the Japanese. In November 1946, Pa led a strong contingent of Argyll officers who attended a dinner at the Royal Marine Barracks at Eastney and drew up the plans for a formal affiliation between the two organisations. This affiliation still thrives.

One of his first acts as Colonel of the Regiment had been to discuss the plans for a memorial to all who had fallen in the War. The decision was made to record their names in a Roll in the Scottish National War Memorial at Edinburgh Castle, and to raise subscriptions for establishing cottages for those who had been disabled. It is interesting to note that the cost of a cottage was £1,050. Although Pa continued to take an interest in this project, he persuaded Major General Gervase Thorpe, his predecessor as Colonel, to take on the chairmanship of this demanding venture.

He was able to visit the 1st Battalion at Osgodby Camp in Lincolnshire in 1945. They had been training to join the force which was to retake Malaya and Singapore, but the atom bombs ended the need to defeat the Japanese forces in the Far East by conventional means. This did not let the Battalion off the hook, and they were earmarked instead for Palestine. Pa visited them shortly before their departure. Lieutenant Colonel *Squire* Webb had just taken over command.

The 2nd Battalion received three visits. He went to Germany where they were temporarily based in Wesel, in the Ruhr, where he presided over the return of the Colours after their period in safe keeping in Stirling Castle throughout the war. It was a hectic three day visit with two lectures to give, a ceremonial parade to return the Colours, and entertainment in the Officers' mess one night and the Sergeants' mess the next, besides visits to two detached companies.

The second visit was just before Christmas 1946 when they had moved back to Scotland and were stationed at Buchanan Castle, and were heading for Christmas and New Year leave.

The third visit was a sadder one, as the announcement had been made on New Year's Day 1947 that the 93rd were to be among the first batch of army units to be placed in 'suspended animation', and the men would be posted to other units. The ceremonial laying up of the Colours, once more in Stirling Castle, took place in heavy snow on 5th February, a week before he left for Palestine. Pa was the Inspecting Officer at what was hoped to be a temporary demise of the Battalion he had first joined, but it was to prove permanent.

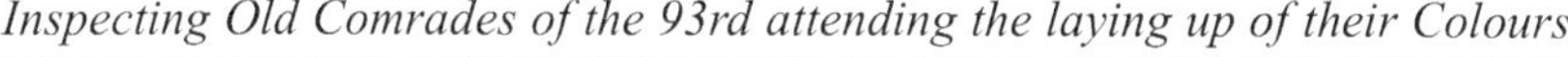

Inspecting Old Comrades of the 93rd attending the laying up of their Colours

In July 1946 there had been a happier gathering, when the survivors of the Old 93rd, who had eventually been taken prisoner in Singapore, after fighting with great distinction in the Malayan campaign, held their first reunion. Brigadier Ian Stewart who had commanded them in that campaign took the chair, but Pa spoke as Colonel of the Regiment both after a pre-dinner lecture, and at the dinner itself.

He was not able to spend too much time visiting the many Argyll battalions and training units which were deployed from Austria to Moray. Very soon after his appointment as Colonel, however, he came to Stirling for the official home-coming of the 7th Battalion. Like the 2nd Battalion it was to lose its regular soldiers, but was to be reconstituted in its pre-war role as the Territorial battalion centred on Stirling. He was also able to meet a contingent from the Regiment when they came to London for the Victory Parade in June 1946. He visited Regimental Headquarters at Stirling on a number of occasions, including one when the King and Queen, and the two Princesses, came to the Castle on 27th June 1946.

His period in London came to an early end when he was promoted to Lieutenant General to become the General Officer Commanding (GOC) in Palestine. Knowing that he would be unable to carry out his duties as Colonel while he was abroad, he entrusted them to Brigadier Harry Clark. He was able to keep a close eye on the 1st Battalion since they were one of the units in the large army that he commanded. Sadly for Pa, however, by the time he arrived, its commander, *Squire* Webb, had fallen foul of the pro-Jewish press (and also of the Secretary of State). He had been replaced by Cluny Macpherson, with whom Pa had taken part in many athletics meetings back in the early twenties.

One evening, *Squire*, who later became my father-in-law when I married his daughter Belinda, had gone round all the posts that the Argylls were manning in Jerusalem, and moved all the ones that had established themselves in the same position as the previous evening's curfew enforcers. When the time switches that operated the awnings over the shop windows came on, to roll them up for the night, a series of explosions occurred which would have killed or wounded a lot of the jocks if *Squire* hadn't done the rounds and shifted them.

When he got back to his HQ he was surprised to find half the press corps waiting for an interview, obviously hoping for a lot of gory stories. Not only were they disappointed to find there had been no casualties, they were more than peeved when he told them to wait in the guard-room, and he would give them individual interviews. The last ones were American, pro-Jewish correspondents who came through about breakfast time, having spent a tedious night, as they said, 'under arrest', and had missed their deadlines. They were very angry and demanded that he should be removed. This wasn't supported by the C-in-C, but he was over-ridden by *Manny* Shinwell, the Secretary of State, and *Squire*'s tenure as CO was formally brought to an end.

Ma and Pa always found *Squire* amusing company during his visits to Finlaystone. It was amazing how he could get away with very *risqué* stories and limericks, that were accompanied with gales of laughter, which came out of a very tall but rather thin face with a prominent moustache and a mouth which he himself said had one of the first sets of free army false teeth.

After *Squire* left Palestine, one of his appointments was to supervise the disbandment of a British led battalion in Burma, in circumstances nearly as chaotic as those in Palestine. Pa was greatly amused to get a telegram from Squire some months later saying "My second in command is called U Win".

The outstanding regimental event that occurred shortly after he reached Palestine was the appointment of Princess Elizabeth as Colonel-in-Chief of the Argylls. While he had to leave the formalities to Harry Clark, he took a close interest in the arrangements for the presentation of a regimental brooch to the Princess when she met many representatives of the Argylls, past and present, in Edinburgh on 15th July 1947. It was modelled on the pattern of brooch that he had given Ma as a wedding present. Princess Elizabeth's visit to Edinburgh was just five days after she had announced her engagement to Lieutenant Philip Mountbatten who joined her as she met the representatives of the Regiment for the first time.

HRH Princess Elizabeth visits Stirling Castle, 1947

Pa was able to get home for a short time in late September to be present when Princess Elizabeth paid her first formal visit to Stirling Castle, and received the Freedom of Stirling on behalf of the Regiment. During the same visit he attended the parade marking the return of the Colours to the 7th Battalion, now reforming as a Territorial unit. Both occasions were marked by heavy rain, so perhaps Palestine had more to offer.

He returned from Palestine for another brief trip when he and Ma were invited to the Princess's wedding in November. This not only involved the wedding ceremony itself but included an afternoon party at St James's Palace on 17th November, and an evening party at Buckingham Palace on the 18th which was attended by many of the royal families of Europe and heads of government of the Empire and allied nations. It was a happy coincidence that, when I was Colonel of the Gordon Highlanders, Belinda and I were invited to attend similar celebrations when Prince Charles, the Colonel-in-Chief, married Diana.

Although he felt that the distance between Scotland and Gibraltar made it necessary to appoint a Deputy Colonel for the Argyll and Sutherland Highlanders, Pa continued to take a close interest in regimental matters, even to the extent of signing a letter explaining which the correct pattern of regimental tie was, after the amalgamation of the 1st and 2nd Battalions. He usually timed his occasional visits to Scotland to fit with regimental activities. Thus, in 1953, it coincided with the presentation of New Colours to the 1st Battalion. The parade took place in the garden of the Palace of Holyroodhouse, and Pa accompanied the Queen who presented the Colours.

The 1st Battalion, which I had joined in 1953, was seldom static for more than a year during this period. Pa was unable to see them off when they were recalled at very short notice from exercising at Catterick to pack their bags in Edinburgh and sail four days later in HMS *Implacable* to keep the peace in British Guiana, in September 1953.

He was, however, also at home shortly before the Battalion landed back in Britain in November 1954, having accompanied the Queen when she took the salute at a parade to mark the Centenary of the Battle of Balaklava, in October. Representative companies of the Regular and Territorial battalions and the Depot assembled for inspection at Stirling Castle, the 1st Battalion contingent being found from the advance party, who were preparing to take over the camp at Elgin. The following day he read the lesson at a service in the Church of the Holy Rude in Stirling.

HM Queen Elizabeth at Balaklava Centenary parade, 1954

Military commitments did not altogether cease when Pa retired from the Army on leaving Gibraltar. He remained Colonel of the Argylls, both of Scotland and Canada, and was also earmarked to take command in Scotland should the GOC be called away on an emergency. Besides the routine matters of regimental policy and selection of potential officers for the Scottish regiment, these commitments entailed a number of visits to both formations. Notable among them were his trip to Berlin to visit 1 A&SH and a visit to Hamilton when the Queen presented new Colours to the A&SH of Canada, and to the other Scottish-Canadian regiments of which she was Colonel-in-Chief.

The Berlin trip included visiting a number of War Graves with retired Canadian General Don Agnew whom he had known since 1937, and who was now Director of the War Graves Commission for Europe. Ma and Judy accompanied him, and they drove (sometimes at a rather funereal speed) all the way to Berlin. Ma used to criticise my driving for its speed and to compare it with that of Don, who never had to use the brakes. If you travel on empty autobahns at much less speed than the rest of the traffic, this isn't difficult!

When they arrived in Berlin, and stayed with Barclay Pearson, the CO, and his wife Heather, the ceremonial and social part of the programme was pretty intensive, but there was still time for some highly competitive tennis with their hosts.

Pa jokes with Captain Barry Gardiner, Berlin, 1956

The Canadian visit included a parade in the main sports arena in Hamilton with massive crowds watching as the Queen carried out the presentation of Colours. Pa was at her right hand and featured in a number of papers in a particularly striking picture entitled *The Smiling Queen*.

The Smiling Queen

His final duty as Colonel of the Argylls was to say farewell to the Battalion at Liverpool in January 1959 as it embarked for Cyprus, to take part in the last phase of the campaign against the EOKA terrorists led by the Greek Cypriot Colonel Grivas.

Since he no longer had any official status he was free to campaign against the threatened disbandment of the Argylls under the next phase of reductions in the Army in 1968. He chaired the *Save the Argylls Campaign*. Among the leading members were Colin Mitchell who had left the Army shortly after returning from his very successful tour in command in Aden in which the press gave him the nickname *Mad Mitch*. One of the others who participated, not always to Pa's satisfaction, was the Duchess of Argyll. By mobilising a huge number of supporters, the campaign collected a million signatures, and Pa led the delegation which delivered the papers to Parliament.

Although the Conservatives had promised to retain the Argylls if they returned to power in the forthcoming election, the disbandment process had gone too far by the summer of 1970. They were able to save a company at that time, but the problems in Northern Ireland soon afterwards demanded an expansion in the infantry, and, much to Pa's satisfaction, the Battalion returned to full strength in 1972.

When the Argylls were stationed in Belfast in 1978, Pa stayed with me in Lisburn and visited the Battalion headquarters for lunch. During the meal a bomb went off in a factory nearby, and he was given a flak-jacket and went with the Commanding Officer to see what was done during the follow-up operation. He was like an old war-horse revelling in the smell of cordite one last time.

Pa at site of Belfast bomb, 1978

One of Pa's other responsibilities, as Chairman of the Board of Her Majesty's Commissioners for the Queen Victoria School in Dunblane, also helped to keep him in touch with military matters. The school, which is funded by the Ministry of Defence, offers a boarding school education for about 270 children of Scottish servicemen. In Pa's day, the emphasis was on education that would equip boys with the skills to join the forces. He would be surprised that it now trains both girls and boys and that the Principal is a lady, largely as a result of decisions taken during my subsequent time as Chairman.

Queen Victoria School Grand Day: The Inspection

CHAPTER 7

Palestine (1947-1948)

by
Andrew

Peace was not to last long. Pa received a letter from the War Office, dated 24th October 1946, that read "Sir, I am directed to inform you that you have been selected for appointment as General Officer Commanding (GOC), British Troops in Palestine and Transjordan *vice* Lieutenant-General Sir Evelyn H. Barker, KBE, CB, DSO, MC to another appointment."[xxix] This arrived just two days after a British Government decision to withdraw General Barker from Palestine after allegations that he had engaged in an extramarital affair with Katie Antonius, the widow of an eminent Arab author, and following his public expression of strong personal anti-Semitic feelings in the aftermath of the bombing of the King David Hotel.[xxx]

Ma had expected to accompany him. But, after the heavy baggage had been packed and sent off, much to her surprise, Pa informed her that she would not be allowed to travel. The War Office had decided late in 1946 that 'no families' were to accompany British troops in Palestine, but, for some obscure reason, the decision was classified as *secret*. And so Pa, while aware of the prohibition, was unable to tell his wife, and watched helplessly while Ma spent all her clothing coupons – for clothes were still rationed in Britain – on summer clothes, and, no doubt, helped her pack them as well as all sorts of other supplies. She therefore stayed at Finlaystone while he left to take up his duties, alone, on 13th February 1947.

On his way to Palestine, Pa stopped in Fayid, in Egypt, for briefing by General Sir Miles (*Bimbo*) Dempsey, Commander-in-Chief, Middle East Land Forces, his immediate boss and good friend – as well as my godfather. Pa visited Dempsey in hospital and received his briefing in the form of a pencilled scribble on the two sides of a piece of scrap paper, which has been copied in the photograph below. The fact that the paper is so well-worn suggests that Pa must have kept it in a pocket in his uniform and referred to it from time-to time in the coming months during which he seems to have followed the instructions to the letter. The brief is remarkable for its conciseness yet completeness:

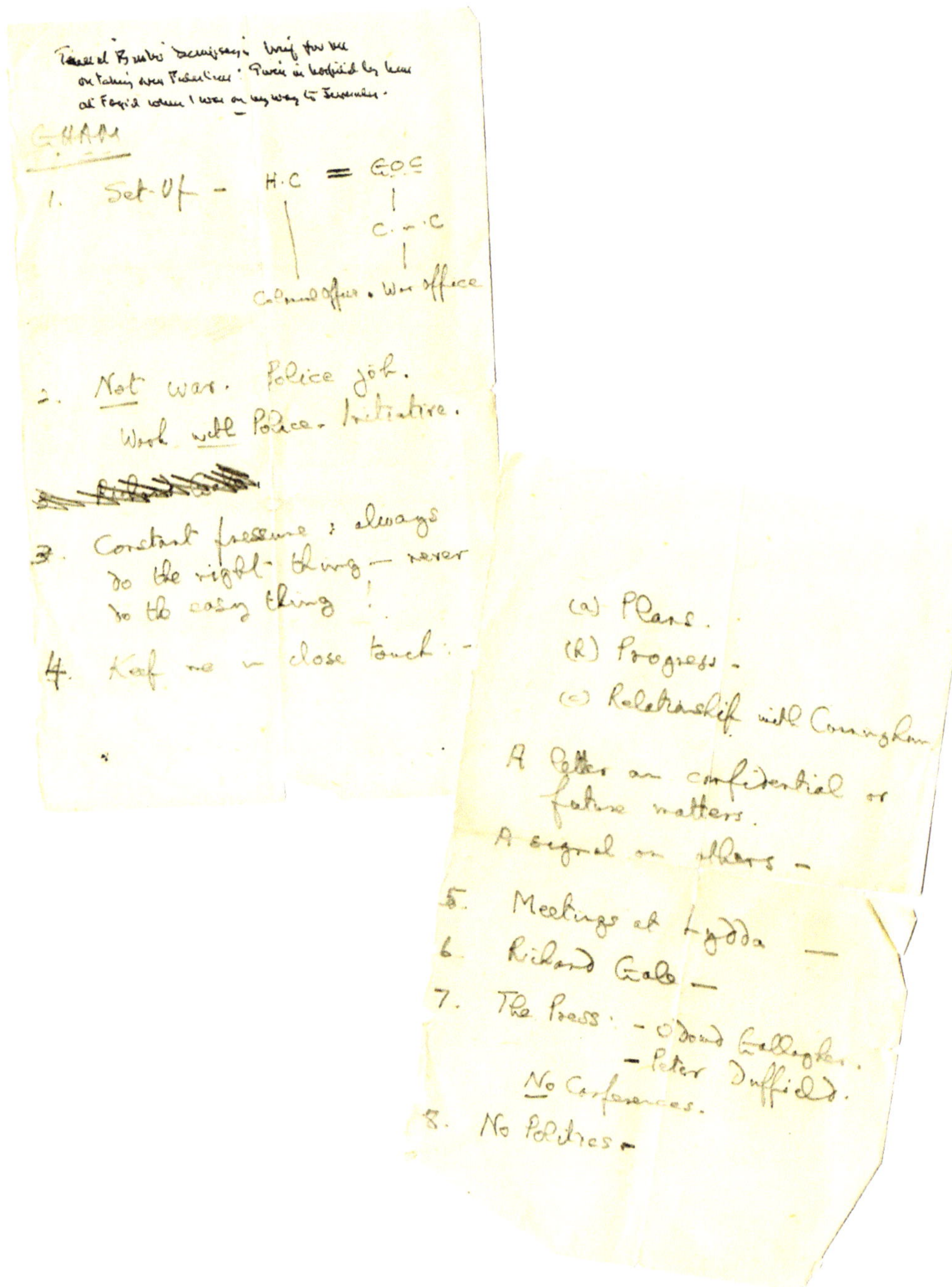

Pa can be seen in a *Pathe* news clip, disembarking on an airstrip near Jerusalem from an Avro Anson, inspecting troops of the 2nd Battalion Royal Lincolnshire Regiment and hurriedly getting into a car to head to Jerusalem to take up his new duties.[xxxi] It is not clear whether he was yet aware that, on the previous day, his predecessor, before leaving Palestine, had approved the death sentences on 3 Jewish men who would have to be executed on his watch.

When he began his assignment, several British newspapers commented on his selection for the job. One wrote that:

"General Gordon MacMillan brings to perhaps the most unpleasant job which has ever fallen to the lot of a British general two valiant qualities. He is first, foremost and all the time a soldier, regarding politics as the cemetery of a military career. Secondly, he is completely fearless. He won an MC with two bars in the First World War and a DSO in the second. Quiet, efficient, yet capable of divine wrath when the need arises, he is a great leader and is both loved and respected by his subordinates. He is also a master of the unexpected."[xxxii]

In the *Daily Mail*, Robert Jackson, in an article entitled 'The *Babe* takes over', wrote that

"When the job of attempting to bring order to Palestine became vacant, the wiseacres maintained that the difficult task would go to someone who was in "disgrace" or to a strong-arm man not afraid to use strength.

"Major-General Gordon Holmes Alexander MacMillan, CB, CBE, DSO, MC, is certainly not in disgrace, whatever that may mean. He can be tough, but his reputation as a soldier rests on efficiency rather than toughness. "Dreadful," exclaimed MacMillan, when a colonel sacked from Palestine said the Jews would get far rougher treatment than they had ever had before MacMillan arrived. "I hope that's not the sort of thing people are saying about me."

"MacMillan is an exception to the rule that generals do not usually look like regular soldiers. Generals resemble butchers, clergymen, actors, grocers, farmers and undertakers, but hardly ever soldiers. He is tall and spare, has an incisive tenor voice and the manner of a man who from youth has had his orders obeyed.

"He is not particularly good-looking, but his smile is ready and charming. A leg wound from shell splinters in Normandy makes him move a little more stiffly than he once did, but all his actions are still quick.

"The general who looks like a general takes a soldier's view of his appointment to Palestine. There is a job to be done and he has been picked to do it. Any comments? You can almost hear the question as he used to ask it in his precise voice at the end of a Staff College Lecture.

The General who looks like a General

"You can say this," says General MacMillan. "I am looking forward very much to going to Palestine. I have never been there before, but I know a great deal about the work. I have seen my predecessor, General Barker, and he has put me in the picture. I think things are going to quieten down in due course, but that is a soldier's view!"

The article went on to say "On leaves at home in Scotland he shoots when he gets the chance, but in spare moments is called on to help in the garden. His wife is an expert gardener and all the children have inherited her green fingers, but the general takes orders in the garden.

"I am just the labourer," he says. But MacMillan's labouring, like all his other work, is done efficiently and methodically. "The general is very good in the garden," says his wife, in an unsolicited testimonial. "He is hard-working, quick and very reliable. I can even trust him to hoe without supervision. I know that all the weeds will be hoed out, but not a single flower." A general like that is just what Palestine needs today."[xxxiii]

On the day following his arrival, the Secretary of State for Foreign Affairs and the Colonies, Ernest Bevin, told the House of Commons that His Majesty's Government had decided that the moment had come to place the question of the future of Palestine before the United Nations.[xxxiv] This decision was to have huge implications for British troops in Palestine because it became the prelude for the eventual end of the British mandate there and for an increasingly violent struggle between Arabs and Jews for control of the territory, that subsequently turned to open warfare. Pa must have quickly found himself revising his view that things would "quieten down".

Following the end of World War I and the surrender of the Ottoman Empire, Britain was granted a mandate by the League of Nations on 23rd September 1923 to rule Palestine and Transjordan, that had formerly been part of Ottoman Syria. A major purpose of the mandate was to put into effect in Palestine the Balfour Declaration of 1917 which stated: "His Majesty's Government view with favour the establishment in Palestine of a national home for the Jewish people, and will use their best endeavours to facilitate the achievement of this object, it being clearly understood that nothing shall be done which may prejudice the civil and religious rights of existing non-Jewish communities in Palestine, or the rights and political status enjoyed by Jews in any other country." Britain transferred many of its powers over Transjordan progressively to local Arab rulers, culminating in the creation of the Hashemite Kingdom of Jordan by King Abdullah I on 25th May 1946.

Britain established a full civilian government in Palestine under the authority of a High Commissioner. Throughout Pa's tour of duty, the responsibility fell to Sir Alan Cunningham, a Scot and former Lieutenant General who, like Pa, had been for a while Commander of the 51st Highland Division during World War II. His ancestors had also been owners of Finlaystone.

In 1947, the population of Palestine consisted of 1,845,000 people, of whom about two thirds were Arabs and one third Jews. Law and order were maintained by the Palestine Police (including 4,000 British staff), and by the British Army. At the time of Pa's appointment, there were about 100,000 troops stationed in Palestine, a force of almost the same size as the entire British army in 2010.

Political decisions and events in 1947 had a fundamental impact on the role of the army in Palestine and on the extent to which it could realistically be expected to maintain law and order. Bevin's announcement to the House of Commons marked the beginning of a process that was to lead to a decision, on 27th September 1947, to terminate the British mandate on 15th May 1948.

The United Nations Special Committee on Palestine (UNSCOP) was formed in May 1947 and arrived in Palestine to carry out its investigations on 14th June. Pa was quite scathing about the work of UNSCOP. Referring to its visit to Palestine, he wrote, "Neither I nor any of my officers were required to give evidence in person before the Committee. Most improper attempts to influence me to commute the death sentences [on the 3 Jews, confirmed by Barker, for their part in the attack on Acre Jail] were, however, made to me by more than one member of the Committee, even while the case was *sub judice* and before the proceedings of the Military Court had reached me, notably by the Representative of Guatemala whose approach and attitude were not worthy of the high ideals of the Institution which he represented. Such suggestions… could only bring its [the committee's] activities into contempt and disrepute as far as the Army was concerned."[xxxv]

The UNSCOP report, approved by the UN General Assembly on 29th November, called for a partitioning of Palestine, a recommendation that was strongly supported by the US government but bitterly opposed by Palestine's Arabs and considered unworkable by Britain. As Pa noted, "As soon as the Partition Plan recommended by UNSCOP was announced, the Jews became hysterically jubilant and the Arabs were stunned that such a solution could be possible, involving, as it did, the gift to the Jews of such large areas of purely Arab population."[xxxvi] Some historians consider 29th November as the date on which civil war between Arabs and Jews began.

Violence between the Jews and Arabs and by the Jews against the British authorities escalated rapidly. By late 1947, the British began reducing troop numbers in anticipation of the final evacuation that had to take place immediately after the end of the mandate. The practical result was that the capacity of British forces to keep the peace and enforce law and order was diminishing just as the demand for their engagement was growing rapidly. An increasing proportion of their capacity had to be applied to protecting themselves and preparing for the evacuation.

Throughout Pa's time as GOC, there were divergent views between the Civil Administration and the Army command in Palestine, on the one hand, and the political and military authorities in London, on the other, as to the appropriate response to the escalating violence. Within two weeks of his arrival, he and the High Commissioner, under pressure from Field-Marshal Montgomery,[xxxvii] then the Chief of the Imperial General Staff, took the decision to impose, for a short time, 'statutory martial law' on Tel Aviv and parts of Jerusalem. The aim was to round up extremists amongst the Jewish population who had been responsible for some of the worst 'outrages'.

Some 10 days after the end of this operation, the High Commissioner and GOC were summoned to a Cabinet meeting in London, presided over by the Prime Minister, Clement Attlee. Sir Alan provided an overview of the situation, noting that "The Jewish terrorists, whose strength was about 6,000 to 7,000 or 1 percent of the Jewish population, were continuing their activities and persistent pressure must be maintained." He went on to refer to the need to enlist the support of the moderate Jewish population to curb extremist activities, and admitted that the imposition of statutory martial law had been a mistake in Jerusalem, in that it restricted movements and economic activities and hence risked alienating moderates. "The GOC expressed agreement with the High Commissioner's survey. There was complete accord between the civil and military authorities in Palestine. The morale of the troops is high."[xxxviii]

The same Cabinet meeting approved recommendations made by the Chiefs of Staff for retaining the existing civilian government, intensifying military pressure against terrorists and the selective re-imposition of 'statutory martial law'. They asked for further thought to be given to a proposal to establish summary military courts to deal with specified offences.

This meeting helped to clarify the rules of engagement for British forces in Palestine. Both Sir Alan Cunningham and Pa, however, must have been relieved that the much more vigorous measures to root out terrorism, known to have been favoured by Montgomery (and proposed by him to an earlier Cabinet meeting in January 1947) were not even proposed to the Cabinet: they would almost certainly have led to very damaging counter-attacks on British troops at a time when the priority, in their minds, was to assure a safe British withdrawal. Subsequently, Montgomery, in his memoirs published in 1958, wrote scathingly of Cunningham's handling of the situation in Palestine, inducing the latter to write a letter to the Daily Telegraph, stating "He criticizes my methods of dealing with terrorism… He argues throughout that the Civil Administration was preventing the Army from doing its job. This is quite untrue…– His Memoirs incline me to believe that bees buzz in bonnets, however eminent."[xxxix] These were sentiments that were, no doubt, shared by Pa.

Pa took up the theme of terrorism at about the same time in an address to army officers in Palestine which may be as relevant now in the 21st century as it was then. "I have given orders that the word *Terrorist* be abolished in order to make clear our position… We deal only with breakers of the law, and, when a murder has been done, we seek the murderer. *Terrorist* has a two-fold implication: it invests the criminal with glamour and implies that he inspires terror in someone. No murderer or dabbler in explosives is glamorous and it is ridiculous to even suggest that such people are frightening the British Army."[xl]

It is necessary to explain that much of the responsibility for maintaining law and order within the Jewish and Arab communities effectively resided with their local paramilitary forces, with whom the British Army and the Palestine Police had quite good working relationships, though the extent of mutual trust varied over time. On the Jewish side, the mainstream militia group was the Hagana which, together with the Palmach, its commando group, subsequently became the foundation on which the Jewish Defense Force was built. In the 1930s, Jewish leaders had imposed a policy of restraint on the Hagana vis-à-vis the British, which drove the more militant elements to found the Irgun (or Etzel), and similar motives led to the creation of the equally militant Lehi (or Stern Gang) in 1940. Because of Britain's war with Nazi Germany, both Irgun and the Stern Gang lay low during the Second World War, but, as soon as peace was declared, they renewed their attacks on the British. Most notable amongst these was the attack on the King David Hotel in Jerusalem, that housed many of the offices of the British Army, in July 1946, leaving 91 dead. As a consequence of this, the Jewish Agency and the Hagana distanced themselves from the two extremist forces.

This was fortunate for Pa as members of the Hagana were responsible for thwarting two of three recorded attempts to assassinate him in 1947. These are described in some detail by Nachman Ben Yehuda in the following excerpts from his book, entitled *Political Assassination by Jews*.

> "MacMillan was a tough minded commander and intended to implement a tough policy against the pre-state underground Jewish groups. One of his first acts was to demand that the British troops would stop referring to members of Lehi, Etzel and Hagana as 'terrorists'…. Another of his acts was to sign and confirm the death sentence on Meir Feinstein (from Etzel) and Moshe Barazani (from Lehi). Lehi decided to assassinate MacMillan. The responsibility for the assassination was given to 'Uzi the Red' and Ezra Yachin.

"The first assassination attempt was made about two weeks after MacMillan signed the death sentences in April 1947….. A powerful mine was planted underground (on Saturday night) in one of the curves of the Jerusalem-Tel Aviv road…. A few of Lehi's members rotated in observation, waiting for MacMillan to show up. Unfortunately for Lehi, the British discovered the mine and dismantled it.

"A second attempt focused on planning to use a cart (used by baggage movers). The plan was to fill the cart with explosives and to detonate it in Jaffo Street in Jerusalem…. A short time before the bomb was supposed to be detonated, a small unit of Hagana members came by and told the two Lehi's operators to dismantle the mine. The Hagana's goal was not to arrest Lehi's members but to prevent the assassination.

"A third attempt was made on the third and fourth of July 1947 when a powerful mine was discovered by Hagana members on the road from Jerusalem to Tel Aviv. The police was notified and the mine was dismantled.

"Yachin's account… conveys the clear impression that at that time (probably April-July 1947), he was literally obsessed with the idea of assassinating MacMillan and approached his local commander in Jerusalem with various ideas about how to do it, including volunteering to put himself in some dangerous and risky situations. All his suggestions were rejected by his commander."[xli]

In spite of the prevailing tensions and dangers, Pa seems to have been able to take time off occasionally to shoot quail and wildfowl around Huleh, Jericho and Nablus, often in the company of his ADC, Hughdie Spens.[xlii] He also found some time for tourism, visiting a number of the holy places including the Church of the Holy Sepulchre and its various chapels, and the tomb of Moses. In a short summary of his impressions[xliii], he noted that "Although the whole of Palestine is filled with relics and buildings of intense historical interest and antiquity, many of them are cheapened by the mercenary outlook of their custodians."

Pa can also be seen looking, in a *Pathe* news clip, quite relaxed, presenting the prizes at a horse show held at Samakh, beside the Sea of Galilee, where riders from the Palestine Police, the Transjordan Frontier Force and Lancers compete in *tent-pegging*.[xliv] Moreover, living, as he did for most of his time in Palestine, in the King David Hotel, which housed the Officers' Mess, must have been more convivial than staying alone in the GOC's official residence.

In spite of the considerable pressures under which he was working, he took particular interest in the activities of the 1st Battalion of the Argyll and Sutherland Highlanders. Records show that Pa visited them on a number of occasions for dinner in the Officers' Mess and celebrated Balaklava Day with the Sergeants. He took full advantage of the Battalion's presence in his Command to get to know them better.

Pa with 1 A&SH Officers, Palestine

His visits were not always merely social occasions, and in the last days while the army was moving into the final positions round Haifa and Jaffa, he inspected the posts which the Battalion was manning.

He also had the opportunity to entertain the Moderator of the Church of Scotland, Dr Matthew Stewart, and his Chaplain, the Reverend John Fraser, during a visit they paid to the three Scottish regiments serving in Palestine. He told them a good deal about the last weeks of the Mandate which were fast approaching, and they commented that they could "well understand the pride which the regiment takes in claiming as one of themselves a commander of such distinction, a man with such qualities of head and heart."[xlv]

At some stage during his time in Palestine, Pa visited Amman to pay his respects to King Abdullah, and to thank him for the assistance given to the British Army by the Arab Legion and the Trans-Jordan Frontier Force. It is believed that Pa gave the King a pair of field glasses, and perhaps a regimental print of the harbour at Balaklava. After lunch the King rang a bell to summon a lackey and told Pa that he wished to give him a rug. When Pa showed signs of hesitation, the British Resident,

Alec Kirkbride, reportedly said, "Don't be a fool: Alan Cunningham took two!" For many years, 'King Abdullah's carpet' graced the floor of the drawing room at Finlaystone.

With King Abdullah of Transjordan, Amman, 1948

On almost every day of Pa's time in Palestine, there was some kind of incident. Many were gun battles between Jews and Arabs, instigated by one side or the other, and often ending with a temporary truce, arranged by the British Army, and the confiscation of weapons. Much of the Army's time was taken up, working alongside the Police, in *cordon and search* operations, aimed at apprehending extremists and recovering arms. But the Army itself came under frequent attack, especially by Jewish extremist groups, requiring that a large number of soldiers had to be engaged in guard duties to protect sensitive targets.[xlvi] It also came in for much verbal attack from the two sides as each claimed that the army had sided with the other. And both Arabs and Jews did their best to disrupt the territory's railways, especially the route to Egypt through which many of the army's supplies arrived and were eventually to be evacuated. Between 1st January 1947 and 30th June 1948, the British Army lost 13 officers and 161 other ranks, and a further 37 officers and 382 other ranks were wounded.[xlvii]

While many of these events were of a routine character, several, either at the time or later, with the benefit of hindsight, caught the attention of the local and international press, which was usually highly critical of the British handling of affairs: this was particularly the case when British actions conflicted with implicit US policies, especially in relation to Jewish immigration into Palestine.

The events that attracted most international attention during this period included:

The execution of 9 Jews, members of the Stern Gang and Irgun between April and July 1947, following convictions in military courts. These were followed by reprisals, including the kidnapping and murder of two British sergeants – which, in turn, sparked a rampage by British troops in Tel Aviv (causing 5 Jewish deaths), and widespread anti-Semitic violence and rioting in Britain.[xlviii]

The arrival of *SS Exodus 1947*, under Hagana command, with 4,515 illegal Jewish immigrants on board on 18th July 1947, when it was boarded in international waters by the Royal Navy (resulting in the death of 3 immigrants) and escorted into Haifa. In a change of British policy, under which illegal immigrants (65,307 of whom arrived on 47 ships during 1946-48) had until then been shipped to refugee camps in Cyprus, the *Exodus* passengers were to be returned on British vessels to France from where they had sailed. After they had refused to disembark in France, they were taken to Hamburg and placed in camps in the British occupied zone of Germany. These events coincided with the UNSCOP visit and may have contributed to their recommendations on partition and to US support for this.[xlix] (Pa would have been amazed to find that, nowadays, photos of the *Exodus* event are included in Yad Vashem, the Holocaust Museum, alongside pictures of the most dreadful atrocities inflicted on the Jewish people during and before the second world war.)

The court martial on 2nd October 1947 of Major Roy Farran, a former special forces soldier who had joined an anti-terrorist squad set up clandestinely within the Palestine Police Force. He was accused of murdering a 16 year old Jewish boy who was abducted while handing out leaflets in support of the Irgun. Farran's acquittal, on the technical grounds that no body had been found and hence there was no proof of murder, enraged Jewish public opinion and undermined much of the tacit support that had until then been given to the British by moderate Jews.[l]

Following the UN resolution on Partition of 29th November 1947, British troop numbers were progressively reduced and there was a parallel scaling down of the Civil Administration. On 28th March 1948, Pa formally stated that the growing demands of the incipient evacuation process were severely reducing the Army's capacity to react properly to the escalating hostilities. "The tasks of troops in every sector are made more complex, not only by the increase in Arab and Jew activity but also by the reduction in strength and effectiveness of both the civil police and the Government Administration… Effective military action can no longer be taken to forestall, break up or punish large scale attacks by either community."[li]

Acting consistently with his stated position, some two weeks later, on 9th April, Pa claimed that his troops were "essentially non-functional"[lii], and refused a request by the High Commissioner to send soldiers into the Arab village of Deir Yassin to halt a reported massacre that was being carried out jointly by members of the Irgun and the Stern Gang with the tacit support of the Hagana. This left at least 107 villagers, many of them unarmed women and children, dead. It was strongly condemned by moderate Jewish leaders but the accounts of the horrific scenes in the village also ignited panic in the Arab community, setting in motion what was to grow into a massive wave of emigration.

Four days later, a Jewish convoy, carrying medical staff to the Hadassah hospital on Mount Scopus, above Jerusalem, was ferociously attacked by Arabs – intent on revenge after Deir Yassin – and over 70 Jews were killed in a fierce day-long battle. Some British soldiers, led by Major Jack Churchill, had appeared quickly on the scene, but were unable to arrange a truce and, reportedly, their offer to evacuate some members of the convoy in an armoured personnel carrier was refused.[liii] On his way to Kalandia airport that morning, Pa came close to the battle scene but then withdrew, after being fired on by a Jewish armoured car. His own report notes: "Jewish convoy en route to Hadassah Hospital attacked by Arabs at Sheikh Jarrar. The GOC's car was hit but no-one was injured."[liv]

The delay in authorizing substantive British intervention was consistent with the position taken by Pa in relation to the Jewish attack at Deir Yassin just four days earlier, and with his wish to prevent further loss of British lives in the days immediately preceding the start of the evacuation. He was, however, strongly criticized by the Jews for being aware of the outbreak of violence but not immediately authorizing intervention by the Army, which eventually arranged a truce, after using heavy weapons against the Arabs, at 4.00 pm. Some Jewish commentators also allege that British police had colluded with the Arabs and were aware of the planned ambush.[lv] To all intents and purposes, however, civil war had broken out and there was little that could be done to prevent serious clashes between two forces so intent on seriously damaging each other and on gaining control of key strategic points, without placing extra demands on already over-stretched troops.

In the first half of April, the Army shifted its headquarters from Jerusalem to Haifa and began to move troops into the area in preparation for the beginning of the main phase of the evacuation that was scheduled to start from 15th May, immediately after the end of the mandate and when the citrus harvest – which required the full capacity of the port of Haifa to handle export shipments – was over. The logistical task was immense as it involved moving 70,000 personnel and an estimated 210,000 tons of military stores and equipment, spread around the country, out of Palestine, partly overland to Egypt but largely through the port of Haifa.

Pa was billeted in the Carmelite monastery, overlooking Haifa. He got to know the nuns and found that they were expert needlewomen. He persuaded one of them to restore his Pipe Banner, as the tartan backing, on which Ma had embroidered his crest and the Regimental crests soon after their marriage, had begun to deteriorate. The beautifully restored banner still hangs at Finlaystone in a double-sided glass frame that allows both sides to be seen.

Until late April, there was considerable confidence amongst the Palestinian Arabs that, once the British had left, they, with the help of the regular armies of neighbouring Arab States, would be in a position to take charge of most of Palestine. The Arab League's Army for the Liberation of Palestine had been building up its strength in Palestine since early March and had been quite successful in some engagements, only to find itself deprived of weapons and ammunition by its Damascus-based commanders and paymasters.[lvi] Amongst the Arab leaders, however, only King Abdullah of Jordan recognized the military strength of the Jewish forces and was also willing to see some form of homeland for the Jews, while hoping to play a role in the oversight of any State that might emerge.

On 25th April, General Sir John Glubb (*Glubb Pasha*), the British-born commander of the Jordan-based Arab Legion that had been assisting the British Army in Palestine, wrote to Pa, stating that "The situation is developing in a manner rather different to that anticipated, and it looks as though the Jews may have complete possession of all Palestine before May 15th. In these circumstances the Trans-Jordan

Government will probably not be prepared to implement their scheme for the re-occupation of the Arab areas of Palestine on May 15th. The purpose of this letter is to warn you that we may want to take the whole of the Arab Legion out before May 15th, not leaving any detachments behind."[lvii]

Pa annotated this "As long as they are leaving we can get them out and inform the Jews."

Five days later, on 30th April, King Abdullah wrote personally to Pa: "We hear with great anxiety of heavy Jewish attacks on Jerusalem. It is not just that the Jews be allowed to conquer Jerusalem with the British Mandate still in force and while Britain refuses to allow Arab forces to intervene in defence. Beg you to stop Jewish attack with British forces, Abdullah."

In response, Pa wrote to the King: "I can assure you that no efforts are being spared to bring about peace in Jerusalem. Security forces are in control and Jewish attacks have ceased at the moment. Arab artillery is, however, firing and unless it also ceases it will be hard to maintain truce. British forces will resist any further acts of aggression in Jerusalem wherever they may come from. I trust that Your Majesty will counsel patience among Arab forces at least until Mandate has ended on 15th May."

Shortly before the British Mandate formally ended and Sir Alan Cunningham had left Palestine, David Ben-Gurion declared the establishment of the Jewish State of Israel on 14th May 1948. This provoked an immediate reaction from Arab states, and served as the starting gun for all-out war.

In this very dangerous situation, Pa was required to operate under the terms of a Government Directive that ordered him to:

"Be responsible:

For the orderly evacuation of our forces;

For the evacuation of stores..... You will ensure that no weapons or ammunition are abandoned in Palestine in serviceable or repairable condition.

...The basis of the powers which you may exercise will be that of Commander of a military force in occupation of a foreign territory.

You have no responsibility for the preservation of law and order in any part of Palestine except as required of you for the protection of our forces and for the purposes of evacuation."[lviii]

In 1978, in a television interview about the evacuation, Pa explained that "There were four principles laid down. One was that it was vitally important to maintain the security of Haifa which was going to be the main port for the evacuation of our troops and stores. The second was to cooperate closely with the civil administration, and the third was to make sure that there was no interruption to our lines of communication, that were to Haifa and to Egypt. The last one was that we would have to stay in Jerusalem until the end of the mandate." He went on to note that "As the British withdrew in the North toward Haifa, in the South toward Egypt, Arab and Jew were left facing each other. A war between Arab and Jew now seemed inevitable."[lix]

For security reasons, General Sir John Crocker (Pa's commander during the initial stages of the liberation of Tunisia), who had succeeded *Bimbo* Dempsey as Commander in Chief Middle East, and Pa had, in fact, unsuccessfully urged Sir Alan Cunningham to move from Jerusalem to Haifa on 5th May "unless an earlier date is forced upon us by unforeseen circumstances."[lx] This was in response to an earlier letter from Sir Alan to the Colonial Secretary , in which he wrote "In regard to the soldiers' suggestion that we should go to Haifa, I do not wish to put this forward myself, though if the soldiers consider it for security reasons, it would have to be considered. To abandon Jerusalem to become a battlefield and then to go on sitting in Haifa unable to function, would to my mind be even more damaging to British prestige than all that is happening so far."[lxi]

The day-to-day management of the evacuation process was delegated to Major-General Hugh Stockwell. He saw the need to avoid confrontation and so deployed his troops in Haifa "in a manner that would not interfere with Hagana's deployment in the city." This encouraged the Hagana to make a rapid strike to take over the city on 22nd/23rd April, triggering the evacuation of the city by all but about 3,000 of its 50,000 Arabs. According to Sir Henry Gurney, the Colonial Secretary, Stockwell's pragmatic tactics "enjoyed the full backing of his superiors – Cunningham, Gurney, MacMillan. Their approach, which was in flagrant contradiction to the policy of their superiors in London, notably Foreign Secretary Ernest Bevin and the CIGS, Field Marshal Bernard Montgomery, derived from their conclusion that it was no longer possible to execute the evacuation and bring about calm simultaneously and fully."[lxii]

Gurney went on to observe that "London did not like what occurred in Haifa, to put it mildly. Foreign Secretary Bevin, viewed the events there as a gross mistake by the Administration and more especially the Army… They… opposed MacMillan's desire to protect his remaining forces and what remained of his status by helping the United Nations to take control of Palestine."[lxiii]

On 15th May, when Pa formally took over responsibility for British interests in Palestine, he wrote to Ma:

"My very own Darling one,

We finished off yesterday very successfully. I lunched on board HMS *Euryalus* with H.E..

The inhabitants of Haifa are at present behaving well and I think that the Municipal Council will be all right but the new Jewish Government have appointed a 'District Commissioner' and it may be tiresome, if under the direction of Tel Aviv, he incites the Haifa people to give trouble. I hope that this does not occur as I have a lot of troops and could give them an awful crack if necessary – but don't want to do so."[lxiv]

Largely because of Stockwell's controversial action, the very complex evacuation process went smoothly, without a single loss of British life.[lxv] It ended on 30th June in the following way: "The GOC then said goodbye to the British Consul-General and just after 12.39 descended the port steps, the last man of the British forces to leave Palestine. As his launch left the steps, 15 guns were fired in salute by HMS *Phoebe*. The last RAF patrol flew by in salute. The motley collection of craft in the anchorage – liners, LSTs and Z-craft – set off to their destinations as each was ready. As HMS *Phoebe*, with the GOC aboard, was preparing to leave, sixteen aircraft from HMS *Triumph* flew by in salute, in perfect formation. As HMS *Phoebe* steamed out, the two destroyers and frigate that had preceded her in line ahead turned about and steamed by, each ship giving three cheers for General MacMillan.

Thus, with dignity, without incident and entirely according to plan, ended thirty years of British occupation and of British labours for Palestine."[lxvi]

Pa had made a particular point of being the last British serviceman to leave Palestine and quite often referred to this in later years. Oddly enough, Judy subsequently met a senior naval officer who described his predicament when, as a young midshipman, he was detailed to cast off the launch but had been ordered by Pa to board ahead of him!

As an additional touch, the Argylls sent a small detachment ahead and provided the Guard of Honour for Pa when he reported to General Gale in Cairo to hand over his final report and to prepare to leave for the United Kingdom.[lxvii]

Subsequently, in reporting on the period of his tenure as GOC, Pa wrote "The even temper, forbearance and impartiality displayed by all ranks in the Army in Palestine was quite one of the most remarkable features of this period."[lxviii] It was, however, an extraordinarily difficult period for him and all the other soldiers involved. Hugh Stockwell's biographer, Jonathon Riley, sums up the situation as follows: "For the British, Palestine was a salutary lesson. The Army had been pushed into a campaign ill prepared for an insurgency, and military successes in 1947 …had failed to translate into wider success when it became clear that the government had neither the will nor the authority to continue governing Palestine."[lxix]. In spite of this, however, Stockwell, in a hand-written note to Pa, was able to refer to the "very happy and entertaining time under your command."[lxx]

Inspecting Guard of Honour from 1A&SH on return to Egypt from Palestine

Pa's actions throughout the period were, however, clearly consistent with Dempsey's initial instructions. When he was given these instructions in early 1947, Britain's future in Palestine was very unclear. During his first year, however, the political context evolved very rapidly, with the British decision to place the issue before the UN (February), the decision to end the Mandate (September), the UN General Assembly adoption of the UNSCOP recommendations on partition (November), and the eventual unilateral declaration of the State of Israel (May 1948). With each move, the violence between Arab and Jew escalated as did the number of direct attacks on British targets, and the demands on the British Army and the Palestine Police grew commensurately. While initially they were still able to fulfill their task of maintaining law and order, this became less and less feasible, as troop numbers were progressively drawn down and preparations for the evacuation began. As Commander of the troops in Palestine, Pa saw his mission evolve from one of keeping the peace to one of maintaining a semblance of authority and of assuring the safe evacuation of British civilians and military personnel from a country whose citizens were intent on war with each other. This exposed him to fierce criticism from both Jews and Arabs, and it strained his relations with the British political and military establishment in London that was, in his view, unable to appreciate the complexities and realities of the situation on the ground. Both he and the High Commissioner were very much aware that, towards the last days of the mandate, the Army was extremely vulnerable to attack and that, the more it sought to intervene, the greater would its vulnerability have become.

It is in this context that his decision to shift the prime objective of the Army from that of maintaining law and order to ensuring the safe evacuation of British personnel and stores in the last months of the mandate seems to have been entirely justified by the outcome. This was, in the words of Princess Elizabeth, Colonel-in-Chief of the Argyll and Sutherland Highlanders, a "difficult task most honourably fulfilled."[lxxi]

Postscript

We also have a 'worm's eye view' of the closing episode from 2nd Lieutenant Michael Spurgin R.A. in a letter written to his mother in June 1948. At that point Michael was unaware that thirteen years later his sister, Jane, would marry the General's eldest son. Michael wrote as follows:

"Yesterday Gen. MacMillan G.O.C. Palestine came to visit the Regt. to say goodbye and pat us on the back for all the work the British Army had done in this country. He told us how, when the plan was made to withdraw, it was estimated that there would be 250,000 tons of stores to get out by August 1st, and that the army itself would be out by that date. He pointed out that already 254,085 tons had been evacuated and the personnel would be out by July 1st. This, he pointed out, was because the Jews and Arabs had not molested us as much as was expected, and also the efficient way the R.E.s took over stevedores' duties on the docks after the Jews had taken over Haifa. The General then went on to tell us what preparations had been made for the final withdrawal, so that the Jews could not take advantage whilst our backs were turned.

All our stores have been loaded – vehicles and all, and it only remains for us to embark on the Empire Test, which leaves Haifa in the next day or two (most unfortunate since I did want to be one of the last troops to leave Palestine)."

CHAPTER 8

Gogar Bank (1949-1952)

by
John

Once back in Scotland again, Pa was able to attend more directly to regimental matters, before he took up his next appointment as GOC Scotland in January 1949. He was, incidentally, the first Argyll to hold that appointment.

National Service was still current, and the troops in Britain were largely a back-up for the much stronger forces which were serving overseas. Much of the army was in stations where former colonies were making the sometimes painful transition to independence, while an equally strong force was concentrated in Germany where the Cold War was being regarded with increasing anxiety, since the blockade of Berlin had made it clear that Stalin was a threat to be reckoned with. The outbreak of the Korean War in August 1950 added an extra urgency to the tasks of supporting the forces overseas. A special dimension that concerned Pa was the deployment of 1 A&SH from Hong Kong to Korea as one of the first two British battalions to join the war there. The other was the 1st Battalion of the Middlesex Regiment whose forebears had served alongside the 93rd throughout the First War, and later, during the Second World War, had supported the 1st Battalion as a Machine Gun regiment in North Africa and Italy.

After the last minute decision that Ma could not accompany Pa to Palestine, it was unfortunate that the chance to enjoy an accompanied posting at Scottish Command was delayed for several months because Gogar Bank, the house that went with the job, needed a major overhaul.

This didn't stop Ma getting to grips with its walled-in garden which sloped down to the two banks of the Gogar Burn, while she was grounded at Finlaystone. The ex-Palestine Police Wolseley that Pa had bought and shipped home made a great many journeys to Gogar Bank so heavily laden with plants from the Finlaystone border, packed in old ammunition boxes, that the front wheels had a very casual contact with the road. Spring was a very good time to perform this operation, and the resulting planting became known for a great many years as 'Lady MacMillan's garden'. Many of the stock plants were still there in 1988, when I and my family came to live at Gogar Bank, when I, too, served as GOC Scotland.

Pa must have made use of this time to get to know his new estate. Scotland was still full of military units, many of them in transition from their wartime roles to a shape more suitable to the days of peace. His office was in Edinburgh Castle, and with the appointment went a large 1930s Rolls Royce, which had been presented to the army commander at the beginning of the war.

One of his earliest embarrassments was to have to fight for funding to have the car given the overhaul that it needed after eight years of service. Since it had been a gift, no-one had taken it officially on to the Army's establishment, and he was told that he would have to pay for it himself. He had to be very persuasive, pointing out the wonderful service it had given at minimal cost to the taxpayer, before he was granted the money to make it fully roadworthy.

David recalls that Corporal Mills, the army driver who drove the Rolls Royce, did not use a key to start it. He grew one of his thumb nails to use instead.

Once the repairs to Gogar Bank were completed, we were able, for the first time since 1939, to enjoy a fairly normal family life – at least during the school holidays – with both our parents present. Pa's duties were far less demanding than they had been in Palestine and throughout the Second World War, and so he found time to be with his children – whether depositing Andrew from the Rolls on his way to the Castle at Angusfield House School in Edinburgh; doing *The Times* crossword most evenings with George, or playing a round of golf occasionally with me. Sometimes, he felt the need to be firm, as when he refused to allow David to accept the repeated invitations of Sergeant *Craigie* Heron, the butler, to go to the speedway races at Meadowbank stadium.

It was also a time when Pa was able to see more of his mother. As David remembers. "Soon after we came to Gogar Bank, Pa's mother, Granny MacMillan, came to live in a residential hotel in Edinburgh to be closer to her son and see more of his family. She had been widowed in the mid-1930s and had lived what must have been rather a sad life in various residential hotels in London before coming to Edinburgh. Pa had apparently written every day to his parents during the First World War, and to his mother during the Second World War. She worshipped him. Unfortunately, she tended to over-fuss about him which he sometimes found rather irritating.

"We used to go to her hotel in Edinburgh and played different card games with her and some of her elderly friends. Many years later, when one of these friends died, she left us a legacy and a note recalling the fun and the noise which had cheered them all up during the card sessions."

Indeed, life for the GOC was far from unpleasant. The status of the army had always been high in Scotland, and there were many opportunities to enjoy the free time that peacetime soldiering permitted. Many distinguished land-owners invited him to shoot; the subscription to the Headquarters Sporting Fund entitled him to membership of Dalmahoy Golf Club, as well as membership of two rough shoots, for £10 per annum; and the spread of units throughout Scotland required him to travel the length and breadth of the country. No doubt there were also many important decisions which he took, concerning the changing need for many of the wartime establishments, and the deployments and barracks which would be needed in the longer term.

Gogar Bank was also a convenient place for many of his old friends to come and stay, and one of the most regular was General Dick O'Connor. On one occasion he turned up a bit earlier than expected and, when Ma returned, she was surprised to find this very distinguished general being paddled down the burn by David in a tiny rubber dinghy.

David's recollections of Gogar Bank were mainly about cows: "There were some fields around the house and Ma thought it would be good to have a house cow so that she could provide her children with fresh milk. She enlisted an elderly widow, Mrs. Leslie, who lived in a nearby cottage on the place, to care for the cow. I also helped to look after it and milked it during the holidays. I took some very good pictures of Jean, a cross Jersey, with my Brownie box camera. I do not think that there has been another boy at Aysgarth who had a framed picture of a cow next to his parents on the dressing table in the dormitory.

"At this time I was becoming interested in all things to do with farming. When Aunt Buster, Ma's younger sister and very good fun, once came to stay, she was sitting in the drawing room, sewing, when I came in and tried to make polite conversation. I started with a question: "Do you know anything about udder clap?""

Pa was supported at Gogar Bank by two successive ADCs who became great favourites of the family, not least for taking David and Andrew on outings in their sports cars! The first was Colin Mitchell – later to be known in the popular press as "Mad Mitch" – who was still unfit for more active service, having been wounded in Palestine. He was easily raised to a height of indignation, but I think the highest point was when he was in his room in the Officers' Mess in the Castle, and a guide addressing a group of tourists under his window said "Of course, before the War there were soldiers in Edinburgh Castle. Now there's just Scottish Command."

When Colin heard that the Argylls were leaving Hong Kong and going to Korea, he immediately asked to be sent back to the Battalion. Pa agreed and a very tall cavalryman, Robin Stormonth-Darling, was found at short notice to replace him as ADC. I'm sure he was a very good ADC to Pa, but he was also good fun to be with and played quite a large part in the life of the whole family.

There was also the matter of 'ceremonial'.

Installation as Governor of Edinburgh Castle

The GOC is appointed His Majesty's Governor of Edinburgh Castle for the duration of his tour of duty. One aspect of this is the need to have a standard which can be flown from the flag pole over the Castle entrance when the Governor is in the Castle, but, to be entitled to a standard, the incumbent must have Arms. At some point between the wars, Pa and Ma had spent a holiday looking at MacMillan tombstones in Argyll, and had come to think that Pa was the heir to Duncan MacMillan of Dunmore, who had registered arms in 1742. Unfortunately, their notes were destroyed in the bombing of the furniture store in London. When he ventured to suggest to the Lord Lyon, Sir Thomas Innes of Learney, the custodian of all heraldic issues in Scotland, that he might be entitled to Duncan's arms, his case was dismissed for lack of evidence. Sir Thomas duly authorised a new Coat of Arms, and Pa paid the required fee.

For reasons which are unexplained, the actual Installation ceremony did not take place till 13th November 1950.[lxxii] While the event was fairly low-key compared with later Installations, we came to know the main features well, as a re-enactment formed one of the features of the Edinburgh Military Tattoo the following year. After nine or more occasions when he hosted the Tattoo, Pa must have known it word perfectly.

The story of the standard did not end there. During his time as Governor, the self-appointed Bard and Historian of the Clan MacMillan, the Reverend Somerled MacMillan, persuaded the Lord Lyon that Pa was the correct person to hold the post of Clan Chief. At some point it emerged that Duncan MacMillan had been recognised by the Lord Lyon of his day as the Chief of Clan MacMillan. By definition, then, as his recognised successor, Pa turned out to be Chief of Clan MacMillan too.

David vividly remembers that "Somerled would turn up on his bicycle from Edinburgh at very short notice and drone on for hours about the Clan, reciting the verses that he had composed, alternately in Gaelic and English. He interrupted this only by the rendering of mouth music while pretending to play the bagpipes, pumping his arm up and down, which he thought he was good at. We had to sit and listen to this and try not to get the giggles."

The upshot was that Pa found himself entitled to a different Coat of Arms, so he went to the Lord Lyon and asked him to put the matter right. He was slightly irked to find that Sir Thomas didn't apologise for getting it wrong in the first place, making the point in his high-pitched voice that "I never revoke arms once granted". He then demanded a considerable additional fee to matriculate the correct Arms.

When Pa asked what would happen to the one that was no longer valid, he was told to pass it to his second son. This saved me any expense many years later when I became Governor in 1988, and caused some amusement as the Lord Lyon at that time was Sir Thomas's son, Malcolm. He would only believe the story when he was shown the parchment with his father's annotation on it to say that it had been passed on. This must have been tiresome for Malcolm, as he lost a potential fee.

Pa's first duty as Governor was to receive a key for the United Services Museum in the Castle so that he could reopen it after its closure during the War. His main ceremonial activity during his time as

GOC was undoubtedly the Tattoo which took place, during his first year, on alternate evenings in Princes Street Gardens and on the Castle Esplanade. This had been restarted in the time of his predecessor, General Sir Philip Christison, as a very small event, showing off the skills of the many elements of the army stationed in Scotland. The highlight was the piping and military music provided by the large number of bands from the regular and TA units. During Pa's time, the stands were built on the Esplanade, but at the beginning it was a matter of a few arm chairs for the VIPs and standing room for the remaining spectators.

Besides being a show case for the army in Scotland, the Tattoo also provided an excuse to bring a number of influential people from Whitehall to Scotland and to make them aware of what was going on north of the Border. On one occasion Ma was faced with a difficult point of etiquette when the Secretary of State for War, the Secretary of State for Scotland, and the Lord Provost were all invited to dinner at Gogar Bank. Shinwell was clearly important in his own eyes as the top man in the military hierarchy, the Scottish Secretary reckoned he was as good as the King of Scotland, and the Lord Provost, as Lord Lieutenant, represented the King. History doesn't relate what the solution was.

HRH Princess Elizabeth pays first visit to 1A&SH at Colchester, 1949

The Regiment continued to feature strongly in Pa's life. At the end of October 1948 he took the salute at a parade in Colchester to mark the formal amalgamation of the 91st and 93rd. In January 1949 he was in Colchester once more accompanying Field Marshal Wavell, the senior

Highland Colonel, on a visit to the 1st Battalion, and in June he and Ma were back there when Princess Elizabeth paid her first visit to the Battalion. At the last minute, this had been brought forward by a week as the Battalion had been given very short notice to leave Britain once again to strengthen the garrison in Hong Kong. Despite rain varying from intermittent to tropical ferocity, the Princess carried out the inspection of the troops on parade, visited a number of families in their quarters, took tea with the officers and listened to Retreat – from the shelter of her car – without suffering ill-effects afterwards.

The 7th Battalion was chosen to do its annual camp in Germany, and Pa went to Duisburg to visit them in July 1949. He flew from Edinburgh, leaving at 5 am, spent the afternoon visiting elements of the battalion training, and flew back to Hendon where he arrived at 7pm, changed into a tail coat and dined with Princess Elizabeth that evening. His visit to the 8th Battalion at Scarborough was equally brief, but included a parade to present a Long Service and Good Conduct medal to a private with 21 years of service – though history doesn't relate why he was still a private after that long period which had included the war years. He was also a frequent visitor to Stirling Castle, the Regimental Depot, either to discuss regimental business or to escort visitors such as the Secretary of State for War.

This year also marked the beginning of his long association with Queen Victoria School, Dunblane. As GOC, he was ex-officio the Chairman of the Commissioners, and he took the salute on Grand Day in July. His interest continued for many years after he had left the Army but remained as one of Her Majesty's Commissioners. But the highlight in 1949 was the visit that he and Ma paid to Canada. He had just been appointed Honorary Colonel of the Argyll and Sutherland Highlanders of Canada, one of the regiments affiliated to the Argylls. They were away from 21st June to 5th July and were able not only to spend five days (in sweltering heat) with the Canadian Argylls in Hamilton but also to visit many old friends in Ottawa, Kingston and Montreal. One instance of the attention paid to them both was the loan of a large Buick and driver, provided by the Canadian CGS, in which they covered over 1600 miles. The Hamilton Highland Games, a Tattoo with 21 Pipe bands, cocktail parties, dinners, a ball, cruises on Lake Ontario, and ceremonial parades made for a very full and entertaining programme.[lxxiii]

Closer to home Pa continued to be involved with the development of the regimental War Memorial project to build homes for veterans, and was invited by General Gervase Thorpe to open the first of the houses to be completed. This was a group of four cottages at Stenhousemuir, on land gifted by Colonel Chris Sherriff. The opening was done with due pomp, including a Guard of Honour and the Pipes and Drums of the 7th Battalion, and was supported by a strong contingent of officers whom Pa had known from both the World Wars.

Reading past copies of the *Thin Red Line*, it is hard to see how Pa found time for his other responsibilities as GOC Scotland. He is reported as attending Regimental dinners and garden parties (usually too wet to be in the garden), accepting the Honorary Colonelcy of 554 Light Anti-Aircraft Regiment (TA), which had been the 9th Battalion of the Argylls at the outbreak of the war, and becoming involved in a long association with Tourville, in Normandy. This small town had been liberated by the 2nd Battalion during the first battle fought by the 15th (Scottish) Division, and the Mayor of Tourville wanted to commemorate the liberation by constructing the memorial to the Division on a site in his part of the battlefield. The unveiling unfortunately coincided with the trip to Canada, but in later years Pa kept up a correspondence with the mayors of Tourville, and visited on at least one occasion.

His Argyll activities were not all work, as he represented the Regiment at cricket against the Black Watch in both 1949 and 1950, where his successful batting and bowling received a mention from the correspondent. He was even reported as curling, but for the Lowland Brigade, against the Highland Brigade. He had come to the rink for lunch, but was pressed to take part when the lowlanders found they were a man short. He can't have disgraced himself, as they won!

Developments on the other side of the world were to concern him in his regimental capacity for the year that began in August 1950. The 1st Battalion was sent at very short notice from Hong Kong to join the hard-pressed American and South Korean forces that had been driven into a small perimeter around Pusan in the south of Korea. The 'Brigade' consisted only of the two battalions, the Argylls and the Middlesex Regiment, with the minimum of transport, stores or other supporting arms, and notably with the kit they stood up in, which was eminently suitable for the summer, but far from adequate when the severe winter weather began.

Their arrival coincided with the lowest point in the campaign, and on 22nd September they were given the task of taking high ground, known as Hill 282, to secure the route up which the US forces would advance. The successful assault on the hill was achieved and North Korean counter-attacks were being contained while the wounded were being evacuated with great difficulty down the steep slopes. Disaster, however, struck when three American aircraft that had been called to support the position mistook the signals and dropped napalm, and strafed the two Argyll companies with machine guns. The extraordinary gallantry of the Battalion second-in-command, Major Kenny Muir, enabled the stretcher bearers to evacuate all the wounded while the survivors fought off the enemy who took up the opportunity of confusion to mount powerful counter-attacks. The Argylls fought until they were down to virtually the last round of ammunition, and they were compelled to withdraw from the summit. Major Muir was killed repelling the counter-attacks, but his gallantry was posthumously recognised by the award of the VC. The punishment they inflicted on the enemy must have done a great deal of damage to the North Koreans as they withdrew from the hill top during the night.

Pa was at Finlaystone when he was telephoned about this disaster, and I remember how deeply he felt it. The Americans were quick to apologise for the error and Pa had correspondence with the Consul General in Edinburgh, and the Commander of the US Bombardment Wing whose aircraft were involved, but this can have been small consolation to the relatives of the three officers and ten Other Ranks killed on 23rd September and to the 58 who were wounded. The affiliated regiments and many others who had been closely associated with the Argylls also sent messages of sympathy, all of which needed acknowledgement. No doubt he also visited many of the wounded in hospital, as well as the bereaved. (There would be no funerals in Scotland for those who had fallen in Korea.)

He will have continued to keep in as close touch as possible with the campaign in Korea, which saw the Battalion travel and fight right up to the north of North Korea, only to find the Chinese intervening and forcing the United Nations forces back to the starting line, along roughly the line of the pre-war border. While the Battalion was involved in a number of serious engagements, notably at Pakchon, their worst enemy was the weather, and although there were further casualties they were never on the scale of Hill 282.

They were eventually relieved, arriving back in Hong Kong on 28th April 1951.

He next saw them as they passed Gibraltar in September 1952 aboard the troopship *Empire Halladale*, heading back to Britain after an eventful three years in the Far East.

In the summer of 1951 Pa was once more hosting Princess Elizabeth when she joined the Officers and their wives at the tea party at Brown's Hotel preceding the Officers' Regimental Dinner. He was also able to renew his acquaintance with the Argyll and Sutherland Highlanders of Canada whose Pipes and Drums came over to take part in the Tattoo in August.

Shortly before Pa left Scottish Command, in early 1952, King George VI died and Princess Elizabeth succeeded to the throne. This produced a minor matter of etiquette as she had to confirm her willingness to continue as Colonel-in-Chief, which she did, thus giving Pa several more years of regular contact with her. The first of these after the accession was on 8th April when he kissed hands on his appointment as Governor of Gibraltar, a month before he left to take up his new post.

Before leaving for Gibraltar, he had performed yet one more regimental duty, when he took the salute at a parade at Stirling Castle when the 7th Battalion Pipes and Drums, and contingents from the 8th Battalion, the Depot and the Cadets celebrated the raising of the Regiment on 9th March.

With CO 1 A&SH, Lt. Col. Jim Church, when Empire Halladale passed Gibraltar, 1952

CHAPTER 9

Gibraltar (1952-1955)

by
Judy

Pa arrived in Gibraltar on 9th May, 1952 to take over as Governor from General Sir Kenneth Anderson. He finished at the end of March 1955, handing over to General Sir Harold *Dixie* Redman. His three years in the job, and in particular 1954, had been eventful ones. He arrived in a Gibraltar that was still going through some teething pains, following the introduction of a limited kind of democracy in the form of a Legislative Council, but where the Governor still held considerable power. There were a number of pressing issues facing the Rock, such as the need to redevelop the port and to provide more housing to alleviate severe overcrowding. This was accompanied by a growing acknowledgement of the requirement for both some form of social security, and some means, other than the weekly lottery, of raising revenue and funding these projects. His tenure saw celebrations for the Coronation on 2nd June 1953 and the 250th Anniversary of the capture of Gibraltar on 4th August 1954. There were also three Royal visits, by the Queen and Duke of Edinburgh on 10th/11th May 1954; Princess Alice, the Princess Royal, from 27th September until 3rd October 1954, and the Duke of Edinburgh on 26th/27th March 1955.

There had also been the unexpected to deal with, in particular the aftermath of the sinking of the troopship *Empire Windrush* when she caught fire off Algeria, on 28th March, 1954, which saw 1500 military, family members and crew arrive in Gibraltar 24 hours later, requiring clothing and accommodation before transportation back to Britain.[lxxiv]

In addition, he had seen a number of personal milestones go past, such as the death of his mother on the 1st April 1953, his promotion to full General on 12th January 1954, and his 25th wedding anniversary on 10th August 1954. Colouring the whole were difficulties with the Franco-led Government in Spain, as Franco reasserted the Spanish claim to the Rock.

Inspecting the Coronation Parade, Gibraltar, 1953

In Pa's initial speech to the Legislative Council, dated 9th May 1952, he pledged to be guided by the spirit of the Constitution conferred on Gibraltar by King George VI in 1950, which stated it was designed to secure "peace, order and good government in Gibraltar". He further added that he was anxious "to enhance and enlarge the happy relationships which are traditional between the Colony and its neighbours on all sides."[lxxv] It was this latter concern that took up much of his time in office. An early indication of trouble ahead had come in August 1953, when Franco accused the UK of reneging on a promise to hand over the Rock after World War II if Spain remained neutral during the war. A telegram from the Madrid Embassy held in the British National Archive, quoted the Generalissimo as telling the *Arriba* newspaper: "If the hopes of the restitution of the Rock held out to Spain during the war are not fulfilled, no one should doubt that we will use every means to put an end to this offensive situation."[lxxvi] Franco was further incensed by the news that the Queen and Duke of Edinburgh were to visit Gibraltar at the end of their six month Coronation tour, and it appears to have been this that led to increasing difficulties at the border, where there would be frequent go-slows and unexpected closures on the Spanish side, causing long queues. In his final speech to the Legislative Council of 25th March 1955, Pa refers to this as "what has been called 'The 14th Siege of Gibraltar'."[lxxvii]

The background to the claim that Britain had promised to restore

Gibraltar to Spain was investigated by Britain in 1949 and the conclusion was reached that surviving documents showed that the British Government position of the time was defined by War Cabinet decisions of June 1940, in which it had been agreed that the Spaniards could be told they "should be ready after the war to discuss any matter of common interest" between the two countries although "this offer should omit any specific mention of Gibraltar". It appears that Churchill was one of those said to have given assurances to Spain on the issue of Gibraltar, at a lunch party in the Spanish Embassy during 1941, although, when asked about it during the investigation, he stated that "while he might have made favourable comments on the position of Spain in the Mediterranean, it was quite untrue that he had at any time given any formal pledge to Spain."[lxxviii]

Pa made regular visits to the Provincial Military Governor at Cadiz. Despite the pressure from Madrid, first General Barroso and then General Cuerta were on good terms with Pa and, like him, appeared to see that Franco's attitude was in neither side's interest. As Gareth Stockey in his book, *Gibraltar – A Dagger in the Spine of Spain*[lxxix] argues, the relationship between Gibraltar and the Campo area around it was one of mutual interdependency. Gibraltar needed access to fresh produce and a workforce, and southern Spain was very poor and needed the income Gibraltar provided. Some 14,000 Spaniards came into Gibraltar daily and valued their jobs, considering themselves the lucky ones. And the sale of fruit, vegetables and other produce as well as the money from tourists visiting Gibraltar on liners and then entering Spain, were important sources of revenue in an area of high unemployment.

One indication of the friendly relationship between Spain and Gibraltar up until the Royal Visit was that the Spaniards provided a private beach for the use of the Governor, a twisty drive up the Mediterranean coast, to which initially we would take picnics on Sundays. It was guarded by a Civil Guard who kept other people away. Undoubtedly his must have been one of the most boring jobs in the world and he must have been glad of the flat back to his hat, making it possible to lean comfortably against the bathing hut for hours on end. These visits sadly ended when, to show his disapproval of the increasing difficulties at the frontier, Pa stopped crossing the border except when he finally left to drive home the following year.

I was told that many local Spaniards even loved the British Royal family and that the humblest home around the bay was likely to have a picture of the newly wedded Princess Elizabeth and Prince Philip stuck up on a wall. Locally there did not appear to be much of an appetite for a squabble. It is also interesting that Pa noted in a letter to Jock Colville, Churchill's Private Secretary, dated 21st April 1954, that he saw some signs of acquiescence to the Royal Visit within the Spanish media, writing "Franco's press is now putting more emphasis on the beauty and excellence of the Queen and commiserating with her at being forced to come here by Sir Winston Churchill as an insult to Spain. Even this story is beginning to lose its press value and no longer cuts any ice with the great majority of Spaniards." He goes on to say that "there are indications that, unless some new fuel is provided, the Franco-Falangist rockets are going to go off like damp squibs instead of V2s."[lxxx]

Preparations for the Royal Visit took up a lot of Pa's time during early 1954 and, in his final speech to the Legislative Council[lxxxi], he notes it as one of the "outstanding events" of his time in Gibraltar, along with the Coronation celebrations. The programme for the visit included tours of the underground installations, the City Council Waterworks, and a visit to the apes. Here the Duke was given monkey nuts to throw to the apes, but chucked them instead at the clamouring crowd of photographers saying "And that will do for you lot" as he climbed back into the car.

The Queen and Prince Philip meet the Apes

There was also a dinner at the Governor's Residence, The Convent, for which a full rehearsal was held a week previously (a photograph of which appeared in "Life" Magazine)[lxxxii], as well as lunch with the Legislative Council.

The Convent. Ceremony of The Keys

Churchill was extremely concerned about the Queen's safety and had decreed that she was not to wave to the crowds from The Convent balcony in case a sniper took a pot shot at her. In fact she insisted on doing just that, not once but twice, much to the delight of her enthusiastic subjects. On the second occasion, Pa stood in the doorway behind her and noticed that her Garter Sash had been pinned at the waist by an Argyll regimental brooch. When she rejoined him, the Queen asked if he had noticed anything and when he told her he had spotted the brooch, she was delighted. Pa was very touched by the thought that had gone into planning every detail months before, as they had set off on their trip round the world.

Prince Charles and Princess Anne were flown from England to meet their parents on the Royal Yacht in Malta for the final part of the tour, and a programme also had to be arranged for them. The inhabitants of the Rock made a fine doll's house for Princess Anne and a large replica of the Rock with *Hornby* train lines running through and round it for Prince Charles. They were set up in a building near where Britannia was tied up, and the Queen and the Duke arrived a little late for dinner, saying they had been playing trains with Anne while Charles amused himself with the doll's house.

The visit culminated in a private investiture on board Britannia for Pa and Robert Ferguson, his Military Secretary at that time, who received a KCVO and MVO respectively.

Jock Colville wrote afterwards that "The Queen told the Prime Minister that her visit to Gibraltar had been an unqualified success and that not only were the arrangements admirable but they were also enjoyable. I imagine that this was by no means always the case during the six months of the Tour! I heard too from the Duke and from Michael Adeane glowing accounts of Gibraltar."[lxxxiii]

In an interesting sub-plot to the Royal Visit, the prospect of which so enraged Franco, a substantial correspondence exists regarding the top secret possibility of Churchill, at that time Prime Minister of Britain, flying out to meet the Queen at the end of her 6 month world tour. This appears to have been suggested by the Queen, and Churchill was enthusiastic about the plan, although Pa had deep misgivings. These misgivings were threefold. Most importantly, he was concerned that even a whiff of a visit by Churchill would result in conditions for Gibraltarians thereafter becoming more difficult, drawing an analogy with how visits to the trenches by Generals during the first world war, and the extra movement they occasioned, usually resulted in increased shelling of the trenches, making life afterwards even more unpleasant for those occupying them.[lxxxiv] In his last speech to the Legislative

Council before leaving Gibraltar in March 1955, Pa stated that "whenever I have had to take a difficult decision, I have always asked myself first "What is going to be the best for the good of Gibraltar",[lxxxv] and this may be one of the occasions of which he was thinking, as it cannot have been easy to advise against what Churchill obviously wished to do.

His second concern was that, if it was even suspected that Churchill was going to visit, the border would be closed, meaning that Spanish labour required for the operation of Gibraltar could not enter, and nor would those British living in the South of Spain and wishing to come to Gibraltar be able to enjoy the visit. He also suggested that, if a plan to allow Spanish workers to stay in Gibraltar the night before the visit to ensure that they were able to work during these days, were put into action, it was likely that reprisals would be made against the families of those workers that did stay.[lxxxvi]

Finally, there were domestic issues, such as the shortage of suitable cars, and the size of The Convent dining room, so that, in order to accommodate Churchill at dinner, he would "have to fling someone out, which in this case would be an ADC. I fear I could not include anyone else with him."

Despite these robustly expressed misgivings, Churchill decided to go ahead with the visit. Confirming this, Colville wrote "Although I well understand your apprehensions, I hope that in the event they will turn out to be less well-founded than you have reason to fear, more especially as this is indeed going to be the most top secret operation of all times and it is proposed that the Prime Minister should land in Gibraltar without a single soul knowing about it. ... At present the only people who know at all about the project are The Queen (who originally suggested it), Michael Adeane, the Foreign Secretary and Jock Balfour" (who was then Ambassador in Madrid). "Sir Winston does not even know that I have told you although in the course of the next day or two I shall have to seek permission to do so!!" The visitor was given the code name *Kirkwood* – apparently in reference to the name of his valet – and arrangements were put in place as much as was possible without giving anyone a hint that the Prime Minister was to visit.[lxxxvii]

On May 5th 1954, Pa received the following telegram from the Secretary of State for the Colonies addressed "Immediate Governor Gibraltar".

"TOP SECRET AND PERSONAL. No. 71. Following for Governor from Colville. For reasons which I will explain by letter the arrangements about which we have been in correspondence are cancelled. End."[lxxxviii]

The letter which followed from Colville explains that "The Prime Minister cancelled his plans because things looked like getting difficult at Geneva and there was a distinct possibility that the French Government might fall, with possible grave consequences for Europe."[lxxxix] And that Sir Winston, who was due to travel home on board Britannia with the Queen, did not feel that he could be absent from Britain whilst Eden, the Foreign Secretary, was also out of the country. It seems possible, if Churchill's visit had gone ahead, given his role in the ill feeling that existed between Britain and Spain, Pa's fears may have been realised as Franco was likely to have found it particularly provocative.

This was not the end of the saga, however, as it transpired that, despite the declaration that this was to be "the most top secret operation ever", there had been a number of security breaches, and, once the Royal Visit was safely behind him, Pa wrote again to Jock Colville on 12th May, 1954. His anger is evident as he complains that he had been surprised to be asked by Ma, on the evening of 5th May, if it was true that the PM was coming when the Queen was to come. "Having just had your signal cancelling all the arrangements, I replied, "Certainly not. Who told you this ridiculous story?" It then transpired that she had been asked this question by Mrs. Jaime Russo, who attended the wedding of her brother Captain Zulueta to *Boy* Browning's daughter about two months ago and had been told by *Boy* Browning." (Sir Frederick Browning was a retired general, married to the author Daphne Du Maurier and close to the Royal Household.[xc]). This was followed by the Colonial Secretary also being asked by Mr. Joshua Hassan, the Chairman of the City Council, if the PM was coming and, on the following day, Ma again being asked if the story was true, this time by her chiropodist as she had her corns done in preparation for the big visit. Pa's concerns were that, because the Russo's lived in Spain, this story was likely to have circulated there as well, and that by doing so, the safety of both *Kirkwood* and the Queen, was likely to have been compromised. He also worried that "if Franco even now suspects that *Kirkwood* had intended to come and then cancelled his arrangements, he can claim to have stopped his visit." He finishes this section of his letter by saying, somewhat stingingly, "I have not told *Boy* Browning but in fairness to him I think he should be informed in case he blurts out any more secrets in future to nice young girls"![xci]

A second breach of security had also occurred because Coastal Command had failed to cancel the flight booked for Churchill and continued to send signals indicating that a "very special VIP" was inward bound to Gibraltar on the 10th May, requiring Pa to double check with Colville on the 9th May, that the visit really was cancelled.[xcii]

The security breaches were not Pa's only complaints. He had obviously been hurt to be called to London in March 1954 and required to explain his security measures to 10 Downing Street, feeling that "The method in which this was handled made it clear to me that the PM had no confidence in my ability to handle the Royal Visit." This feeling was exacerbated when he was reminded that "the safety of Her Majesty was of paramount importance," by the sending out of an additional policeman from London to double check the security arrangements in the week preceding the visit, and by Churchill's refusal to take his advice that to come out to Gibraltar during the Queen's visit would be to increase the security risk. He concludes by saying "The morale in Gibraltar is terrific and we can turn a blockade of Gibraltar into a blockade of Spain, but if I am to do this I must be given a clear cut policy and support in its execution. If I am not to be trusted, I am perfectly prepared to be told to go and if the PM no longer wants me I'm ready to go at once. Indeed if he wishes to make a change, he should do so soon, as the Franco campaign will steadily worsen and he may feel he ought to have a good general in command instead of one he does not appear to trust."[xciii]

Colville's reply is a wonderful example of emollience. He "was much distressed" by Pa's letter, firstly because it was he who had told *Boy* Browning about the visit, and secondly because he saw that Pa felt "very much aggrieved personally on other scores." He assured Pa that any actions taken by Downing Street were entirely caused by increasing anxiety as the visit grew closer, and were "not in any sense due to lack of confidence in the measures you were taking." "The Prime Minister did not once say to me anything which cast reflections on you personally," and "although reflections on your management of the situation may have seemed to be implied by the action at this end, nothing of the kind was intended."[xciv] Colville wrote again on 18th May, 1954, saying that he had had a letter from "Browning who is overcome with horror and remorse," and suggesting that the matter be left there as "when people eat humble pie to this extent and say they are sorry, I for one do not like pushing matters any further, and I hope that you feel the same."[xcv] Pa appears to have agreed and to have been placated as there is no further correspondence on the matter.

As alluded to previously, the system of Government under which Gibraltar's 28,000 inhabitants lived was enshrined in a Constitution dating from 1950. This established the Legislative Council, which included five members elected by proportional representation. The

President was the Governor, who held a casting but not original vote, and there were three official members (Colonial Secretary, Financial Secretary and Attorney General), plus two nominated members, one unofficial and one official, both Gibraltarians, giving the locals a majority of seven to three, and making the proportion of elected to unelected members equal. The Governor also chaired an Executive Council made up of the heads of the Services, plus the official members of the Legislative Council. The civil government machine was bulky to say the least, with no less than 19 committees and boards, such as the water committee, lottery committee, midwives board and City Council, plus 50 senior government officials in 12 different departments. In addition there were coordinating committees between the three Services, which each liked to do things its own way, causing considerable duplication of administration and services, such as water and light.[xcvi]

The Governor still held wide powers as he could refuse assent to Bills passed by the Legislative Council, and had powers of reservation on Bills concerned with external relations, religious discrimination and discipline of the Armed Forces, whilst being required to recommend any financial Bills. Kenneth Anderson, Pa's predecessor, had told him, "I have been far more a civilian Gov. than a soldier, for many constitutional and other changes have taken place recently and I found it best to play an active part rather than leave all to my Colonial Secretary. Until recently the Gov. was theoretically all powerful and laws were made on his fiat alone. With the new Leg. Co. I have become less dictatorial! … My immediate task is to pilot thro' Leg. Co. the first income tax bill in Gib. and our first step in real social legislation – Workmen's Accident Insurance. The former has caused a lot of headaches!"[xcvii] At this point Gibraltar had no direct taxation, except for a tax on trading profits, up to a maximum of £400, introduced in 1950. With no import duty imposed, goods could be bought at prices a half to a third of those in Britain, meaning that Gibraltarian shops did good business from those who were passing through. The only other source of revenue was an astonishingly popular State Lottery, held once a week, at which a population of 28,000 bought up to 13,000 ten shilling tickets.[xcviii]

Social legislation was promised for 1951,[xcix] as the flip side of no taxation was that there was no social security in any form, such as pensions or sickness benefit. It is notable that Pa, as he was leaving, told the Legislative Council "I am sorry about certain developments and advances which I would have liked to have seen completed before I left Gibraltar. In particular the Social Insurance Scheme…"[c]

Pa appears to have had more success, recorded in the same speech, with the help of a Gibraltarian delegation to the Colonial Secretary, in eliciting funds for building "300 new flats or houses over a period of 5 years, and secondly a major scheme of Port Development, which will include provision for a deep water quay, from which oil and water can be piped to ships alongside."[ci]

That many of the problems that Pa faced in Gibraltar were intransigent is confirmed by a letter from his successor, *Dixie* Redman, who wrote to Pa after having been in the job a couple of months, "I do not need to worry you with the different problems which are current. They are just the same problems that you were struggling with when you were here, in fact the list of points for me to discuss in London was exactly the same list as the one you have used on various occasions."[cii]

On a personal level, my parents' first impressions of Gibraltar delighted them and they wasted no time in getting established and throwing themselves wholeheartedly into the job. The warm and friendly welcome of the people, the heat of the early summer sun, the vibrant colours of the Mediterranean flora, and the delicious smells that wafted into the house in the evening – orange blossom, stephanotis, datura and belladonna lilies – gave them a happy feeling.

The Convent had been described to them by Kenneth Anderson as "a dear old house"[ciii] which he was sure they would love, and he was right: they did. It was rambling and pleasant and the flock of Spanish maids that met them were smiling and helpful. The food was beautifully cooked and it was served by well turned out, polite, army waiters. The dining room was impressive but comfortable, and the drawing room was cool and well-proportioned with French windows opening on to a balcony, which overlooked a large enclosed garden. Plumbago and bougainvillea climbed all over the railings and it was a lovely place to stand and lean on the balustrade and enjoy the view. The garden was flat but full of a variety of plants of different heights and shapes, and a squash court, tennis court and small swimming pool were tucked away amongst the greenery. The ground floor was mainly offices and the living quarters were above.

The timing of this appointment was ideal for our family. George, now aged 22, was studying to be a school master and was soon to leave Cambridge and teach at Wellington; John, 20, was at Cambridge and destined to join the Army; I was 16 and in my last year at West Heath, and David and Andrew were at Eton and Aysgarth respectively. We were all of an age at which we could travel independently and we all still expected to spend the holidays with our parents.

It turned out to be a very popular place to visit for our friends, who particularly enjoyed the summer months and all the outdoor activities.

In those days, foreign trips were rare and long distance travel to other continents for holidays was almost unheard of. Regular commercial flights had only just begun and, on Andrew's and my first visit, our Vickers Viking had to land at Bordeaux to refuel and again in Madrid where we had a leisurely lunch under a pergola while the plane was again refueled: the journey took most of the day. Arriving by air was most spectacular: the plane would seem to be heading for the water when the end of the runway would appear below and the forbidding steep North Face of the Rock would seem alarmingly close to the side.

Our parents were very relaxed with us and keen that The Convent should feel like home and not oppressively grand and formal. However important the guests, we all sat in the drawing room and had meals together in the dining room, and I think they enjoyed the fooling around that went on in the holidays.

The Convent from the garden

When we first arrived, Pa could not wait to show us round and the first two afternoons were spent touring the Rock with him in an open Humber, of the type that had been used by senior officers during the Second World War. We drove up out of the town and stopped to look down on the scene below. He pointed out the vast harbour with its moles where there were frequently a number of warships tied up. Nearby was the dockyard and, towards the mouth of the bay, was the tiny harbour at Rosia, where Nelson's body had been brought ashore after Trafalgar, before being returned to Britain in a cask of rum.

At the southern tip of the land was a lighthouse and a flat area called Europa Point where the Garrison had playing fields, except they were anything but fields, there being no grass anywhere: they were flattened gravelly mud, painful to fall on but much used. Pa played hockey there in the winter months and survived despite the terrain and the fact he was in his mid-fifties. He never took to water sports in the way his family did but loved his tennis games on The Convent court and played squash regularly with Jock Edington, his ADC.

Continuing our tour, we visited the apes, very much a tourist attraction, despite being flea-ridden compulsive thieves. They had an army minder called Gunner Portlock who was so attached to his charges that, when his wife gave birth to his own child, he was unable to be with her as he was assisting one of his apes with a difficult confinement. The theory was that, if the apes fizzled out on the Rock, the British would also leave. Churchill felt the apes' survival was so important for morale that he had more imported from North Africa during the war, a story which was fictionalised in Paul Gallico's novel *Scruffy*.

From the apes, we visited St. Michael's Cave, a natural cathedral with spectacular stalactites and stalagmites in the heart of the Rock, and then we drove through a man-made tunnel which brought us out at the Eastern side. This side was very sheer and the road ran along the foot of the cliff close to the sea. There was a small straggle of houses on that side called Catalan Bay, where the community was remarkably cut off from the main population, and one got the feeling they were happy to be so. Much of this side of the Rock was a water catchment area, where the rain fell on a huge area of asbestos-cement sheeting and poured down the rock side before being channeled into underground storage tanks, carved out of the limestone.

The catchment areas involved another trip the following day. Here Mr. Montegriffo reigned over his catchment kingdom and it amused us that in English he would have been *Mr. Mount Tap*. He was pretty serious and filled us with a mass of statistics. This water and what was caught on the roofs of houses provided the Rock with its supplies. If the season was very dry, water-bearing tankers would have to come into the port and top up the reserves.

Pa was a fund of information about everything we passed and clearly loved showing off all the detail that he had already acquired. During his 3 years in Gibraltar, he must have done the tour umpteen times and never appeared to tire of showing it all off to visiting friends and VIPs alike.

Despite there being no grass, the Rock was by no means barren. A walk called Mediterranean Steps was especially interesting with a variety of plants to look at. In mid-winter the ground was covered with paper-whites with their overpowering smell, and at Easter we would pick prickly armfuls of Spanish gorse, covered in gold flowers, and fill long troughs with it in front of the choir stalls in the King's Chapel, attached to the house. At some point in the season there would be a mass of red hot pokers and large fleshy purple flowered mesembryanthemums. A pair of peregrine falcons was often to be seen hovering where the cliffs dropped steeply down to the Mediterranean, and, on the bare rock, lizards would sun themselves until disturbed.

The Rock is honeycombed with tunnels and underground rooms, in addition to the massive water storage tanks. In the war these served as the military headquarters and also housed a large hospital. They were still being used in the fifties by the army for a number of purposes, including vehicle repair workshops. Further tunneling in the rock supplied the boulders used to lengthen the airstrip so that it could handle the increasingly large civilian and military planes that were used in international travel. By the time we left Gibraltar, we could fly non-stop from London by Vicker's Viscount!

Pa's position as Her Majesty's Representative in Gibraltar meant that his public appearances were inevitably formal affairs, performed with dignity and correctness, so it was especially lucky that his staff saw the funny side of most situations and, though professional, were able to inject a large amount of light entertainment into life in The Convent.

Charlie Forrester, the Assistant Military Secretary – or AMS – had spent the war as a prisoner of the Japanese in Hong Kong and was a Major in the Gunners. He and his family were already on the Rock when Pa arrived, and when his regimental friend, Ozzie Younger, was ill and could not take up the job, Charlie was appointed in his place. Jock Edington, Pa's ADC, was a young Argyll who had been wounded in Korea and was not considered fit enough to return to regimental duties. Both had similar senses of humour and revelled in the comparatively carefree jobs in which they found themselves. They had adjoining offices across the passage from Pa's and were the centre of much laughter and high jinks.

In addition, Pa had a Gibraltarian Permanent Honorary ADC, named Bobbie Capurro, who was invaluable on my parents' arrival. He was a retired Colonel and knew everyone and all there was to know about the Rock. He also spoke Spanish fluently and would act as interpreter when required.

When the Executive Council met in Pa's office, the Big Wigs would leave their brass hats and homburgs in the outer office in the care of the deferential AMS and ADC, little suspecting that, as soon as they had all arrived and were deep in council, their headpieces would be tried on by Charlie and Jock who would impersonate the owners, much to their own amusement, before replacing them where the Admiral, Air Commodore, Chief Justice, Colonial Secretary, Head of City Council etc. had placed them on arrival. Unfortunately, one day the meeting was unusually short and they all reappeared sooner than expected. Jock and Charlie managed to get back behind their desks before they entered to collect their hats but had not had time to put them neatly back where they had come from. A bewildered bunch of chaps searched and were a little puzzled as to why things were not exactly as they remembered but could not believe that the two officers so busily writing at their desks could know anything about the muddle. Hats recovered, they were politely escorted to their cars by Jock and Charlie and waved away before they confessed to His Excellency who went chortling back to his office.

Lesmoir Wimberley, the daughter of a Scottish General, Douglas Wimberley (who, like Pa, had served in both World Wars), arrived towards the end of 1952 to be Ma's Personal Assistant, and completed the Home Team, joining in the fun of it all with gusto. Lesmoir later married Jock, and my parents remained close friends with them and with Charlie and Diana Forrester all their lives.

John recalls that Jock and Charlie's favourite game was that of ringing others up, pretending to be someone who had an urgent matter to raise with H.E.. Later Lesmoir was admitted to the circle of pranksters. They very nearly caught Ma out on one occasion, pretending to be a Jewish family, who would be greatly honoured if she would attend their daughter's wedding. Her suspicions were aroused when the bridegroom asked that she would do them the honour of being in the inner sanctum of the tent for the ceremony and she sent Lesmoir down the corridor to peep round Jock's door, before putting the ball back into their court by saying that she would have to see the ADC before she could accept, as she did not yet have the latest fixtures entered in her diary.

This game backfired when a man rang down a crackly telephone line from Portugal saying "My name's Audley Money-Kyrle and I'm a friend of George and John's from Cambridge. I'm with St Barbe Baker, you know, *The Man of the Trees*, and we are going across the Sahara planting peach stones. We'll be arriving at the Border on the Bank Holiday, and would be most grateful if you could ensure that we get through the check point." "The boys really must learn to do better than that if they want to take part in our game," thought Jock, and put the telephone down. Luckily he was having a glass of sherry with us before lunch on the holiday, instead of taking the day off, when a call came from the border check point asking if anyone would come and see this strange party through, as they were expected by the Governor. Jock could move fast when he had to!

The Forresters returned to UK before the Royal Visit and were replaced by Robert Ferguson and his wife Eve. Robert was a Northumberland Fusilier and had been a prisoner-of-war in Italy, where both his legs were broken when all the POWs ran out of their huts to wave at the RAF flying over, only to have a bomb dropped on them. He had already done a spell in Gibraltar, and they were more than happy to return. Once more my parents were lucky and the Fergusons became lasting friends and the happy atmosphere at The Convent continued.

Charlie left many amusing memories behind including the time when he made the mistake of seating Mrs. Hassan, the wife of the Head of the City Council, whose command of English was very limited, next to Pa at dinner and, again, after dinner in the drawing room. They had both gallantly struggled to communicate throughout dinner, but were disconcerted to find themselves next to each other also for the rest of the evening. Pa was unamused and made this plain to Charlie later. Next morning he found on his desk the lines written out 100 times, 'I must remember if I can, not to put H.E. next to Mrs. Hassan'. How could he stay cross?

Charlie's eyebrows were exhibited on the yacht club bar long after he had gone home. Jock often dined there and was fed up with one, Peter Smith, who bragged that he had the longest eyebrows on the Rock. Jock bet him that he was not the eyebrow champion and disappeared, returning with Charlie. Their eyebrows were duly plucked out and flattened and attached with drawing pins to the side of the bar. When measured, Charlie's won hands down, as anyone could have told Peter they would.

On arrival, Robert and Eve Ferguson and their sons, George (6) and Ricky (4), came to lunchtime drinks. George was very chatty and told me and Val Scott, a friend who was visiting, that Ricky was recently out of hospital having been hit by a car. We expressed concern, whereupon George explained that Ricky was very lucky because the car in question was a Rolls Royce. We thought at the time that this was a rather astonishing remark from a six year old and only later realised that it was exactly what Robert would have felt. If you have to be run over, make sure it's a Rolls and not a Skoda that does the deed.

Robert revelled in being a snob and, surprisingly, it somehow added to his considerable charm. Where objects were concerned, he loved quality and where people were concerned it was the Quality that he loved. Military Secretary in Gibraltar over the Royal Visit, followed by Princess Royal's Visit and a second one by the Duke of Edinburgh, was a job dreamed up in Heaven for him, and he had a high old time hob-nobbing with the big wigs. Nobody could have enjoyed it more. I sat next to Robert when the Queen and Duke dined at The Convent and he was most gratified to see that Her Majesty scooped the sugar out of the bottom of her coffee cup and ate it off her spoon!

Soon after his arrival, Robert had to accompany Pa on one of his visits to the Provincial Governor in Cadiz. While Pa and Bobbie discussed things with the General, Robert and his opposite number exchanged pleasantries and Robert was flattered when the other admired his ceremonial sword and he explained that it had belonged to his father. The Spaniard beamed with delight and, pointing to his own rows of medals, exclaimed "See all these, they belonged to my Grandfather!"

Robert was a perfectionist and when he left the army he took up cabinet making and made several beautiful period doll's houses, one of which ended up in royal hands. The last time we saw him and Eve, they had moved into Amesbury Abbey, a very up-market nursing home. Both were pretty frail by then and Robert had had a bad stroke and could scarcely walk, but was happy to tell us that at the Abbey everybody was Somebody!

A later addition to the team was Nigel Crowe, who came to take over as ADC but overlapped with Jock during the Royal Visit and was assigned to the royal children and their nanny. Nigel escorted them to the apes and found Prince Charles was already a good conversationalist with an excellent grounding in the Old Testament. On hearing that Nigel had just come from Egypt, he enquired if he had met Moses? Told that he had not, the Prince felt sure that he would have come across the Pharaohs.

Jock and Lesmoir both left after the Royal Visit and shortly afterwards announced their engagement. Jock went to join the Argylls in British Guiana and Lesmoir returned to Scotland to organise their wedding which John and I attended in Perth in December. John stood in for Lesmoir's brother Neil, who could not get home for the wedding from Germany, and I was one of their bridesmaids.

After Lesmoir's departure, Jean McMicking came in her place. Her father, General Neil McMicking, was in the Black Watch, and he and his wife Peggy were old friends of my parents. Their son, Thomas, had been a contemporary of John at Aysgarth and Eton; Jean had been a year above me at West Heath, and their younger son, David, and my brother David went through preparatory and public school together. As army officers, John and Thomas were forever taking over from each other when their respective regiments followed each other in various parts of the world.

Jean was in Gibraltar when the Princess Royal came for several days in the autumn of 1954. She recalls how the Princess Royal fainted at dinner one evening and had to be carried out of the dining room, a task which Robert found difficult due to her slippery knickers making it impossible to get a firm grip of the Royal Form!

Pa would spend most mornings at his office desk until lunchtime, then do *The Times* crossword and read in the drawing room during the siesta period. It must have suited him well to have time to read more without feeling that he should be out helping Ma around the place. At The Convent, there was a massive staff so there was no requirement to lift a finger. (My parent's silver wedding card was signed by no less than 31 members of house and garden staff, both civilian and military, and this did not include the staff that manned the governor's barge – a large motor launch – or the personal staff such as the AMS and ADC.)[civ] He would return to his office for a bit around 3 pm to sign letters etc. and, in the early evening when it was a little cooler, he would take some form of exercise. He much enjoyed tennis and his regular doubles partners were Diana Forrester, Jock, and Lady Gaggero, who very much liked to be asked and was about Pa's age.

During the previous Governor's time, an ammunition ship, the RFA *Bedenham*, had blown up in the harbour, doing considerable damage and killing 13 people. Lady Gaggero was unlucky enough to be hit by some debris and had a small bit of shrapnel removed from her buttock. She did not like to be beaten at tennis and, if this looked like being the case, the other three would avoid catching each other's eyes as they waited for the tell-tale limp and the inevitable comment about her wound playing up. Even Pa struggled not to giggle.

Ma's days were full as well, as she had decided that The Convent garden needed attention. Over the years, various VIPs had planted trees around the garden but most of the plaques had either been lost or been muddled up. She had a few trees moved to better positions and created a wide herbaceous border down each side of the main path. Finding that a lot of South African bulbs enjoyed the Gibraltar climate, she introduced ixias and spiraxias and other interesting plants. Water was scarce, but the bathwater was saved in a barrel on wheels, so newly planted material was given a drink of slightly soapy liquid to get it going. Deciding that the path should lead to a focal point, she designed and oversaw the construction of a sort of folly. It consisted of two curved white stone benches backed by a crescent of tall narrow Cypresses, with, in front of them, a semicircle of black and white smooth, shiny pebbles set into the ground in a pattern. These pebbles were collected over time from beaches in Spain by us as well as by long-suffering visitors under Ma's supervision. The whole effect was well proportioned and pulled the garden together nicely.

Ma also felt strongly that the garden should have a lawn and so planted one, painstakingly hair-pinning all the shoots to the ground to get it to root and grow together. It was a particularly tough variety of creeping grass supposed to survive in dry conditions and, by the time she left, it was beginning to resemble a lawn, but I don't recall that it ever got tall or thick enough to need mowing. Before leaving, she also founded the Gibraltar Horticultural Society, with Cecilia Hankey as its first Secretary. It got off to a good start, putting on an annual flower show, in which David was very upset not to win the miniature garden prize. The Society was well supported and is still going strong.[cv] George recalls that she also established a rota of ladies to do flowers at the hospital each week.

When not in the garden, Ma was never idle: after lunch, when everyone was having a siesta she would sit in the sunroom beyond the drawing room working on a tapestry. She found the light good and preferred to stitch rather than snooze. The tapestry was a fine copy of a flower painting in the V. and A. and she had a stool frame made to put it on when finished. In fact, it was decided that it was too good to be sat on and it now hangs as a picture in Finlaystone.

Latterly, another ploy was looking ahead to our return to Scotland and considering the setting up of a flower arranging business which we could do together. To this end she had some very handsome walnut pedestals made by Michael, the handyman, and found a pottery over the border to make a large quantity of vases, rather rough copies of ones she already had. There are still some around and they proved invaluable when we did set up as florists, travelling the length and breadth of Scotland arranging flowers for weddings, balls and other functions.

In the front hall of The Convent was an official visitors' book, in which people coming to Gibraltar could sign their names so as to draw attention to their presence. The book was examined by the staff to check who had signed it that day and whether they should be invited to a meal, a cup of tea or drinks. Indeed, I don't remember many evenings when the family dined alone. A lot of entertaining went on in The Convent, which my parents did very well thanks to the great team they had to help them. Santos, the Spanish chef, was excellent and the variety of fresh produce meant the standard of fare was very high. We had come from Britain where vegetables and fruit were still completely seasonal and things like peppers, eggplants and melons were unheard of. Here, cooked with olive oil, accompanying a whole new range of fish – tuna, sword fish and red mullet, to name a few – it all seemed pretty exotic. Having a glass of delicious, light, dry sherry before lunch and dinner became an easy habit to adopt.

The only ingredient that Ma particularly missed was fresh milk. This was remedied by the Infanta Beatriz, a great grand-daughter of Queen Victoria. She and the Infante Alfonso de Orleans y Borbón, were part of the Spanish royal family, unrecognised by the regime of General Franco and living the life of country aristocrats on their estate near Sanlúcar de Barrameda. They were among the first of the locals to come to Gibraltar and introduce themselves to my parents and thereafter came and stayed quite regularly.[cvi] They were most hospitable and frequently entertained my parents and parties of guests to lunch at La Botánica. The Infanta was a keen farmer and, on hearing that Ma was looking for a cow, said she would like to give her one. She personally walked down her byre, selected the best milker and despatched her to the Rock.

General Redman gave a wonderful description of one of the Infante's visits to Gibraltar in a letter to Pa. "We had the Infante through yesterday, returning by ship from Rome with two grand-children. What a fine old man he is, simply full of personality and a law unto himself with his deafness of which he seems to be rather proud; his fine up-standing bearing, his real courtesy, his wonderful command of languages and his appreciation in small quantities of absolutely neat gin. He leaves with me a picture to be remembered and his long Packard with trailer simply full of relations and nannies and driven by his chauffeur in RAF uniform (but minus the Verey pistol which had been left behind by mistake) made a wonderful departure."[cvii]

Upon arrival in Gibraltar, Chula took up residence in the large, steep and partially uncultivated garden at the Mount, half way up the Rock, which was occupied by Admiral *Mick* Mickelthwait who had offered it up to Ma to house Gibraltar's only cow. We had cleared lots of stones so that some forage could be grown with which to feed her. A soldier with a farming background was responsible for the daily milking, and the milk was shared between the Admiral, the Governor and the Colonial Secretary. At times Ma, somewhat to Pa's embarrassment, could be seen leading Chula to the Spanish Border to rendezvous with a bull. When *Life* magazine did their article on Gibraltar to coincide with the Queen's visit, they photographed Ma following Chula along the roadside. The caption read, "The Rock's only cow follows its owner in hunt for scarce grass."[cviii] If Ma noticed the slip it certainly had not concerned her so, when first a massive bunch of anthuriums arrived and then a flustered representative of the magazine flew in from Madrid to apologise personally for the dreadful mistake, she was left wondering what the fuss was all about. *Life* need not have panicked that they were about to be sued as that thought would have never crossed her mind.

Ma took Spanish lessons and would practice speaking on her daily visits to the market where she would purchase flowers from a blind flower seller at the entrance. There was usually a lovely selection of lilies, carnations, tuberoses and bundles of gladioli. On one occasion she was approached by an agitated young naval officer who asked her for advice. What would be a suitable bunch to send to a lady? Ma asked if the lady lived in a big or small house and on being told she lived in a very big house recommended a large bunch of gladioli and moved off to the vegetable stalls. On returning to The Convent, she was amused to find the gladioli had beaten her to it and had a thank-you letter from an Admiral who had dined with them the night before, attached to the bunch. That night it was my parents' turn to dine with the Admiral on his flagship. The Admiral was surprised, when he introduced Ma to his embarrassed-looking Flag Lieutenant, that she smiled and said they already knew each other. Years later, when Robin was Commander at Greenwich, a senior Captain on the staff told me that he had been that naive young officer all those years ago.

Both my parents added to the Gibraltar sound-scape in ways that were not universally popular. Pa sent for Piper Robson of the Argylls to play Reveille under the bedroom windows every morning and Ma inadvertently acquired a pair of pea fowl. They were shown to her on a routine visit to the poultry part of the market and had clearly been brought in from Spain with her in mind. They lay on the ground with their feet tied together, looking very sad. She resisted for two days but gave in on the third day and released them into The Convent garden, hoping they would not dig everything up but look decorative as they pranced among the hibiscus, the male fanning out his lovely tail for all to admire from the drawing room balcony. In fact, they preferred the hen run and only appeared in the garden on rare occasions, generally leaving a trail of moulted feathers behind them.

When Prince Charles and Princess Anne visited the Rock with their parents they had tea in The Convent garden with George and Ricky Ferguson and the peacock feathers really appealed to them. After dragging the feathers through puddles and mud, they were just what their parents did not want waved in their faces when they came to take them back to the Yacht. Meanwhile the demonic screeches of the pea birds echoed up the Rock, daily disturbing the peace of the siesta, and the skirling of the pipes at 8 am, as Piper Robson made sure we all awoke to the strains of *Hey Johnnie Cope*, reverberated round the town, falling largely on unappreciative ears.

Sometimes the *Levanter*, a big black cloud, would hang above the Rock for days at a time when an east wind blew, making it humid and heavy, while some miles up the coast the sun shone and the atmosphere was less sticky. Prior to the difficulties at the border, this was a good time to retreat to the Governor's Beach in Spain. The Rock was always noisy and crowded and it seemed peaceful on the beach, miles from anywhere. We would spend all afternoon swimming and splashing and would come home pink and salty after a happy break.

The countryside in Spain was so different from Scotland. Olives and almond trees dotted the landscape and the hills rose high on the inland side of the road. Bee eaters had nests in holes burrowed into the bank by the road, and high hedges of aloe and prickly pear surrounded small fields. White egrets sat on the backs of cattle feeding off ticks, and pigs were tethered or watched over by small children. There were large cork woods and on the road we would pass strings of donkeys carrying the cork bark in nets on their backs. Little villages lay up terrifying zigzag roads and Ma would lead expeditions to them in search of honey or oranges for marmalade. Once we went to Ubrique, a remote village devoted to leatherwork where they produced beautiful cigarette boxes, suitcases and jewel boxes in shiny green, dark red and blue skin. Ma later took the silver hairbrush set she and Pa had given me over several Christmases and birthdays to Ubrique, and had a dressing case made to fit them. I still have it.

This was also a very sociable time for Ma and Pa. Early on, they went with a cricket team to Rio Tinto for a weekend to play against the Rio Tinto company, much enjoying the trip. Later there was a return match in Gibraltar. They visited Jock and Francis Balfour at the Madrid Embassy, with the former becoming a good friend and ally to Pa. They were also invited by the Grahams to spend a weekend 'roughing it' in the Douro, the port growing area of Portugal. It turned out to be anything but roughing, as they were treated like royalty and wined and dined in style. (Nearly 40 years later Ma returned to Portugal when her grandson, Alastair, married into another port family and we travelled to their wedding in Oporto and came across the Grahams once more.) They forged strong links with many of the sherry families in Jerez and frequently visited bodegas, taking their guests to see how sherry was made and to have lunch with the Domecq, Gonzalez, Osborne or Williams families. Guy Williams had served for many years as British Consul in Jerez, and had played a role in setting up *The Man that Never Was* hoax that contributed to the relatively weak resistance to the allied invasion of Sicily in which Pa had participated in 1943.

Ann and Beltran Domecq took us all to a bull fight. Their enthusiasm and commentary and the general atmosphere made it seem all right at the time and it was only afterwards that we felt pretty sickened.

Pa had several days shooting at Guadacorte and Vejer, the former of which was owned by the Marquis of Bute, who came out annually by sea, passing through Gibraltar. When Pa was shooting at Vejer, he was a bit embarrassed that he only shot one bird all day, particularly as there had been a continuous barrage of gunfire. He was therefore amazed when everyone toasted him as Champion after the last drive and it turned out that nobody else had shot a thing![cix]

Journeys back to the UK were relatively few and far between for my parents, and when Pa's Mother died in Edinburgh in April 1953, only George was able to attend her funeral, although Pa had seen her not long before she died. By this time plans for celebrating the Coronation were taking up a lot of Pa's time as it was only a few weeks away. It is interesting in the light of his Palestinian experiences that one of the few letters of condolence that Pa appears to have kept is one from the Jewish Community in Gibraltar.[cx]

George was still in the UK a few days after Granny MacMillan's funeral and was able to listen to the Boat Race, in which John rowed in the winning Cambridge crew, on a taxi's radio outside Oxford station on his way to be interviewed at Wellington where he took up a post as 'Usher' that autumn. In Gibraltar we all crowded round a crackly radio to listen to the race. Only Great Uncle Jack represented the family, following the boats in a launch.

P&O and British India liners still called regularly on their way to and from Suez and beyond, taking about 3 days from Tilbury, with Gibraltar as the first stop out and last on the way home. It was a route that was used as much if not more than the 'plane, but my parents insisted on driving when they went home for their month's annual leave. They would hope to get to the Channel in 3 days. Usually they had passengers, George, Jock or me, and it was a pretty miserable experience. The Spanish roads were un-tarred and dusty and we invariably got stuck behind a large, slow and smelly lorry for miles on end. Ma was always dying to stop to look at flowers, buy fruit or simply have a look at something of interest as we sped along. Pa was deaf to all entreaties and only stopped every 2 hours to change drivers and check the tyre pressure. As we set off again, we would each have one boiled sweet and press on. Finding a suitable place to stop for a picnic lunch was never easy, and, when we did, it consisted always of ham in a bun and a large tin of grapefruit segments shared among the party. The route varied, but, as we shot past everything with no time to appreciate where we were, I am not sure why we bothered. Once we crossed the Channel from Lydd to Le Touquet by air, travelling with the car in the same Silver City plane: rather a good way to start the journey back.

It was on one of these trips home, in June 1953, that Pa spent an afternoon with other representatives of the colonies and Commonwealth countries, planting an Oak on behalf of Gibraltar in Windsor Great Park as part of a stand of Oaks to commemorate the Coronation. He was presented with the spade that he used, a medium sized stainless steel one. He passed it straight on to Ma and she never used any other. Its blade is now half its original length, but we still use it for planting though it's no longer any good to dig with.

At some point many years later, somebody picked up some acorns from under the Gibraltar Oak in the Great Park and sent them to Ma and she grew them on; one, now itself a sizable specimen, is growing in the McNeil, the field lying between the main road and the Langbank drive at Finlaystone. It was planted to replace a beautiful old oak which had been struck by lightning a few years earlier.

The family Visitors' Book[cxi] reminds me just how many people came to stay at The Convent. They included a mixture of relations and old regimental friends, interspersed with a quantity of Scottish aristocrats who my parents had got to know while at Gogar Bank. There were also a mass of official guests including the Colonial Secretary, Field Marshal Montgomery, Douglas Fairbanks and Sir Malcolm Sargent to name but a few, plus The Sultan of Zanzibar, one of his wives and 12 year old daughter, who came ashore for the day on their way to the Coronation.[cxii] To our horror they set their hearts on dressing their daughter for the Big Occasion in something bought in Gibraltar's Main Street. Lesmoir accompanied them into the town and they returned delighted with a hideous shiny bottle green dress which was most unbecoming and nothing like as suitable as her national costume.

When the Supreme Allied Commander Atlantic, who was a senior American Admiral, was visiting Gibraltar and rang to suggest a time that his wife could call on Ma, her reply was disconcertingly honest, "I can't see her then, I'm having my beard removed." This was not at all the answer he had expected and he confided to Lesmoir that his wife would never have said a thing like that, but that he found it refreshing.

He must have felt that some of his initial misgivings were justified, when, as David recalls, Pa went to pay his respects to the Admiral. Bill Logan, one of Ma's more eccentric cousins, was staying at the time. Not only was he the loosest of loose cannon, but did not ingratiate himself to Pa by always calling him *Corporal*. Pa was invited to lunch on the American flagship in the harbour. The party set off with the army driver and Robert Ferguson in the front and Pa and Bill in the back. The car had the Governor's flag up, General's stars showing. They arrived at the ship, tied up on the mole. As the car stopped, the guard of honour turned out to welcome them. Pa got out to inspect the guard, while Bill bounced out of the other back door and ran up the gangway, and, when he got to the top, he shouted, "Hurry up Corporal, there's loads of grub up here". Apparently, after the initial shock, Bill managed to charm the Americans. What Pa had to say about it is not recorded.

The Convent housed the incoming Bishop of Gibraltar, Thomas Craske, when he was installed in December 1953, and when a Parliamentary Delegation came out on a fact finding trip, they too were all put up at The Convent. We also housed 15 survivors of the wreck of *Empire Windrush*, who stayed on the night of March 30th, 1954.[cxiii] Lesmoir and I both took families shopping in Main Street, when the survivors were brought in. Pa had only 24 hours to prepare for their arrival and enlisted the help of the local St. John's Ambulance Association. Everyone was allotted a helper to get them clothes and other essentials to last till they reached the UK, and they were all accommodated with families around the Rock till they were evacuated by air or sea. They arrived very shattered after a terrible ordeal, many of them with young families. A nice Captain with a wife and 4 children, whom Lesmoir looked after, explained how wrong it was that servicemen were not taught to swim when joining up. He recounted how he had literally had to throw them overboard because they were more scared of the water than the flames. He had clearly worked hard and had burns to show for his efforts.

Pa was a bit annoyed by Lady Mountbatten, President of St. John's Ambulance, who flew out, arriving as the survivors were coming ashore and after the preparations had been completed. She did the gracious lady act, completely ignoring the hard work that everybody else had put in, and Lesmoir was amused to overhear one rescued wife say to another "She ain't aged that well, has she?"

Most of our parents' friends chose to come in the autumn or spring to escape the British climate and enjoy a little warmth. Lots of them would arrive and stay a few days before holidaying at a Spanish hotel for a couple of weeks. They would return for another night or two and go home by air or liner.

The Earl and Countess of Stair – Jack and Violet – came twice and were unforgettable.[cxiv] Both were elderly and massive, she stately and serene, he outwardly gruff but really good fun. They loved nothing better than to go on trips into Spain with Ma. The expeditions were often in search of early spring flowers as, like Ma, they were keen horticulturalists. On one particular afternoon they went to locate an eagle's nest. The birds were flying around the top of quite a high hill and, long before they got near the top, Violet ran out of puff and Ma had to escort her back to the car to rest and wait for the others to return. As Ma retraced her steps she was alarmed to see the vast figure of his Lordship lying flat and still on the hillside. Convinced he must have had a heart attack, she scrambled on up the hill towards him. As she approached, much to her relief, he sat up and explained that he had been playing dead to see if the eagles would swoop low over him and give him a closer view of themselves.

Navy days. Pa transfers by jackstay to HMS Broadsword

The Stair family name is Dalrymple and HMS *Dalrymple* was visiting Gibraltar while they were staying and invited Jack to spend a day at sea on board. The crew were impressed how nimble the old boy was when it came to getting around the ship and christened him Lord Ladder. One evening when the Stairs and my parents returned to dine with the Captain, Jack stalked up the gangway and looking rather fiercely at the Captain said "I understand some of your chaps call me Lord Ladder". The Captain started to apologise on behalf of his chaps when Jack cut him short and said "Meet her Laddership". He mesmerised the small Fergusons one morning by turning into a giant. He slung a long overcoat over his shoulders and faced an open door. With the help of a walking stick he gradually raised his hat and somehow the overcoat at the same time so that from behind he looked like a very, very tall man peeping over the top of the door.

The Stairs were among the signatories on a card sent to Ma and Pa for their silver wedding, signed by lots of friends who had been to stay with them over recent years at Gogar Bank and The Convent.[cxv] There was a covering letter from Dick O'Connor explaining that they all felt so grateful to my parents for the hospitality they had received from them, that they were presenting them with a portrait of Pa that had been spotted by the Wimberleys in a gallery in Dundee, as a thank-you from them all.[cxvi] A few years earlier an artist had written to Pa explaining that he had painted his portrait from a photograph and would very much appreciate it if Pa could look in on his studio when next in London so that he could see the colour of his skin, hair and eyes before he completed the painting. My parents did go and were offered the finished picture for fifty guineas. Educating 5 children stretched their resources as it was and they declined the offer, feeling that it was something they could live without. By the time it reached the Dundee Gallery it was priced at a hundred pounds but, divided between so many, it became a different proposition and the perfect silver wedding present to give them. He is wearing battle dress and must have been in his late forties. The picture has hung ever since at Finlaystone.

Our younger friends, too, were made welcome and it was good that on the whole they came in the summer holidays and were able to enjoy sailing, water-skiing and picnics on the Governor's barge. When nothing special was happening we would go to Rosia harbour, to the officers' swimming club. A narrow winding stair led down to a pier with a couple of diving boards on it. A low concrete building housed two changing rooms and a small bar behind which Mr Politza presided. He was caretaker, barman, jelly fish catcher and general factotum, and I think he had to put up with a lot of teasing. It was decidedly scruffy, but a great meeting place for the young and that was where we met and made our friends. Jock taught me to dive and he would often swim out of the bay with his harpoon and mask in search of fish. No one worried about sunburn then and we would drag 'biscuits' – rather hard cushions – on to the changing room roof and doze in the sun as we dried off. Often we would end up having a midnight swim after a party when the water would light up with phosphorescence.

A bunch of us gave Pa a few anxious hours when we got a lift on the *Zeebrugge*, a fast launch belonging to the RAF, to Tangier. We spent the day exploring the souk and eating in a Moroccan restaurant before returning to the harbour for the trip back. When we reached the *Zeebrugge*, we were surprised to find it battened down and no sign of life, but eventually managed to rouse a sleepy serviceman who told us that it was too rough for them to make the crossing and that we should come back in the morning. As some of the party were due to fly back home from Gibraltar the next day, we had to find a way of getting back in time. Eventually we came upon a very scruffy little cargo boat, the *Plymstock*, with a shady looking crew and a mangy guard dog. After much discussion amongst the crew they agreed to take us and drop us in Gib. on the understanding that we remained throughout the voyage in the saloon. Somehow we managed to send a message to the Rock telling them we were on our way and when to expect us. It was a miserable trip, rough, smelly and stuffy, but we were so relieved to have found a means of getting back we did not really mind. We arrived in the early hours of the morning, as the *Plymstock* was extremely slow, and were met by Nigel in the Governor's barge to be told that the *Plymstock* was on the black list as it belonged to smugglers and was not at all the sort of boat with which the Governor's family should associate. Luckily we were not held to ransom and there were no repercussions, but Pa breathed a sigh of relief when we reappeared unscathed, without causing an international incident. In our defence, we had not had the benefit then of reading a letter which Kenneth Anderson had written to Ma and Pa in which he had told them that Gibraltarians were "very likeable people, but inclined to go off at intervals like overcharged siphons! A typically southern Med. race, of extremely mixed racial origin: very keen commercial brains and run neck and neck for 1st place in black-market and smuggling activities – which flourish in this corner of the world (Tangier being the home of the super-racketeer and Spain being full of skilled players.)"![cxvii]

As well as friends who came from the UK, for the last few months in Gib., Ma acted as guardian to Chen after her family returned to England. Her parents were Peter and Gwenllian Pelly. He was Captain of the Dockyard and Sal, Chen and Clare were their 3 daughters. Chen was about to sit her School Certificate and it was agreed that it was a bad time for her to leave Loreto Convent and start in a new school back home. She was a bit younger than me but became a great friend, and still is, having married an old school friend of Robin's. On our return to Finlaystone, she and Jean both remained very much part of our lives and were 'slaves' at different times.

I have a feeling that our parents enjoyed it when we were all around in the holidays. It introduced a touch of normality into a rather unreal world. They seemed to appreciate that our youthful high spirits needed an outlet and were remarkably tolerant. Apart from some hot mornings picking stones off the Admiral's garden where Chula, the cow, lived, there was very little constructive work to do, so lots of time on our hands to cook up jokes. George used to go to Ronald Torrie to be read Greek, and I had some Spanish lessons and helped to do the flowers in the house but, with both parents pretty busy, we were left to our own devices much of the time. As a large family, we were used to being teased and at times annoyed by our siblings and did not take it to heart and *Loss of Face* was not in our vocabulary. Consequently our jokes appeared to be funny and never intended to be cruel, but in retrospect they must have appeared to others to be unkind.

When George brought a fellow 'usher' from Wellington to stay, the friend definitely felt hard done by. On arrival David and Andrew suggested he might like to send a telegram home saying he had arrived safely. Sandy was touched by their consideration when they pulled out a chair for him, until when he sat down a very rude noise resounded round the drawing room and it dawned on him he had been tricked into sitting on a whoopee cushion, much to the merriment of the rest of us. After a few days, David realised that Sandy much enjoyed his gin and, after one normal gin and tonic, he refilled Sandy's glass several times with ice, lemon and tonic only, wandering by to check at intervals that Sandy's drink was to his liking. The penny eventually dropped and poor Sandy took it very badly, even making an official complaint to Pa that he had been made a fool of in front of the girls. Dave was told to lay off and remarked to Pa that he felt Sandy asked for it. I think Dave's view was that, as a school master, he was fair game and would know how to react.

Another time, when Nigel Crowe arrived to take over as ADC from Jock, he found no bed in his room but a beautifully constructed nest with a verse pinned to it. It read:

> *I've never seen a nesting crow.*
> *I never hope to see one.*
> *But if you really want to know,*
> *I'd rather see than be one.*

Again, all meant as a friendly joke but, for a newcomer, possibly a little unnerving.

However, during the visit by the Parliamentary Delegation, a joke from David broke the ice. They were out most of the time, only reappearing in the evenings for dinner. When Labour MP, Norman Dodds, a Yorkshireman and somewhat ill at ease in the strange surroundings, was seated next to Ma one evening, he discovered a large revolting slug in his salad. Ma quickly came to his rescue and, as she removed it, explained that it was plastic and out of her son's Christmas stocking. Norman looked relieved and exclaimed, "I never thought this would 'appen to me in Guvernment 'ouse Gibraltar" and then added "But I do understand the kiddies' antics." – a remark which we remember to this day, and which greatly endeared him to us – not least because by this time, David was already at Eton and was not entirely appreciative of being thought a 'kiddie.'!

Before Pa took over, General Anderson had suggested that he might find life a little quiet and a bit routine, with the Ceremony of the Keys, Queen's Birthday Garden Party, Legislative Council projects and after-dinner speeches coming round regularly.[cxviii] As it turned out this was by no means the case, and Harold Redman, writing to Pa a little while after he had taken over, observes "There seems to be an awful lot of activities to catch up with and I have come to the conclusion that you both must have been pretty busy in your time here."[cxix] It may have been partially because of this that, when Pa was asked both by the CIGS and the Colonial Secretary[cxx] if he would like to stay on a bit longer, he declined. His foremost reason to go, after 3 years, was that he and Ma felt they must return to Finlaystone by April 1955 at the latest. This was because a decision had to be made by George's 25th birthday on June 20th as to whether he was going to keep it as his future home. Granny Houston had left it in trust for him, as her eldest grandson, till his 25th birthday. George was in no position to give up teaching and retire to Finlaystone, so my parents felt they must see if it was feasible for them to keep it going until George would be in a position to take over from them. They thoroughly enjoyed their time on the Rock and had made many good friends, but it was time to think about Pa's future and return to Scotland and leave on a high note with nothing but good memories.

The governorship of Gibraltar had provided a very happy and fitting end to an army career that had begun in the grim trenches of North East France nearly 40 years earlier.

Leaving Gibraltar, 1955

CHAPTER 10

Retirement: Finlaystone

by
David

with help from
Liv, Judy, Chen, Blynda and Alice

Between our time at Gogar Bank and arrival in Gibraltar, Granny Houston died in her sleep, aged 86. Under normal circumstances, Finlaystone would probably have been left to her second son, George Blakiston-Houston. He, however, had drowned in Auchendores Reservoir at Finlaystone in 1925, aged 25, while swimming in its cold waters to retrieve a duck that he had shot, causing great shock and sadness in the family. This meant that everything at Finlaystone was split in 3 ways between Uncle Johnny[cxxi], Ma and her sister, Aunt Buster. The home farm, Burnside, stayed with the house and gardens, along with the surrounding woodlands. All the farms were valued and split in three ways. All the furniture, paintings, china and other household contents were divided in the same way.

I think that some time before Granny died I heard a conversation between Ma and Uncle Johnny which went like this: Uncle Johnny: "I do not want Finlaystone. Do you think George would like it?" Ma: "I am sure he would love it." The upshot was that the house and its surroundings as well as Burnside and Langside farms, came into Ma's possession in trust for George. Ma received a one third share of Bogside farm and bought the other two thirds from her brother and sister.

After the house contents had been divided up, there was a public auction in the spring of 1952, when all that remained was sold. All the arms and armour in the hall, which ranged from chain mail to bows and arrows, swords and fire arms, went for a pittance. As Ma and Pa had few belongings after the blitz, they bought most of the things they wanted, including some now valuable furniture. I remember us all putting pressure on Ma to bid for one of the last lots, when the money must

179

have been running low, and she bought the billiard table for £15. If she had not got it, we would have missed out on many wild games of billiard fives and lots of fun in later years.

The decision to make Finlaystone the family home after Pa retired in 1955 cannot have been an easy one, because Ma and Pa were very much aware that it would be extremely expensive to run and that their own resources, consisting mainly of Pa's army pension and income from Ma's investments, were modest in relation to the needs. It would also take a lot of very hard work on their part. The house was briefly put on the market, but withdrawn by them when the offered price was too small and they learnt that the only potential buyer would have demolished the building. But what probably induced them to take the plunge was that, with the exception of Pa, we had all lived there for 10 years and loved the place.

Pa was keen to take on some jobs that would immerse him in an active way in Scottish life, and hopefully also bring in some extra income. He soon found himself quite busy, even if not very well paid, serving as chairman of a variety of institutions. It seems that he was regarded as a *no nonsense* chairman, who prepared himself very thoroughly before meetings and tolerated no deviations during discussion. Ma, as we shall see later, took a number of initiatives to raise the level of income generated by the gardens.

The first job that Pa picked up was to be appointed Chairman of the Greenock Harbour Trust. He took up the assignment in 1955, as the Trust celebrated its 200th birthday, and ended up being its last Chairman, when it was taken over by the Clyde Port Authority in 1966. The Trust was responsible for the management of all the ports and dry docks in Greenock and for collecting dues from ships that docked in them. Greenock had had a long history of rivalry as a port with Glasgow, but Glasgow maintained its supremacy for many years by dredging the navigational channel in the Clyde estuary ever deeper to enable larger ships to come and go. Pa's office was in the imposing neoclassical Customs House, built in 1818 right beside the river.

Perhaps because of this connection with the shipping community on the Clyde, Pa was approached in 1958 to serve as Chairman of a consortium of Clyde shipbuilders, formed to finance and build a large dry dock in Greenock. The thinking behind this idea was that the larger ships which were then in demand could not be launched and fitted out in Glasgow shipyards, because the channel was not deep enough to take such ships with their engines installed. The Firth of Clyde Dry Dock, at 305 metres long, was to be able to take the largest ships envisaged at the time: these would be launched in Glasgow and towed down the river, to be fitted out on the lower reaches. The shipbuilders involved included Connell's, Scotts', and John Brown's: the engine makers, Kincaid, and the pump manufacturer, G and J Weir, were also members of the consortium. The idea was that the members would cooperate, and provide labour to finish ships in the dry dock even if this meant working on a competitor's ship. This was always going to be difficult because there was very strict demarcation between trade unions in shipyards at that time, leading to frequent disputes and strikes.

The dry dock and the adjacent tanker cleaning terminal were forecast to cost about £7 million. In 1959 Pa took a delegation, consisting of members of the consortium and Jack Maclay, Secretary of State for Scotland, to meet the Prime Minister, Harold Macmillan, to negotiate a government backed loan, reported at the time to have been £3 million. Work started the following year and took four years to complete.

After the 'Big Dock' was ready, it lay idle for one year because of labour disputes. In spite of having had a broad agreement from the unions before work started, the Boilermakers Union refused to agree about working practices. From 1964, several ships were fitted out or repaired, but, just 2 years later, the company announced that it would have to close because of financial difficulties. It went into liquidation in April 1967. Pa was very disappointed, and said that he had been told right at the beginning by Sir James McNeill of John Brown's, that the lower Clyde shipbuilders would make sure that the project would fail, and then step in and buy it for next to nothing when it went into receivership. This is exactly what happened.

The dock has continued to operate until now, under various management arrangements. In its early years, it hosted both the RMS *Queen Elizabeth* and the *QE2*. The *Queen Elizabeth* entered the dock on a very windy day in December 1965, guided by 7 Clyde Shipping Company tugs, causing some "anxious moments". A 4-foot notch had been cut in the front end of the dock to allow the sloping bow to fit, and there must have been great relief when the dock gate was closed and rose to finish just one foot below the stern. The fit was extraordinarily tight, with the keel just clearing the sill at the dock entrance by less than 2 feet. The whole event was guided by the use of walkie-talkies on land and on board – reportedly a world "first" for this type of operation.

While in the dock, the ship was refitted to enable it to serve both as an ocean liner and a cruise ship. This involved installing a leisure deck and a heated open-air swimming pool; putting bathrooms in every cabin and extending the air conditioning system to the whole of the vessel. It left the dock in March for a scheduled voyage from Southampton to New York, but with work on 150 cabins not yet finished.

The Queen Elizabeth enters the Firth of Clyde Dry Dock

The *QE2*, launched by the Queen in September 1967, was largely fitted out in John Brown's fitting out basin in the Upper Clyde, but entered the dock for hull cleaning a week ahead of its trials in November 1968. Partly because of labour disputes, work on the cabins and state rooms was running badly behind schedule. Although, by then, he had retired, Pa took us round the ship which was an absolute shambles. Pa was disgusted with the builder's management who he said sat in an office in the bowels of the ship and never bothered to see what was happening above. It was well documented at the time that there was widespread pilfering of materials. The ship left the dock to go on its trials but these had to be abandoned because of an oil leak. They were completed very successfully a month later. However, when the ship set off on its maiden voyage to the Canaries, with still a lot of workers doing the finishing touches at sea, some of the turbine blades broke off in the engines and it had to limp back to the UK. Cunard refused to accept the ship from John Brown in this condition, but its chairman was careful not to blame the dry dock.

As far as I know, in spite of the amount of work and stress involved, Pa was never paid anything for serving as Chairman of the dry dock!

Pa got much more pleasure from his appointment, from 1956 to

1965, as the first Chairman of the Cumbernauld Development Corporation. As in the case of his Harbour Trust job, his office was also in a particularly fine building: Cumbernauld House had been built on the site of a former castle, to designs by William Adam, the foremost Scottish architect in the early 18th century.

Lord Muirshiel turns the first sod at Cumbernauld New Town

One of Pa's first duties was to lay the foundation for the town on 15th February 1956. The Corporation was set up as a *quango* to build a new town with a target population of 50,000, aimed at relieving the pressure on housing in Glasgow, so as to allow redevelopment to take place there. As Pa explained in a speech in 1957, "The charter which has been given to us is to produce a self-sufficient community with its own commercial and industrial facilities, and its own church and social community life".

The Corporation retained several renowned architects who designed a town which excited a great deal of interest at the time. In its early days, the Corporation received numerous design awards. Cumbernauld was described as "the most coherent and internationally renowned realisation of the new patterns of community design", which included a separation of cars from pedestrians, with pedestrian ways linking all houses to the main shopping centre – the first shopping mall in Britain. It was also the first town in Britain to feature roundabouts. Apparently Pa was very anxious that no washing should be visible, so drying areas were created under the blocks of flats, where washing could be hung – probably also another first!

Pa explains the design of Cumbernauld to the Queen

Pa focussed much of his attention on trying to persuade industries to set up in Cumbernauld. The first success came when *Burroughs Adding Machines* decided to open up a factory in 1958 that eventually employed 3,000 people, only to close after almost 30 years as a result of competition in the computer industry. I remember him coming back from a meeting one day and announcing over lunch that the American chairman of *Loveable Brassieres* had told him that he had found his *Shangri-La* at Cumbernauld. This must have been very good news as I had never heard Pa mention that particular garment before!

Sadly, in 2001, Cumbernauld – or, more precisely, only its "megastructure" town centre – was given the "Carbuncle Award" for being the most dismal place in Britain. In spite of this, the town is now growing faster than most towns in Scotland, employment is high and delinquency below average. Perhaps the problem is that architectural tastes change!

Of the various part-time jobs that Pa took on after retirement, the Chairmanship of Erskine Hospital Executive Committee probably provided most interest and gave him greatest enjoyment. He served in this role for 25 years, from 1955 to 1980.

The hospital had been set up in a disused country house as a charity in 1916 to provide specialised medical attention for Scottish servicemen who had been injured during the First World War. Some were short-term patients, many of whom had artificial limbs fitted, but the hospital had a large number of long-term resident patients – both men and women. Those that required regular treatment stayed in wards, but the hospital also built 50 houses in which patients requiring less intensive medical care could live with their families.

Princess Anne visits Erskine Hospital, 1971

Pa was a regular visitor to the hospital, and took particular interest in patients from the Argyll and Sutherland Highlanders, of whom there were many, as well as ones who had been under his command during the Second World War. He quite often took us with him. What made Erskine different from most hospitals, and interesting for us, were the workshops which were originally created to make wooden legs and other limbs, drawing teachers from amongst the skilled artisans who worked in the Clyde shipyards. The range of products made by patients was gradually diversified, for sale through shops at the hospital and in central Glasgow.

Harry Diamond, a journalist and fundraiser, was elected as an Executive Committee member in 1973. He had this to say in his autobiography: "It would only embarrass them if I said any more about them but I have to record that the chairman and commandant when I joined the hospital, General Sir Gordon MacMillan of MacMillan and Colonel David Boyle, were men of outstanding ability, dignity and humanity, and their contribution to the hospital is incalculable"[cxxii]

Margaret Thatcher visited Erskine shortly before Pa's impending retirement was announced. She wrote:

Dear Sir Gordon,

I read of your retirement, and remembering my special visit to Erskine Hospital in January I wanted to write and send you my very best wishes.

The success of your quarter century of Chairmanship was very evident when I visited the hospital, as was the affection in which you were held. May I offer you my own special thanks for what you have done, and wish you all the best for the future.

Yours sincerely,

Margaret Thatcher

From 1995, John was appointed Chairman, thus maintaining a family link with the hospital.

Pa's voluntary work also extended to his role as Chairman of the Scottish Police Dependants' Fund which had been formed in 1947 by the Retired Police Officers' Association to provide grants to help families of police who had been killed or injured in action. He also chaired the City of Glasgow Council of Social Service, which had played an important role during the second world war, through its Citizen's Advice Service, in tracing missing service personnel and in arranging for food parcels to be sent from Australia to servicemen in South East Asia. It continues to operate as a Citizen's Advice Bureau, offering help, including legal support, for people facing debt and housing problems, employment difficulties or issues related to their immigration status.

Pa also served as Vice-Lieutenant for Renfrewshire from 1955 to 1972 while his good friend and neighbour, Jack Maclay (later Lord Muirshiel) was Lord Lieutenant. Pa was a member of the Royal Company of Archers – the Queen's Bodyguard for Scotland. He was awarded an honorary doctorate in law by the University of Glasgow in 1969.

Although few of these appointments provided much income towards defraying the costs of running Finlaystone, they enabled Pa to come into contact with a large number of people who were involved in one way or another in Scottish affairs. His continued engagement in regimental matters, described in Chapter 6, provided him with many opportunities to maintain contact with the Army, whereas most of his other assignments brought him to know people in many walks of life with which he was less familiar. Above all, they gave him a chance to feel that he was being useful and able to apply in a civilian sphere much of what he had learnt about management during his military career. Thus, when appointed to run Cumbernauld, Pa had observed to a *Scottish Daily Express* reporter that "Criticism of soldiers getting high civilian posts is unfair. There have been allegations from many quarters that the Army chiefs are not suited for top civilian jobs. But the fact remains that generals by their training have a great deal to do with administration and organisation." He went on to refer to his experience in running operations in Palestine involving 100,000 troops as well as to the civil responsibilities of his service as Governor of Gibraltar. He told me that, when he was appointed to Cumbernauld, another journalist was sent by a paper to interview him: the man intended to portray him as some fuddy-duddy old soldier, and asked him to change into a dressing gown and slippers and sit in a big arm chair in front of the fire in the billiard room! I was not there, but I don't suppose that the journalist's feet touched the ground until he reached the gravel outside the front door.

Ma and Pa were both active supporters of the Victoria League, and Pa was Chairman of the Scottish branch at some time in the late 1950s. The League helped mainly young people from the Commonwealth who came to Britain to study. Amongst visitors that it sent to Finlaystone were two memorable young men from Nigeria who were at Sandhurst and came for a few days and fitted in completely. At lunch one day Ma asked one of them if he had any brothers and sisters. His answer was that he did not know exactly how many but he thought around 30, as his father had many wives. He also announced that he was sure that he was partly Scottish as he was certain his ancestors had eaten a Scottish missionary. A day or two later, the other one, who was quieter, insisted on taking a tray of food up to Ma who was in bed, unwell; he said he must go up and see how Mummy was. Pa very often would say to anyone coming back from working outside, "You must have been working like blacks." Of course the inevitable happened when the two Nigerians came back from working at the sawmill. Everyone got on with them so well. Lilian, who must have been about 6 at the time, said when they left, "Why do I have to be this boring white?"

Although he was declared Chief of the Clan around 1950, it was only after his retirement that Pa was able to devote a considerable amount of time and energy to Clan matters. While the UK Clan Society (founded in 1892 by some distinguished Macmillans, including Harold Macmillan's publishing forebears) was strong and relations with it were cordial, nothing of note happened until 1958, when the Clan MacMillan Society of North America was formed by uniting several strong family groups with the Glengarry and Ottawa Valley MacMillan Society. They invited Pa, Ma and Somerled MacMillan to tour the eastern side of

North America from Halifax to Florida, taking in Hamilton, Ontario, where Pa was invested as Clan Chief with much ceremony, as *The Hamilton Spectator* reports:

"Half an hour before midnight two lines of red flares burst into flame in the centre of the stadium. Fifteen members of the MacMillan family council from Canada and the United States flanked the high-backed "enthronement" chair and from the east entrance of the stadium came the soft mournful music of the bagpipes.

The ancient ceremony which followed lost nothing by being held in Hamilton. Something of the savagery, of the lonesome wildness of Scotland's moors and glens came to life as the flares reflected redly from the solemn faces of those taking part.

It was an impressive ceremony, skilfully produced and faintly reminiscent of the barbaric days when a clan chief was in a state of perpetual war with another and owed allegiance to none. It may be the last we shall see in Hamilton."

Installation as Chief of Clan MacMillan

The next five years were hyper-active, with two large gatherings based at Finlaystone (one of them featuring an extensive tour of Clan sites led by Somerled, chiefly remembered for a very rough crossing from Arran to Ayr), and three trips to North America, where Pa was in much demand as an Honoured Guest at Highland Games. His visit to Grandfather Mountain in 1960 was memorable, because, as soon as Somerled had finished his 'Invocation', the field was engulfed in a deluge which put a stop to the Games. As Somerled's prayer was in Gaelic, some people thought he might have made a mistake in his choice of words and asked for rain.

1985 Clan Gathering at Finlaystone: the Chief and Ma in conversation with
Margaret MacMillan

For at least one of the Finlaystone Gatherings Harold Macmillan, who was out of the country, sent a well-turned message. Pa, of course, read it out. He caused some surprise by ending with the words 'Signed Harold Nicholson'. Ma, who was standing beside him – and the microphone – pointed out the error, which he managed to correct with little or no loss of face, thus: 'My wife tells me that I said "Signed Harold Nicholson". I assure you that the signature on this piece of paper is "Harold Macmillan"'. At the same gathering, we were given a glimpse of what such events mean to Scottish expatriates when John F. (*Lofty*) McMillan, a powerful and much respected figure in the Canadian Trade Union movement, spoke of the fulfilment of his dreams, ending with the words "If only my grandfather could see me now!"

Between 1958 and 1986 Pa and Ma crossed the Atlantic at least ten times (two of them by sea) and put on seven gatherings over here. Their travels were often taxing (as when Ma, after flying all day, fainted at a fund-raising ball in New York); but they appreciated the great kindness they received, and saw the Clan as an opportunity to bring people together – especially across the Canadian-U.S.A. border. They gave a lot, and were correspondingly enriched.

Harold Macmillan's 1959 message sums these feelings up very well:

10 Downing Street,

Whitehall.

May yet another exiled member send his greetings to the Gathering of the Clan MacMillan at Finlaystone. The rising of the clan was once a matter of martial importance – and never at any time in history has any clan had at its head one with greater claims to lead it on any such exploit – but today the Clan is committed to a more faithful adherence to its motto "Miseris succurrere disco – I learn to succour the distressed".

It is a noble ideal, and the opportunities for following it are unrestricted.

In the growth of clan societies in all parts of the world where Scotsmen have settled there is evidence of a renewed awareness of the value of the old system and a belief in the possibility of its adaptation to modern times. In the United States and throughout the dominions the gathering together of people sharing a common affection for their native land is something which cannot fail to touch and inspire us all.

I hope that this will be the first of many gatherings of the clan at Finlaystone and that it will give fresh impetus to the many other societies scattered throughout the world.

Harold Macmillan

August 8, 1959

I have a lot to thank the Clan for, as Ma was needing her wardrobe smartened up to go to Canada and some friends in the South recommended Liv to come and make some dresses for her. If that had not happened, we would not have met.

One of the great advantages of the many assignments that Pa took on after retirement was that they were all part-time and did not require extended times away from home. This meant that he could combine them easily with running the estate and helping Ma in the garden.

Before the estate had been divided up, a part-time factor was retained for its management. About a year after we returned from Gibraltar, Charlie Forrester had assumed some of these responsibilities: he and Diana had lived in the top flat before moving to their own house on the shores of Loch Long. But, after a year or two, Pa took over the work of managing the reduced estate workforce. This consisted of Andrew Riddet, who kept the grounds in order and did much of the routine maintenance on the remaining farms and cottages; Mrs. Riddet and their daughter, Annie, who looked after a large flock of laying hens; Frank Cook, the head gardener, and Jennie Duncan, the land-girl; as well as a forester and Peter Bain, the gamekeeper, whose wife became laundry-maid after Cis McVeigh retired. Although he sometimes seemed to struggle with figures, Pa managed the payroll, collected the rents, paid the bills and kept the accounts with meticulous care, updating the ledger in his office every evening.

I don't think Pa particularly enjoyed gardening, but he took an immense amount of trouble to keep the place tidy, leaving Ma and Judy time to deal with the more glamorous and technical aspects of horticulture. He kept the lawns in immaculate condition, venturing out on his *Brot* to cut the grass as soon as it had grown by an inch or two, leaving the front lawn in neatly striped lines running away westwards from the house. He hoed all the garden paths and trimmed the lawn edges, often cut the hedges, and each year carefully snedded the shoots that grew up from the trunks of the lime trees that lined the drives near the house. On Sunday mornings, before going to church, he could be seen in his suit, pushing a two-wheeled barrow with a large container, emptying the grease traps with a long handled ladle, anointing them with Jeyes fluid, and then walking the contraption down to the bridge over the burn into which its contents were emptied. Sunday was also a day for washing cars.

Pa took charge of the woods and arranged for a lot of replanting of trees, especially after the hurricane that flattened swathes of the Finlaystone woods in January 1968. Many of the fine mixed hardwood stands that are now mature are the results of this work. Much of the actual planting was done by forestry 'slaves', working under his guidance, but he devoted a lot of time to the tedious task of keeping the newly planted trees free from weeds and brambles.

On top of all of these tasks, he also lent a hand in what was essentially Ma's domain, whether through bunching daffodils or looking after the garden shop. All of this was done with meticulous care, with the aim of supporting Ma in their long-term goal of making a go of Finlaystone.

The Shopkeepers

He was particularly busy ahead of the two occasions each year when the gardens were opened to the public in aid of charities. Bill Logan's younger brother, John, always came to Finlaystone to help Ma and Pa with the garden openings. John had served as a Captain in 7th Battalion of the Argyll and Sutherland Highlanders which was sent at the beginning of the war to try to stop the German advance on Dunkirk during the evacuation. John and what was left of his battalion were captured. He spent the war in a number of POW camps, from which he sought to escape. He and his companion, Jack Higgon, made a first escape from Laufen camp by walking out past the sentry dressed as German officers, but their disguise was not sufficiently convincing to take in the guard at the second gate. The Germans then installed a light at the first gate to improve inspection and this became known amongst prisoners as the *Higgon-Logan Memorial Light*. On the second occasion the Swiss Commissioners came to inspect the camp that he was in, and John and another prisoner dressed up in German officer uniforms which they had made. Together with 3 other prisoners, dressed in civilian clothes like the Swiss Commissioners, they went to the main gate and, in his fluent German, he got the guard to turn out. They inspected the guard, giving them a rocket for being scruffy, and made their escape. Unfortunately they were recaptured after five days.[cxxiii]

We never thought that John's efforts towards making the garden openings a success were adequately appreciated. Pa would issue orders to all concerned, with military precision. John would receive his orders as he stepped out of his car, having driven from Stirling. As he kept coming back twice a year for many years, he must have accepted his lot, probably with some quiet amusement.

For garden openings, clan gatherings and weddings, Pa hoisted his standard on the flagpole on the tower. He had once been reminded by his friend Admiral Cunninghame Graham, who lived directly across the river, that etiquette demanded that flags should be lowered at sunset. On one 'special occasion' some of the family were with us for a drink before we were all to dine at Finlaystone. Someone saw that the standard was still flying, though darkness was falling. Putting on a suitably gruff voice, I rang saying "Angus here. I say Gordon, I see you're still flying your standard. You know it's after sunset". A few minutes later we saw the flag come down, and went to the house for dinner. The joke was on us when he said, "I had an awfully nice call from Angus, reminding me to lower the flag. I must write and thank him". A lot of rather hasty back-pedaling had to be done.

Pa enjoyed grouse shooting and had shares in several moors for a number of years with George Kidston, Ma's cousin. He was also asked by quite a few friends to shoot pheasants in the winter. There was a rather idle part-time gamekeeper who looked after what there was of a shoot at Finlaystone. Peter Bain had been a sergeant in the Seaforths and knew exactly how to cope with Pa. He would be seen by Pa wandering about aimlessly carrying a tin. "Bain, what are you up to?" "Looken fr wirms, srr."

Both Pa and Ma seldom went out of the house without the company of their dogs. Of the many golden labradors that succeeded each other, Ma's Gorse and Pa's Gaston are the most memorable. Gaston's excitement on the mornings that Pa got up in plus-fours is unforgettable and the sight of the two driving off, with Gaston in the passenger seat, was most endearing. The atmosphere was generally rather different on their return as Gaston never waited for orders but rushed in to retrieve any bird as it fell and Pa was hoarse with shouting at him. Eventually Pa carried a sturdy peg in his game bag with which to tether his friend and often beat him when he eventually came back from his escapades, treatment that probably compounded his disobedience. Despite all this they were devoted to each other and nobody could dislike Gaston who loved cuddly toys and was in many ways child-like by nature.

Pa's other role was to preside over a household which was filled with people who mainly jumped to Ma's commands, and for most of the time he was very happy to have them around. It must have taken amazing tolerance to have hardly ever an occasion when he could call Finlaystone his home, with all the slaves and us lot being around so much of the time, but he took it extremely well, and genuinely liked most of the people who came while usually successfully hiding his irritation with those who got on his nerves.

At the beginning of the 60's, with quite a full house, there were a lot of people to feed. There must have been a gap between Spanish helpers and Ma wanted to stay in the garden as much as possible. She hit on the idea of getting large hams on the bone, shipped from Ireland on a Clyde Shipping Company boat. Ham was served hot for Sunday lunch, which was good, but, after a number of outings in various guises during the week, it ended up as minced ham on Saturday. One Saturday Ma was in bed with a bad cold and asked Liv to get the remains of the ham and take the last bits of meat off the bone. I came into the kitchen as she brought the ham out. It was moving with maggots. Liv went up to Ma to ask what to do. "Oh, it will all be cooked, it won't do anyone any harm."

In the early 1980s Ma and Pa arranged a dinner party for my birthday in mid-January. Some of the guests arrived very late due to flooding, and so, before dinner started, the dining room fire had been banked up with rather too much wood. During dinner Jane came in and said the chimney was very badly on fire, and that smoke was coming out of a lot of the fire places in the rooms above the dining room. Ma said "That always happens". It was agreed that the fire brigade should be summoned and they duly arrived just when Pa was starting to circulate the port. Most of the firemen went onto the roof but two were left in the dining room with a fire blanket and stood in front of the fireplace ready for something to happen. The firemen on the roof poured 500 gallons of water down the chimney but not a drop came out at the bottom. The firemen enjoyed Pa's offer of port while they waited with us in the unusually warm dining room.

Pa was always very protective about anyone who was at Finlaystone or who worked for him. Just after I started farming I took some lambs into Wilson's market in Paisley with Liv. The next week when I went back to the market, one of the drovers asked me "Who was that teart you were in with last week?" When I came back for lunch I mentioned what had happened as I thought it amusing. Pa heard it at the other end of the table and exploded, and said he was going to ring Wilson's to complain. We managed to dissuade him!

On one occasion Ma and Pa were going on an overseas trip, leaving Judy and slaves behind to look after the place. As soon as Ma and Pa had gone, they started to move some comfortable furniture into the kitchen so they could smoke cigarettes in comfort in front of the *Esse*. To their horror, one of them looked out of the kitchen window and saw a car coming up the drive. The flight to Canada had been cancelled!

I think what Pa enjoyed the most was to have old army friends to stay, such as General Dick O'Connor, Brigadier Jim Cunningham – his best man – Lord Slim, General *Pansy* Robertson and others. This gave him a break from a predominantly female household, where he and Ma had very little privacy.

I am not sure that he was quite so keen on the visits made to Finlaystone by many of Ma's relatives. Ma was always delighted when her elder brother, Uncle Johnny, would come to stay. He had been a career soldier like Pa, but with quite different experiences. In the First World War he had been in a cavalry regiment which had been mechanised. Between the wars he spent time in India with his regiment: a lot of polo, pig sticking and big game hunting went on. He also had an eventful time in Australia as an ADC to a state governor. In the Second World War, he was given the job of forming The Rhodesian Armoured Car Regiment. One story from that period was that he needed to check on the quality of the regiment's footwear. His solution was to order the soldiers to lie on their backs with their feet in the air so that he could inspect their boots.

Pa was never entirely at ease with Uncle Johnny. They had had totally different army careers, and Pa did not have much interest in farming and hunting, and probably did not have much time for the cavalry. I think he also found him disconcertingly unpredictable, which he was, except in his habit of taking notes on everything he saw. Whenever he came to stay he would always come up to the farm with me to look around. The notebook would come out and anything of interest was solemnly documented. Later, during dinner, Ma would enjoy teasing him by asking him if he had taken any notes during his tour of the farm. This always caused some amusement as he tried, unsuccessfully, to find the place in his notebook.

When Liv and I were engaged, Judy cleverly managed to persuade

Ma to get Liv back from London to make all the curtains for the dining room. Judy's arrangement worked well in all directions: I saw more of Liv, Ma got the curtains made more cheaply and Pa did not have to sit beside Ma's friend, who had previously helped with curtain making, at meal times for weeks on end, for whom he had little time. At one point Pa summed up the situation with this somewhat effusive lady, "We kiss, BUT…".

Considering how articulate Pa was, he was remarkably tongue-tied when it came to certain subjects. When I was about to go to New Zealand by liner, the day I was leaving, he asked me to come out on to the gravel where we walked up and down in virtual silence. Finally he blurted out "Mind out for the fairies." Of course I got the message. When Andrew was about to go to Trinidad to study tropical agriculture, the pep talk had changed to "Don't bring back a black girl, she will look awfully silly in the snow." In this case the message did not get through, and it was not long until Pa was having to meet Andrew's Trinidadian girlfriend at the Central Station. In fact he could not have been nicer or kinder to her.

In 1960 we clubbed together to buy a water skiing boat and large outboard engine. We had all learnt to ski in Gibraltar. Quite a lot of the slaves learnt to ski, which gave everybody some light relief and much fun. Ma and Pa were very accommodating in spite of seeing their workforce disappear on a Saturday or Sunday afternoon in summer. The only time they got seriously worried was when the propeller hit a rock off Cumbrae and we had to row back to Fairlie against the tide. We did not get back home until after two in the morning: as there were no mobile phones in those days, they were very relieved to see us.

By the late 1950s Ma had built up the market garden inside the walled-in garden, and had a lot of plants, flowers and vegetables which she took to the Glasgow market once or twice a week, combining this with doing flower arranging contracts in offices, usually helped by one of the slaves.

At about the same time, when the railway bridge over the main road at the bottom of the Langbank drive was being replaced, for several months there was one-way traffic, controlled by a traffic light. We took advantage of this to sell daffodils to people who were stuck in their cars, waiting for the red light to change. This was the origin of a mobile shop that we made, with shelves and a roof. It was towed to the bottom of the Langbank drive and parked in the forecourt on Saturday and Sunday afternoons to catch customers off the A8, to whom we sold home-grown products – vegetables, fruit, eggs, honey, jams, pot plants and whatever flowers were in season. It was usually looked after by the slaves and could do well in good weather. I am sure that quite a lot of the customers came to chat up the slaves on duty.

Later on, Ma sold plants inside the walled-in garden and one of the old stables was turned into a permanent shop. Pa had put himself on a course to learn the art of selling. Apparently at the end of the course everybody had to practice selling to their neighbour whatever they had in their pockets. Pa certainly turned himself into a salesman. He had a full range of patter when people came in. Customer: "Do you have free-range eggs?" Pa: "Indeed we do, and here I have chutney, jam and honey made by Lady MacMillan." When he was not busy he spent his time writing to members of the family who were away. After the shop closed, he would go to his office and add up the takings for the day and announce the success or otherwise at dinner.

Judy was a full-time helper in all the activities until she married Robin Hutton in 1963. One story about their wedding involved Uncle Johnny. He arrived on the morning of the wedding with Aunt Lettice when Judy and Robin, rather than getting themselves smartened up for the occasion, were raking the large expanse of gravel in front of the house to make it look good for the big event. Judy introduced Uncle Johnny, saying "This is Robin." "What are you doing here?" was the reply. Then he took a little box out of his pocket and gave it to Judy as a wedding present. It turned out to be his hearing aid.

Liv and I have spent all our married lives just a few minutes' uphill walk from the 'Big House', and so saw Ma and Pa almost every day for one reason or another, or just because our paths crossed. Liv recalls what life was like in close proximity to her in-laws in the following reflections:

I was asked to go to Finlaystone to make clothes for my future mother-in-law before she left for a Clan gathering in Canada. I was continually sewing in the library when one day David's father came in and said he felt sorry for me sitting indoors when the weather was lovely. He said that I must come back and see Scotland from the outdoors.

At meal times David's parents sat at opposite ends of the long dining room table. At breakfast, letters were read aloud and plans for the day went to and fro across the table. On these occasions, David's father, who was normally very calm, became irritated by his wife's deafness and shouted his messages to her when she did not hear what he had said the first time. I thought it must be awful for her to be shouted at in front of all of us, so one day when we were both weeding in the border, I said that I wanted to tell him not to shout like that as it must be very hurtful.

She turned to me with calm blue eyes and said "If it worries you, I will tell him to stop."

David and I became unofficially engaged and were helped by Judy who persuaded her mother to employ me to make curtains for the many windows in the dining room, so I stayed on surrounded by acres of bottle green velvet, interlining and lining.

We got married at Finlaystone on 24th April 1962. David's father said that he would pay for the champagne if he could avoid having to go to Norway for the wedding, and David's mother said it was much better for my parents to come over and see where I was going to live.

We moved into The Garden Cottage after some changes had been made. One day Ma came up and told me that our garden looked like a dog's breakfast. I said that I knew this, but that I was already looking after her son, half the farm, one child, and did all the cooking, washing and ironing, shopping and paperwork. "Darling, I don't know how you manage, but I'll tell you what: when John is back on leave, he and I will sort out your garden." I thanked her very much, and then came "Pa and I are going to a regimental dinner in London in December. You remember the lovely green silk which Andrew gave me last Christmas. Do you think you could make me something suitable from that?" Of course I had to say "yes", and then she said "I love bartering, don't you?"

Alastair and Lilian were both born at Finlaystone. My bedroom was off the passage near the drawing room. When I was there with doctor and midwife, David and Andrew were in the drawing room with Ma insisting on being a running reporter in between. Alastair was born and looked quite human, with hair on his head. Ma took one look and turned to me, "Do you know I never realised that the cord is just like a garden hose?" and then, after a few seconds, "But I was always at the other end, of course."

When Lilian was about to be born late one evening, we rang the same midwife, who had had enough of a hovering mother-in-law and said, "Switch off all the lights, I will bring a torch." We felt a bit guilty in the morning when Ma came to see us and Lilian was already there. "I am so sorry I was not there to help."

Once when we had a rare weekend off from the farm, we let the dogs out and went back to bed one Sunday morning. We heard foot-steps on the stairs and first saw a black sou'wester and then the rest of David's mother appeared in the doorway, saying "How sweet you look, you really needed a rest."

The King of Norway once came on an official visit to Edinburgh. Some friends of David's parents remembered that I was Norwegian and arranged for us to be invited. In the car going there, I asked David's mother what I should say if the Queen spoke to me. "Don't worry, she won't." The Queen stopped and said something to me, and I cannot remember what I said back. In the car going home, Ma said "I am sorry about that", which was a very satisfactory situation to be in with a mother-in-law.

As David's parents grew older, we began to worry about their driving abilities. After people in the bread shop in Port Glasgow had told me that Ma had done some rather too exciting parking on the pavement, I went to see her about shopping together. I was slightly dreading the discussion, as Pa had been very fed up when I had once suggested something similar to him. Ma was reading the paper and I said my bit: her answer was, "How nice, much more fun to shop together."

When shopping in Port Glasgow by herself, she would put fish, meat, bread and all other things together in a black bin-bag, When it was full, she just dragged it along with her. Near where she parked her Mini there was usually a little group of old men talking. When she arrived they touched their caps with two fingers and said "Good morning Lady MacMillan," and opened the car door to let her and her shopping in.

When we went to Makro 'cash and carry' to do a big shop, we would choose a long flat trolley. Ma would park herself on the front of it and point to what she needed. When I could not reach something there was always a Makro person willing to climb about retrieving what she wanted. They were all rather intrigued by her.

Most mornings I used to see David's father in his office in case I could go to the bank for him when I had to go to Port Glasgow anyway. We would talk about the news and try to set the world to rights, or there would be an obituary of an army friend and he would tell me about him.

The nicest thing that happened after my mother-in-law died was that Lady Maclay wrote to me saying that Ma had told her that we had a lot of fun together, which we did and I certainly enjoyed it. But it was good to know that Ma felt the same!

Ma and Pa had a very single-minded attitude that all their efforts and those of anyone who should come and stay should be directed to the good of Finlaystone. It became a bit of a joke among their friends that it was not wise to arrive to stay before 6pm as it was more than likely you would be put to work cutting something or weeding. Even if you arrived after 6pm, you were by no means safe. After dinner you could easily be expected to assemble the garden catalogue by collecting a page from each pile round the dining room table, or help to make chutney, marmalade or jam. Our good friend Robert Ferguson went one further and always brought a collection of his own shining, sharp garden tools. He was very particular and could not face arriving at Finlaystone and being handed some worn-out, blunt and bent tools to work with.

George retired from his job as a lecturer at Durham University in 1974, when he and Jane and the family came back to Finlaystone, moving into the top flat. They gradually took over the running of the property. Ma and Pa went on working just as hard as ever in the garden and shop. George and Jane started to open the place up for the public to come and pay to visit the woodlands and, occasionally, the house. They also carried out some major much needed refurbishment of the house by rewiring it and re-leading the roof.

In anything written about Finlaystone and Ma and Pa, there should be a mention of Mrs. Hepworth. She came to live at Finlaystone in the early 70s with two school age daughters. Mrs. Hepworth had been running a hotel at Kirkby Lonsdale and had decided to give it up when she was divorced. She was incredibly capable, including cooking, flower arranging, gardening and needlework. She was also efficient and hard working. I think Ma missed her a lot when she retired at the beginning of the 80s, though I suspect that Pa may have breathed a sigh of relief!

Judy

Once they had decided to stay at Finlaystone, Ma and Pa had to work out how to raise income with which to pay the wages and fund its upkeep. George and John had left university and were self-supporting. I had left school and, with poor eyesight and no qualifications, needed to be occupied. David and Andrew were still in full-time education and Pa had no immediate offers of jobs. Since the beginning of the war, the estate had earned income from selling firewood, Christmas trees and holly rings, and snowdrops, daffodils and gentians, but this was not enough to cover the running costs.

Ma had seen that there was an opening for offering large arrangements of garden flowers, tailor-made to suit weddings in churches and cathedrals with receptions in country houses, and other big functions in civic ball rooms or halls. This enterprise would make use of the huge range of mature flowering trees and shrubs and the wide variety of foliage plants growing at Finlaystone and so help to pay for its upkeep. Added to that, it would give both her and me an occupation we enjoyed. We had business cards printed and, whenever a likely engagement notice appeared in the *Glasgow Herald* or *The Times*, Ma would post one off to the mother of the bride and we would wait hopefully for a reply.

Business began very slowly but this gave us time to repair and paint all the windows of the 'Big House' – of which there are almost 100 – during the first summer. We also painted all the drainpipes.

Bookings gradually increased. In the early days, Diana Forrester and Jean McMicking helped us when we needed extra hands, and we discovered that Annie Riddet was a fantastic bouquet maker. Except in winter, when we had to arrange for flowers to be sent by train from Covent Garden and collected by Pa at the station, we mainly used flowers picked from the garden. Two days before a function, Ma and I would tear round, picking all we expected to need and bundling our pickings into 'vase-worths'. The flower room, now George's living room, would be bursting with pails of huge branches of blossom, great sprays of rhodies carefully selected for their shapes, hosta leaves, and masses of whatever was out at the time – osmanthus and other fragrant ingredients making the whole room smell delicious. The day before the function, we would load the van carefully with all the vases, brass pots (carefully wired and polished before being wrapped in newspaper), flower sheets, pedestals, watering cans, a sprayer, secateurs, a hammer and a brush and dustpan. If the event was a wedding, the evening would be spent making bouquets, which would be sealed into bags and packed with tissue paper into boxes. Just before setting off in the morning, the flowers would be taken out of water and wrapped in sheets and loaded on top of everything else in the back of the van.

These jobs were seldom without incident, as when we left a massive bunch of carefully de-leafed philadelphus behind in the flower room. Ma and Annie were travelling in the van, and were half-way to Culross, when they realised they could not smell the philadelphus. The van was high enough to look over most hedges. In due course they spotted a large bush of the shrub in somebody's garden, drew up and rang the doorbell. The owner was delighted for them to attack her plant. While Ma drove on, Annie plucked away its leaves, and it was ready for use on arrival.

If we were doing flowers for a wedding and knew the bride or bridegroom, we would be invited and, once the happy couple drove away, we would put on our flat shoes and remove our hats, and quickly clear up the flowers and stow the vases back in the van before heading home. Very often the caterers were "L'Aperitif" from Edinburgh whose head waiter was Mr. Grey. When George rang to tell my parents that he was engaged to Jane, and planned to bring her up the following weekend, Ma and I were already booked for a wedding that Saturday in Glen Lyon. Ma was desperate to get home for supper to meet her future daughter-in-law, and was upset to find the reception showing no sign of ending in a hurry, preventing us from dismantling the flowers. She explained the situation to Mr. Grey who said, "Leave it to me, M'Lady" and, using the gavel to silence the guests, announced that the Bride and Bridegroom were departing to change. It was a fine summer evening, the marquee quickly emptied, and the guests began to line the drive to wave the newly-weds away, while we rushed in and cleared away the flowers and shot down the drive as fast as we could go!

The flower business combined well with keeping up the garden. As we got busier, it was clear we needed more permanent help and that was when 'slaves' were introduced. One of our first helpers was Sue Stanford who, when asked to witness a signature, wrote "Slave" as her occupation, and the title stuck!

Slaves had to be quite resourceful. David recalls that, at about this time, he and Liv had just got engaged, and Sue asked Pa if she could teach Liv how to drive in his car on the drives. They got up to the lodge on the Kilmacolm drive, and Liv tried to turn round but ran over a large stone. The exhaust pipe came off and she was very worried what Pa might say. Sue said "Leave it to me." They returned to the house and Sue went up to where Pa was reading the paper. "Sorry Sir Gordon, I am afraid your exhaust pipe has come off: metal fatigue, you know." Pa said "Yes, of course."

A job description for slaves is impossible and it is easier to list what they were never asked to do – house work and laundry. Hours were unlimited, days off were rare. Pay was a pittance but the perks were good and the food wholesome. At first, those who applied to come were the daughters of our parents' friends, cousins or our school friends. Others were those who had tried London and did not enjoy it, those recovering from a broken heart, and the odd one who had trained in floristry and wanted some practice. In return for long hours and hard work, they lived as members of the family and joined in everything that happened. At times there were several slaves in residence, including the occasional male slave, who worked in the woods, cleaning and planting trees. Once we had all married, it became difficult to find new slaves by word of mouth and Ma resorted to advertising in *The Lady*, merely stating that "Lady MacMillan needs a Slave". When she turned the walled garden into a plant nursery, many slaves were horticultural students needing work experience.

Chen Pelly, who had lived for a while with us in Gibraltar, looked back on her slave days in an article for an American magazine a few years ago in the following way.

Finlaystone is where I spent the happiest time of my youth, before I was married. In my late teens, I was one of the first of a long succession of contented slaves, and our Slave Drivers were the late Sir Gordon & Lady MacMillan. Every time I return through the gates into the long, well-kept front drive flanked by rhododendrons, I have nostalgic memories of back-breaking days with saws and clippers and spades, shovels and rakes and hoes. And I always remember endless, joyous laughter.

Our duties were enormously varied: sawing down trees, hoeing a field of onions, clearing a dense jungle of undergrowth, raking gravel, weeding flower beds, picking flowers and delivering them in boxes at six o'clock in the morning to the market in Glasgow. At weekends we loaded up a farm trailer and towed it down to the main road behind a tractor, where we set up camp in a lay-by and sold produce from the garden: flowers, plants, vegetables, fruit, honey… Sometimes we gathered armfuls of flowers and foliage and set off for some distant location, to arrange them for weddings and functions and grand balls. It was not unknown for us, having got up at crack of dawn and spent all day making tasteful flower arrangements, to rush off and change into our party clothes, attend the ball and then hang about until the guests had departed in the small hours, to collect up the vases and deliver the flowers to the local hospital. Winter jobs included chopping down acres of Christmas trees, or standing for hours in a freezing cold outhouse, making holly wreathes with swollen, chapped hands.

We slaves lived in the house as family and were treated as such. We got up early, ate a thumping good breakfast, and sallied forth into the grounds where we did our slaving. There was a brief respite for an extremely hearty lunch, returning when darkness fell, to rush up to our rooms, bath and change into respectable clothes and descend to the beautiful drawing room on the first floor, to be given a glass of sherry by Sir Gordon, before sitting down to an old fashioned dinner with 3 courses and coffee. Just like a proper dinner party – night after night. It was a strange life for an 18-year old and, as far as I was concerned, totally idyllic. It was like a very select Adventure Holiday Camp. When we weren't slaving, we played. We water-skied on the Clyde, had riotous games of Billiard Fives in the billiard room, had our own parties with reels and smoochy dancing in the old servants' hall. We had water fights and played practical jokes: apple pie beds stuffed with sprigs of holly, bowls of water balanced on top of half-open doors and, on one occasion, sneaking out during a party and moving all the guests' cars up into the woods. (In those days you could do something clever with fuses in the engine and start a car without a key.) I was number one accomplice in this, and there was an embarrassment when the guests started to depart and we couldn't remember where we had hidden one of the cars.

It is hard, now, to describe how wonderful it was to emerge from adolescence into semi-adulthood under those shrewdly watchful, strict and kindly eyes, with a gang of surrogate siblings, and perhaps there will never be another place quite like Finlaystone because there can never be another family quite like the MacMillans. We adored our Slave Drivers unreservedly and would have done anything in the world for them.

Various slaves met their future husbands at Finlaystone, including Liv who married David, and Blynda and Berta who married John and Andrew respectively. Sari Waldron met Robin's brother, Anthony, while slaving, and became my sister-in-law.

One might have thought that Pa would have preferred to have been able to live at Finlaystone without being constantly surrounded by a bevy of young people. Although slaves must have found it rather daunting to arrive there, he was quick to put them at ease and treat them as though they were members of the family. For those of the family who didn't live close by, there was always open house, and whenever possible they gathered us all together for special anniversaries, such as their Golden Wedding, and Pa's 80th birthday. As Blynda recalls below, he enjoyed being gently teased, whether by slave or family.

The Man behind the Medals

Sir Gordon, Sir G., Pa – these are the names that evolved, and left memories for me of one of the most fabulous people I ever knew.

Arriving as a 'slave' an extremely young and immature 18-year old into my first job, Sir Gordon welcomed and treated me as if I were royalty. I can say that with true honesty as I was at Finlaystone during the Princess Royal's visit, and anyone who met him, no matter what age, was treated with the same respect, from day one until the day he died: in his day that would be described as 'good-manners'!

Memory 1

'Pulling his leg" – pretend pepper-pot battles round the water-jug on the dining room table. Had I blown it and he did not want to 'play'? – then that wonderful twinkle in his eye "No, Blynda, you've got it wrong again, the enemy were here, here and here, we were there behind the flower vase."

Memory 2

Having been put in charge of security for Judy's wedding presents on display on the billiard table. "Blynda have you checked Judy's wedding presents?" Half an hour later, and dressed in suitable hat and flashers-mac, I burst into the sitting room where The General was holding forth to some friend "Come on Sir Gordon, hand it over, I know you've got it". Yes, he really had 'nicked' a fish fork from the bottom drawer of the canteen and concealed it 'about his person' (inside jacket pocket). Without faltering in his conversation with his visitor, he produced it and handed it over to me: I remember to this day the picture on the guest's face.

Memory 3

The slightly scary Grandfather – coming in just before supper to find about 8 grandchildren standing in 2 ranks with 'Grandpa' between them, interrogating them as to where ALL the setting places for dinner had been hidden: it took many months to find everything as they had forgotten where they had put them!

Memory 4

The ideal Father-in-law – always there with a quiet joke, making it very clear that I and the children were always welcome at Finlaystone with or without John, but never interfering, interested in my own mundane day to day life, 100% supportive, and always the perfect guest when they came to stay with us.

When Ma was in her eighties, the Vinery, the biggest greenhouse in the walled garden, collapsed through old age, and she was all for rebuilding it. Eventually, however, she agreed that it was time to start cutting back on her activities, giving up the walled garden to be developed by George and Jane with a tea room for visitors, a fountain and a folly, while Ma and I concentrated our efforts on the rest of the garden. The business had served its purpose, allowing her and Pa to live busy lives, keeping Finlaystone going where there was not only room for the slaves that helped them, but space for their friends and growing family to stay.

Pa and Ma. Pa's 80th Birthday

Alice
Excerpts from a Grandchild's View, written for her Children

When newly married myself and at some military dinner, I sat next to a retired Argyll who recalled my Grandfather describing how, during the First World War, he had had to run up and down the trenches encouraging his men over the top at pistol point, and then the business of entering the German trenches with bayonets fixed – something I found difficult to square with my own memories of him. He obviously felt that his boots from the First World War were lucky for him and he never got rid of them: they sat in the grate of the fire-place in his office.

As a painful reminder of his career in the army, pieces of shrapnel continued to emerge from GrandPa's leg throughout his life. On the first occasion, he went into Erskine Hospital to have the shrapnel removed. Thereafter, as pieces approached the surface, Granny would prise them out with a pair of nail scissors, as they both felt that a quite unnecessary fuss had been made the first time.

By the time I knew them and remember them, when I was about 5, Granny and GrandPa must have been in their 60's and 70's.

I suspect that Granny was never beautiful, but good looking. She always had wonderfully piercing blue eyes, a face that lit up with amusement, and her hair was always immaculately wound up on either side of her head. On one of the few occasions I saw her with her hair down, after the burglar alarm went off in the night, it came down to the small of her back. In old age as she shrank, which she did in a big way, I remember thinking that she had a certain resemblance to Mrs. Tiggy-Winkle. She always retained incredibly elegant ankles and legs, despite having awful trouble with her feet in later years.

Granny's standard dress was sensible lace up shoes or gumboots in the garden, then a dress and jacket or a suit, depending on the season. This was covered most of the time by a large apron, often navy blue with a red edge and a huge pocket that was filled with anything she might require during the day; large quantities of rubber bands of different sizes, plant labels, cuttings, the odd leaf for identification, and latterly a very early cordless phone, the size of a brick. On top of this was usually a *Husky* jacket. The whole was topped off with a red woollen scarf on weekdays, and, for special occasions, a silk one.

When I knew him, GrandPa was largely bald, with a fringe of grey hair around the bottom of his head, cut every six weeks by Jack Smith, the estate handyman, who in a previous life had been a barber. His baldness showed a large dent to one side of his upper forehead, reputedly the result of a car accident in the early twenties. He had a long upper lip with a carefully trimmed moustache of a very unostentatious type.

GrandPa's everyday uniform was a pair of dark brown corduroy trousers, a Bengal striped or checked shirt, tie – often regimental but occasionally a freebie from the Clydesdale Bank – a V-necked jersey and tweed jacket, with a clumpy pair of highland black brogues or gumboots on his feet. He often also wore a *Husky* jacket or waistcoat, over or under his jacket. When outside, he always wore a brown Trilby hat from Herbert Johnstone.

GrandPa lived his life by the maxim 'waste not, want not', and nothing at Finlaystone was ever thrown out until it really, really could not do the job it was meant to do – or any other job to which it might be converted. There was one famous moment during a Victoria League 'nearly new' sale, when a horrified Kilmacolmic voice was heard to exclaim that someone had sent a one-legged pair of corduroys to be sold; this was a cue for much sniggering by those in the know, who had watched Granny patch another pair of GrandPa's corduroys, using the missing leg. Some said that Granny did have the grace to look a little embarrassed, but she did not own up!

As children, neither James nor I could imagine going anywhere better or more fun than Finlaystone. It always seemed to be full of people – and different, often slightly odd, people. Quite what Granny and GrandPa made of them all I cannot remember and probably did not even think about, but kindness and manners meant that they were always included and made welcome. I don't remember GrandPa being desperately comfortable in the company of women, which is not to say that he did not like them and enjoy their company, but having grown up as he had done, I don't think he always found it easy to know what to say to them. I do remember him visibly adoring my mother and loving being teased by the likes of Aunt Blynda. Those who were amusing and interesting saw the best of him, and although he was always courteous, it was sometimes very obvious when he was finding whoever was sitting next to him hard work.

Granny and GrandPa clearly loved family gatherings and got huge pleasure from hearing the hubbub and joking, and seeing their descendants charging around the house. Their ability to put up with mess, noise and disorder was impressive. The passage between the back hall and pantry was frequently a zone for roller skating, scootering and bicycle riding, and games of Dragoons meant that the carpets got scrunched up and were easy to trip over. Granny's only response was to remove the two delicate side tables outside the drawing room, with their valuable Chinese vases, and put them out of the way, so that games could continue without concern.

Most of our generation learnt to drive on GrandPa's mowing machines, starting by sitting on his lap as small children, and graduating to doing the mowing ourselves as we got older. Granny's mini, which was sold for £25 to a consortium of grandchildren consisting of James, Alastair and Richard, after it failed its MOT, was a danger to the public for a long time, as various members of the family practiced their sometimes slender driving skills on the front drive.

I don't remember being asked to work, although occasionally invited to do flowers, but work is what happened at Finlaystone and there were always jobs to be done, some of which were more congenial than others, so we often joined in. We had huge fun demolishing a fallen tree as a whole family one Christmas afternoon, bashed a lot of rhodies, had some fantastic bonfires, spent hours raking grass and leaves and laughed and joked around it all. Granny and GrandPa neither thanked us excessively for our efforts, nor paid us, but one knew it was appreciated, and I think we quite enjoyed being treated as equal members of the team. Thanks to their tuition and the high standards that they set, at relatively early ages we were all quite competent garden helpers, who could name, sort, pick, bunch and pack daffodils for market, writing up the docket for the trader; cut, measure, sell and tie up Christmas trees, make holly rings from scratch, name a considerable number of plants, bag up logs, dip stobs in creosote, and generally make ourselves fairly useful around the place. Equally there were times when we would opt out, ride our bikes around in circles, spend the afternoon in the dingy and pongy room which housed the ancient black and white television, or get stuck into marathon games of Monopoly, Mah Jong or Canasta – and nothing would be said.

For their grandchildren, Granny and Grandpa created an amazing, magical, welcoming place at Finlaystone, showed us what cheerful hard work and high standards could achieve, and gave us fantastic role models for life. They never gave any impression of it being difficult to find blessings to count; they were utterly straight and content with their lot. Goodness shone out of them both. We were incredibly blessed to have known them so well and to have had them as grandparents.

Epilogue

Pa died on 21st January 1986, aged 89, in a car accident when he was turning out of the Finlaystone gate on to the main road below the house.

Ma died on 29th April 1991, aged 85, from massive burns she received when having a bath.

When they happened, these accidents came as shocks to us and all who knew them, but, with the passing of time, we came to see that they had both enjoyed the fullness of their lives: they were both fit and lucid to their last days, and spared the misery of declining powers.

In life, you cannot choose your parents. We were incredibly lucky to be born into this family. While Pa and Ma never spent money on themselves unless it was unavoidable, they were extremely generous to others, and they gave the five of us the best education that money could buy. When we were old enough to go solo they still continued to support us in any way they possibly could, and were wonderfully pleased to see our growing families whenever we came back to Finlaystone.

Their lives epitomized the meaning of commitment to high ideals, bravery in the face of extreme adversity, total integrity and truthfulness, deep respect for each other, tolerance and compassion towards our fellow people, respect for the dignity of labour and the capacity to create happiness around them. They passed these lessons on, not by lecturing but by example.

If you can talk with crowds and keep your virtue,
Or walk with Kings - nor lose the common touch,
If neither foes nor loving friends can hurt you,
If all men count with you, but none too much:
If you can fill the unforgiving minute
With sixty seconds' worth of distance run,
Yours is the Earth and everything that's in it,
And - which is more - you'll be a Man, my son!

(from *If*, by Rudyard Kipling)

References

i For more information on Finlaystone, including many photos, see Finlaystone Country Estate website http://www.finlaystone.co.uk/.

ii "Slavery" at Finlaystone is explained in the final chapter of the book.

iii Victoria Heritage: see website http://vhd.heritage.vic.gov.au/places/show_history/43390.

iv All information on his time at St Edmund's Canterbury has been kindly drawn from the school's archives by Jock Asbury-Bailey and Martin Clifford.

v University of Leeds, Liddle Collection, Reference GS 1032, Gordon MacMillan, Typescript recollections; Extracts from the 2nd Battalion History; Extracts from the 'Ypres Times'; Typed transcript of an interview recorded with Peter Liddle. Also tape of interview (1977). **Unless referred to otherwise, all quotations of Pa's recollections in this chapter are drawn from the above sources.**

vi Record of Service, Army Form B199A.

vii Recollection by David of conversations with Pa.

viii War Diary of 2nd Battalion, The Argyll and Sutherland Highlanders, held in Regimental Museum, Stirling Castle.

ix War Diary of 2nd Battalion A&SH.

x Citations, on Forms/W.3121/5.

xi See Record of Service.

xii Citations, on Forms/W.3121/5.

xiii Ian Campbell, *Diary of the World War* (unpublished typescript), held at Finlaystone, together with MacMillan Papers.

xiv Citations, on Forms/W.3121/5.

xv Ian Campbell, *Diary of the World War*.

xvi Ian Campbell, *Diary of the World War*.

xvii Recollection by David of conversations with Pa.

xviii *Belfast Newsletter*, 12 August 1929 **(All quotations from newspapers, unless otherwise indicated, are from cuttings in the Scrapbook, amongst MacMillan Papers).**

xix *Glasgow Evening News*, 16 March 1935.

xx *The Whig Standard*, 31 May 1935.

xxi *Montreal Gazette*, 17 June 1935.

xxii For a fuller account of this battle, see the Argyll and Sutherland Highlanders website: http://www.argylls.co.uk/history/the-93rd-sutherland-highlanders-1799-1881/new-orleans-1815.

xxiii *Times-Picayune*, 28Dec. 1936.

xxiv **References for World War 2.** The sources used by John in writing Chapter 4 are summarized below.

The main source of original material used throughout this chapter is a personal collection of papers, filed by Gen. Sir Gordon MacMillan (held at Finlaystone, Langbank, Renfrewshire, referred to later as "MacMillan Papers"). Copies of many of these papers are also available for consultation in the Imperial War Museum, and in the Middle East Archive, St. Antony's College, Oxford.

Posting dates and promotions: Record of Service (Army Form B199A).

Awards: Citations and Summary of Awards from Ministry of Defence.

Service in England (1939-42) is pieced together from Training Instructions, from 55 Div, Staff Tables for 9 Corps HQ and War Diaries of 199 Inf. Bde. for the period immediately after he had relinquished this command.

The sequence of events in North Africa is largely based on the War Diaries of the 9 Corps Signal Regiment (National Archives), coupled with *The End In Africa* by Alan Moorehead, and *Tunisian Battle*, by John D'Arcy Dawson. The report on the disagreement between 9 Corps and 34th US Division is drawn from US Official History, *The US Army in World War II: North West Africa* (especially Chapter 30).

The Sicilian campaign is drawn from the *History of 51st Highland Division*, and Current Reports from Overseas Nos. 16 and 19, covering the battles of Baroni and the Sferro Hills (Imperial War Museum).

15th Scottish Division: The *History of 15th Scottish Division* gives the outline. Flesh is added to the bones from the official histories of 2A&SH (Reconstituted), and 5A&SH who were the Divisional Anti-tank regiment, and for the battle of Caumont, the *History of 6th Guards Tank Brigade. Epsom* was also the subject of a battlefield tour John attended in 1962.

49th West Riding Division: *History of the 49th West Riding Division, The Polar Bears.*

51st Highland Division: *History of the 51st Highland Division*; *History of 7A&SH*; *With the Jocks* (KOSB) by Peter White; *So Few Got Through* (1 Gordons) by Martin Lindsay.
xxv University of Leeds, Liddle Collection, Reference GS 1032, Gordon MacMillan.
xxvi Referred to in Zaloga, Steven. J., *Patton's Race for the Seine*. Osprey Publishing, Oxford, 2008.
xxvii Montagu, Ewen, *The Man who Never Was*, Naval Institute Press, 1954: this has recently been published by John Julius Norwich together with Duff Cooper's related novel, *Operation Heartbreak*. Spellmount, 2004.
xxviii Baynes, John. *The Forgotten Victor. General Sir Richard O'Connor, KT, GCB, DSO, MC.*, Brassey's, London 1989.

xxix Wikipedia, biographical article on Evelyn Barker
http://en.wikipedia.org/wiki/Evelyn_Barker.

xxx Gen. Sir Miles Dempsey, Handwritten notes, Feb. 12 1947, Fayid (MacMillan Papers).

xxxi See: http://www.britishpathe.com/record.php?id=54980.

xxxii Unknown newspaper, in MacMillan Papers (scrapbook).

xxxiii *The Daily Mail*, 15 Feb 1947.

xxxiv A fuller statement was made 10 days later. See *Hansard*, Vol 433, No. 55, 25 Feb, 1947.

xxxv Lt. Gen. G.H.A. MacMillan, *Palestine: Narrative of Events from Feb. 1947 until the Withdrawal of All British Troops*, Fayid, 3 July 1948 (MacMillan Papers).

xxxvi Lt. Gen. G.H.A. MacMillan, op.cit.

xxxvii For a fuller review of Montgomery's attempts to toughen the British stance against Jewish "terrorism", see Barker, James, *Monty and the Mandate in Palestine*, *History Today,* vol 59, issue 3, 2009.

xxxviii National Archives, Cabinet 33 (47), Conclusions of a Meeting, 27 March 1947.

xxxix Lt. Gen. Sir Alan Cunningham, Letter to the Daily Telegraph (undated, 1958), a copy of which is in St. Antony's College, Oxford, Middle East Centre Archives, Cunningham Collection, Box5/File 4.

xl General MacMillan, hand-written notes (undated but probably April 1947) (MacMillan Papers).

xli Quoted from: Ben Yehuda, Nachman, *Political Assassination by Jews: a rhetorical device for justice*, State University of New York Press (case No. 66, page 279-280).

xlii See Game Book (MacMillan Papers).

xliii Lt. Gen. G.H.A. MacMillan, *Notes on Palestinian Festivities etc.*, unpublished (MacMillan Papers).

xliv http://www.britishpathe.com/record.php?id=55355.

xlv *Thin Red Line*, 1948, p. 84, *Report of the Moderator's Visit to the 1st Battalion.*

xlvi Major R.D. Wilson, *Cordon and Search – With the 6th Airbone Division in Palestine,* Gale & Polden, Aldershot, 1949.

xlvii Lt. Gen. G.H.A. MacMillan, *Palestine: Narrative of Events from Feb. 1947 until the Withdrawal of All British Troops*, Fayid, 3 July 1948 (MacMillan Papers).

xlviii For a detailed account, see Wikipedia article on "The Sergeants' Affair" http://en.wikipedia.org/wiki/The_Sergeants_affair.

xlix For a detailed account, see Wikipedia article on *SS Exodus* http://en.wikipedia.org/wiki/SS_Exodus.

l See Cesarani, David. *Major Farran's Hat: Murder, Scandal, and Britain's Secret War Against Jewish Terrorism (1945-48),* Heinemann, London, 2008. For a useful review of this book, see Reviews in History http://www.history.ac.uk/reviews/review/856.

li Lt. Gen. G.H.A. MacMillan, *Statement on the Military Situation in Palestine, 28 March 1948* (available in St. Antony's College, Oxford, Middle East Centre Archives, Cunningham Collection, Box5/File 4).

lii Golani, Motti, *The End of the British Mandate in Palestine, 1948, The Diary of Sir Henry Gurney*, Palgrave 2009, p.107.

liii Collins, L. & Lapierre, D., *O Jerusalem!*, Simon and Schuster, New York 1972, Chapter 23.

liv Lt. Gen. G.H.A. MacMillan, *Palestine: Narrative of Events from Feb. 1947 until the Withdrawal of All British Troops*, Fayid, 3 July 1948 (MacMillan Papers).
lv See, for instance, http://www.zionism-israel.com/dic/Hadassah_Convoy_Massacre.htm.
lvi Fauzi Al-Qawuqji, *Memoirs – 1948*, reprinted in *Journal of Palestine Studies*. http://www.palestine-studies.org/enakba/Memoirs/Al%20Qawuqji,%20Memoirs%201948_Pt%201.pdf.
lvii Copies of this and the two following telegrams are amongst MacMillan Papers.
lviii Directive by His Majesty's Government for GOC British Troops in Palestine, covering period from end of mandate and evacuation, May 1948. (MacMillan Papers).
lix Thames Television, An Annotated Transcript of "Palestine", first transmitted by ITV Network, July 1978 (MacMillan Papers).
lx Letter from Generals Crocker and MacMillan to Sir Alan Cunningham, High Commissioner, dated 26 April 1948. (available in St. Antony's College, Oxford, Middle East Centre Archives, Cunningham Collection, Box5/File 4).
lxi Letter from Sir Alan Cunningham to the Colonial Secretary, 12 April 1948 (available in St. Antony's College, Oxford, Middle East Centre Archives, Cunningham Collection, Box5/File 4).
lxii The above quotations are from Golani, Motti, op.cit., p.150.
lxiii Golani, Motti, op.cit, p. 182.
lxiv Gordon MacMillan, handwritten letter, 15 May 1948 (MacMillan Papers).
lxv For a detailed account of events in Haifa at this time, see Riley, Jonathon, *The Life and Campaigns of General Hughie Stockwell*, Pen & Sword, Barnsley, 2006, especially Chapter 13.
lxvi *The Planning of the Evacuation of Palestine*, Notes by the Chief of Staff, Haifa, 30 June 1948. (MacMillan Papers); also quoted in *Thin Red Line 1949*.
lxvii The Thin Red Line, 1948, p. 80.
lxviii Lt. Gen. G.H.A. MacMillan, *Palestine: Narrative of Events from Feb. 1947 until the Withdrawal of All British Troops*, Fayid, 3 July 1948 (MacMillan Papers).
lxix Riley, Jonathon, *The Life and Campaigns of General Hughie Stockwell*, Pen and Sword, 2006.
lxx Letter from Stockwell to MacMillan, dated 10 Dec 1949 (courtesy David Harrison).
lxxi *Thin Red Line* 1948.
lxxii See Pathe News Film at http://www.britishpathe.com/video/new-governor-installed/query/Macmillan.
lxxiii *Thin Red Line* 1949, p103.
lxxiv http://en.wikipedia.org/wiki/MV_Empire_Windrush.
lxxv GHAM, Speech amongst MacMillan Papers.
lxxvi BBC News, 2nd January, 2005, http://news.bbc.co.uk/1/hi/uk/4117495.stm.
lxxvii GHAM, Speech amongst MacMillan Papers.
lxxviii BBC News, 2nd January, 2005, http://news.bbc.co.uk/1/hi/uk/4117495.stm.
lxxix Stockey, G. *Gibraltar: A dagger in the spine of Spain?'*, Sussex Academic Press, 2008. ISBN-10: 1845193016, ISBN-13: 978-1845193010.
lxxx Letter from GHAM to Jock Colville, dated 21st April, 1954, amongst MacMillan Papers.

lxxxi GHAM, Speech dated 25th March, 1955, amongst MacMillan Papers.

lxxxii Life Magazine, 17th May, 1954 available online, accessed 10th March, 2011. http://books.google.it/books?id=IVMEAAAAMBAJ&pg=PA2&dq=17+May+1954+ LIFE+Magazine&hl=it&ei=zKvyTJ_aO8uWOsT0jcAK&sa=X&oi=book_result&ct =result&resnum=7&ved=0CD4Q6AEwBg#v=onepage&q&f=true.

lxxxiii Letter from Jock Colville to GHAM, dated 17th May, 1954, amongst MacMillan Papers.

lxxxiv Letter from GHAM to Jock Colville, dated 21st April, 1954, amongst MacMillan Papers.

lxxxv GHAM, speech dated 25th March, 1955, amongst MacMillan Papers.

lxxxvi Letter from GHAM to Jock Colville, dated 21st April, 1954, amongst MacMillan Papers.

lxxxvii Letter from Jock Colville to GHAM, dated 30th April, 1954, amongst MacMillan Papers.

lxxxviii Telegram amongst MacMillan Papers.

lxxxix Letter from Jock Colville to GHAM, dated 10th May, 1954, amongst MacMillan Papers.

xc http://en.wikipedia.org/wiki/Frederick_Browning.

xci Letter from GHAM to Jock Colville, dated 12th May, 1954, amongst MacMillan Papers.

xcii Telegram amongst MacMillan Papers.

xciii Letter from GHAM to Jock Colville, dated 12th May, 1954, amongst MacMillan Papers.

xciv Letter from Jock Colville to GHAM, dated 17th May, 1954, amongst MacMillan Papers.

xcv Letter from Jock Colville to GHAM, dated 18th May, 1954, amongst MacMillan Papers.

xcvi Ryan, E. F. (1951) *This is the Rock* in Everybodys (weekly), 12th May, 1951.

xcvii Letter from Kenneth Anderson to GHAM, dated 8th January, 1952, amongst MacMillan Papers.

xcviii Ryan, E. F. (1951) *This is the Rock* in Everybodys (weekly), 12th May, 1951.

xcix Ryan, E. F. (1951) *This is the Rock* in Everybodys (weekly), 12th May, 1951.

c GHAM, speech dated 25th March, 1955, amongst MacMillan Papers.

ci GHAM, speech dated 25th March, 1955, amongst MacMillan Papers.

cii Letter from Harold Redman to GHAM, dated 25th June, 1955, amongst MacMillan Papers.

ciii Letter from Kenneth Anderson to GHAM, dated 25th January, 1952, amongst MacMillan Papers.

civ Card amongst MacMillan Papers.

cv www.gibraltar.gov.uk/Weekly_Events.pdf.

cvi Visitors Book, amongst MacMillan Papers.

cvii Letter from Harold Redman to GHAM, dated 28th June, 1955, amongst MacMillan Papers.

cviii Life Magazine, 17th May, 1954 available online, accessed 10th March, 2011. http://books.google.it/books?id=IVMEAAAAMBAJ&pg=PA2&dq=17+May+1954+ LIFE+Magazine&hl=it&ei=zKvyTJ_aO8uWOsT0jcAK&sa=X&oi=book_result&ct =result&resnum=7&ved=0CD4Q6AEwBg#v=onepage&q&f=true.

cix Game Book, amongst MacMillan Papers.

cx Letter from Jewish Community to GHAM, amongst MacMillan Papers.

cxi MacMillan Papers.

cxii Visitors Book, amongst MacMillan Papers.

cxiii Visitors Book, amongst MacMillan Papers.

cxiv Visitors Book, amongst MacMillan Papers.

cxv Card amongst MacMillan Papers.

cxvi Letter from Dick O'Connor to GHAM and MM, dated August, 1954, amongst MacMillan Papers.

cxvii Letter from Kenneth Anderson to GHAM, dated 25th January, 1952, amongst MacMillan Papers.

cxviii Letter from Kenneth Anderson to GHAM, dated 25th January, 1952, amongst MacMillan Papers.

cxix Letter from Harold Redman to GHAM, dated 28th June, 1955, amongst MacMillan Papers.

cxx Letters from Colonial Secretary and CIGS to GHAM, amongst MacMillan Papers.

cxxi See: *I'd Live It Again: Memoirs of Johnny Blakiston Houston* (published privately).

cxxii Diamond, Harry. *Can You Get My Name in the Papers?* Neil Wilson Publishing, Glasgow, 1996 (p. 182).

cxxiii This account John Logan's escapes is based on David's recollections of John's verbal account, combined with those of John's son, Crawford.